THE BLACK MONK of PONTEFRACT

THE WORLD'S MOST
VIOLENT AND RELENTLESS
POLTERGEIST

By Richard Estep & Bil Bungay

Foreword by Katrina Weidman

WITH SPECIAL ACCESS TO EXCLUSIVE ONLINE ARCHIVE

Dedicated to

JEAN PRITCHARD

For her courage and strength in refusing to be cowed by a poltergeist for 50 years.

HOW TO ACCESS ONLINE ARCHIVE

Throughout this book you will see QR codes like the one below. If you have a smart phone or tablet, download a free QR code reader and scan them for access to many exclusive images, videos and recordings. They are a way to digitally enhance your experience and to provide multi-media support for the authors' stories and arguments; but are in no way obligatory. This one shows *Jean Pritchard outside her home* (right) when Colin Wilson's book *Poltergeist!* featuring 30 East Drive, was first published.

CONTENTS

Foreword by Katrina Weidman

Introduction

1. We're Moving House!
2. They've Got a Ghost
3. The Domino Effect
4. I Know What I Saw
5. The Whole House Shook
6. Tidy-Geist
7. Break-A-Leg
8. Shadow Figure
9. Right. Behind. Me.
10. You Whore
11. It Wasn't Me!
12. This House is Evil
13. Living with the Dead
14. Don't Mess with This House
15. Paranormal Lockdown
16. A Very Nasty Thing
17. I've Just Seen the Black Monk!
18. What the Heck is It? Part 1
19. What the Heck is It? Part 2

Acknowledgements

Further Reading

On the top floor of a dilapidated house, at the end of a dimly lit corridor was a dark empty room. It's where it would wait – silently, patiently wait – for me. Several nights a month for years, I would feel its powerful terrifying presence wordlessly taunting me.

On rare occasions I would somehow defy the paralysing fear and make my way to the room, every cell in my body telling me not to, to turn back.

With legs becoming heavier with every step, I'd eventually make it to the door to the room, where I'd tremble uncontrollably outside. I'd lean in to listen to the closed door. I'd truly feel its cold…

Its darkness…

Its heartlessness…

Its hell.

With my heart pounding out of my body, I'd tentatively open the door – I had to see what evil looked like. It was there in the corner, but I couldn't see it. I had to go deeper into the room. But before I ever got close enough to look at its face, the fear so overwhelmed me that I would silently scream and scream until an actual scream woke me from my recurring nightmare.

If anyone ever asks me why I have never spent the night in my own house – I tell them this.

Bil Bungay, owner of 30 East Drive, Pontefract.

FOREWORD

Every place you investigate leaves some kind of mark – a stain that seeps into your soul, and forever changes the way you view reality. Some places challenge everything you've ever known. For me, 30 East Drive was that place.

A haunting that has lasted for decades, it immediately piqued my interest. While always keeping a sceptical lens over my eyes, I went into that house with my mind completely open to the possibilities, but also aware that events which are not paranormal, may have been labeled as such in the past.

What I experienced over the course of several days living in, what the paranormal community has labeled 'The Black Monk House,' has rattled the very foundation of everything I ever thought I knew.

I'm often asked, "What is a ghost? A shadow person? A demon?" The list goes on… I don't have those answers, only speculation. Regardless of the origin or the definition of these terms, I experienced multiple events at 30 East Drive that I can't explain. I can't explain how a door handle would start to turn on its own, when there's no physical hand to do it, and I certainly can't explain the two freshly-planted scratch marks that cut through the skin of my lower abdominals. Yet, these events happened.

If you decide to cross the threshold into this seemingly peaceful house, be aware that you are walking into a world which we know very little about, and because of that I can never fully tell you what you're up against.

Maybe, one day, we will be able to explain how all of this works. Maybe it has nothing to do with what we call 'the afterlife' or what a demonologist would label a 'demon,' but it doesn't change the fact that a phenomenon that defies the laws of science, is happening within the walls of 30 East Drive.

Katrina Weidman
Paranormal Lockdown

INTRODUCTION

Ask any serious student of the paranormal to name the greatest poltergeist cases of all time, and you will invariably be given one of two answers: the Enfield poltergeist, or the Black Monk of Pontefract.

For our money, although Enfield is a fascinating and utterly compelling case that absolutely deserves its place in the pantheon of paranormal research literature, the Pontefract case is an even more curious conundrum, and one that still has paranormal investigators and members of the general public who desire to sate their curiosity, stepping over its threshold to this very day.

On the surface, both hauntings appear to have a great deal in common. For example:

- Each took place in a relatively modest home on an ordinary, unassuming estate, where incomes were low, and life could be difficult.
- Both cases involved young children, at least one of whom was transitioning from childhood into the hormonal flux of puberty.
- The entity at the centre of each haunting appeared to be a deceased male with aggressive, often physically violent tendencies, particularly toward females.
- Both took place at around the same time and gained prominence and notoriety in mainstream national media.

- Each case caused a great deal of strain to the family involved and brought them far more harm than good.
- Each case remains as popular and prominent in the public consciousness today (2019, as we write this) as it was during the initial outbreak. Both the Enfield and the Pontefract cases have spawned movies: in the case of Enfield, a TV mini-series (*The Enfield Haunting*) was supplanted by a big-budget Hollywood feature film (*The Conjuring 2*); the Black Monk also got his chance to appear on the silver screen in 2012 (*When the Lights Went Out*) which triggered a massive surge in the popularity of the Pontefract case, and will be discussed later on in this book.

Both Enfield and Pontefract had very similar symptoms and manifestations: objects appearing, disappearing and hurled directly at people by some unseen force, disembodied knockings, taps, raps and footsteps, the sound of voices, bizarre light anomalies, and as the situation intensified – physical assaults on those who were present in each house.

It must be added that in each case, phenomena were witnessed by impartial and reliable third parties, including police officers and other trained professional observers. Despite the fact that sceptics have attempted to dismiss both Pontefract and Enfield as hoaxes over the years, writing them off as little more than the pranks of overly imaginative children, such arguments simply don't hold water when scrutinised in any detail. For example, WPC Carolyn Heeps of the Metropolitan Police was one of the first to respond to complaints of unnatural disturbances at Enfield. She personally witnessed a solid living room chair rise up into the air and slide across the room, with no visible means of propulsion. After personally inspecting the chair in great detail, she found no explanation for its physics-defying behavior.

Yet there is one thing that clearly separates the two cases. Enfield was almost a textbook example of a poltergeist outbreak; such outbreaks usually last for only a short and finite amount of time. In the case of Enfield, this ran from the summer of 1977 through to their spontaneous conclusion in 1979. Nearly forty years later, the house in Green Street, Enfield, is no longer reputed to be actively haunted; it is once more a private residence, whose occupants like to keep themselves to themselves.

The same cannot be said of *30 East Drive, Pontefract, West Yorkshire, England* (right).

This book is an exploration of the haunting of 30 East Drive. After reviewing the history of both the house itself and the grounds upon which it stands, the authors (both of whom have spent many hours inside the house) will not only share our own experiences there but will also sift through the masses of eyewitness testimony shared with us by those who have investigated the haunting for themselves. We will try to answer that most challenging of questions: Why has this seemingly ordinary suburban house been ground zero for some of the most intense, fascinating, and often downright chilling paranormal activity for the past sixty years?

30 East Drive continues to bewilder, challenge, and sometimes outright terrify those who cross over its threshold today. The Black Monk of Pontefract has been called 'the most violent poltergeist in Europe' by some, and 'the most violent poltergeist in *the world*' by others, yet the truth is that these are both completely subjective labels, open to debate and interpretation. What cannot be argued is this: Something within those ordinary-looking brick walls is a phenomenon which defies easy description, something which seems capable of ignoring the laws of physics as we currently understand them.

Perhaps most frightening of all, while that mysterious something can often seem playful and mischievous, at other times it can be downright nasty and malevolent... indeed, some have gone so far as to use the word *evil*.

Bil Bungay was sceptical of such stories when he purchased the house from the original owner. With hindsight, he would have been well-advised to remember the age-old saying of *caveat emptor:* 'Let the buyer beware.'

You are about to find out why.

CHAPTER ONE

We're Moving House!

Historians know the importance of carrying out extensive research and establishing the facts pertaining to any event, before they ever commit pen to paper. But occasionally, just when you believe you know everything there is to know about a certain event, an entirely new reality presents itself.

The legend of 30 East Drive is well-documented, especially through the exceptional research and writing of *Poltergeist!* author Colin Wilson. The truly phenomenal poltergeist activity that was witnessed by so many people easily places 30 East Drive in the premiership of all poltergeist hauntings ever reported worldwide, if not at the very top of the league itself. But it's the way in which it conforms so comfortably with the general view of how poltergeist hauntings manifest that we are about to challenge: namely, that of 'adolescent children as the prime energy source,' the essential attractant that is necessary for a bored, itinerant poltergeist to latch onto and draw sustenance from, in order for it to create havoc.

As anybody who has spent any length of time at the house has come to expect from this peculiar property, the truth about number 30 is anything but textbook. This is our attempt to set the record straight, as best we can. Our journey begins not with the long-suffering Pritchard family, as most armchair pundits would expect, but with those who preceded them – the Farrars.

Leander William Farrar was demobbed from the army in 1947, was engaged to Barbara in 1948, and married her in 1950, just five short years after the Allied victory over Hitler's war machine. The now elderly *Normandy veteran* (right) was looking for nothing more than a normal life, simply wanting to be able to enjoy the peace he had fought for, and for which so many of his close friends and fellow soldiers of the Royal Signals Corps had died.

A man of limited means, 'Bill' as he prefers to be known, couldn't afford to buy his own house, so had little option but to move in with Barbara's parents, Nancy and Harry Harding, along with Barbara's brother Stephen, almost immediately after his marriage to Barbara.

Fortunately, married couples were eligible to apply for a subsidised council house; it was a simple case of providing the council with proof of marriage, employment, and steady income. But the waiting list was long, and available properties were few, so despite regular visits to the council offices, a suitable property wasn't readily forthcoming.

At around the same time that Bill and Barbara were getting married, the foundations were being laid for a new estate, situated on green fields atop a hill overlooking Pontefract Castle.

Whether the builders of the Chequerfield Estate knew about the historic significance of the hill, with its commanding vantage point over the former Royalist stronghold of Pontefract Castle, is open to debate – but any local historian would have taken care to point out that the land on which the new estate was being built was a former battleground, the site of three bloody clashes during the English Civil War (1642-1651), a conflict that divided King and country, resulting in the execution of Charles 1st and the establishment of a short-lived Republic of England. Indeed, Parliamentarian and eventual Lord Protector Oliver Cromwell himself is said to have at one point overseen the bombardment and gradual starvation of the Royalists defending their castle, which was seen as a key cornerstone in the defence of a royal Britain.

Aside from the obvious strategic vantage point of the hill (it sits some 36ft higher than the ground on which the castle sits, which, given the height of Pontefract Castle's walls, puts it *roughly at eye level with the castle's ramparts*) (left and right), it also offered the bonus of a fresh water supply. This came courtesy of a large medieval well, most likely sunk by the monks from the Priory of St John (founded in 1090) or the residents of Pontefract Priory.

Alternatively, the well may have been emplaced by the owner of an orchard that once stood on the site, although the funds required to build such a well would likely have been prohibitive for a simple apple grower.

The well was said to sit over a spring which fed into a now long-lost stream.

Chequerfield was most likely named because of the chequer trees that grew in the fertile soil there once, rather than after the 'chequered flags' of Saint George that were incorporated into many of the *civil war flags from both sides of the conflict* (right). The battlefield was where hundreds of combatants met one another in hand to hand, sword to sword, pike to pike melee, while also falling victim to a rain of relentless cannon bombardment from the metre-wide ramparts of Pontefract Castle.

But it was prior to that, before the 1588 dissolution of the monasteries and the establishment of Henry VIII as head of a new church, the Church of England, that what was to become the backbone of the legend of the Black Monk of Pontefract began. The story was based upon a wicked monk, who supposedly raped and killed young girls and disposed of their bodies down a well.

It was on this blood-soaked ground that the foundations of the Chequerfield Estate, which was to become the largest post-war council estate in Europe and built to house those living in inadequate accommodation (along with soldiers returning from the Second World War) were being laid.

As Bill and his wife Barbara waited patiently for a council house large enough to house them and their baby daughter to become available, Bill watched the new estate taking shape as he drove around the area, making deliveries for Johnson Brothers Bakery. It wasn't until two-and-a-half years after the birth of their first child that Bill and Barbara were finally rewarded for their patience – with the last house built on East Drive… Number 30.

The brand-new house had 'all mod cons,' as the saying went, the most significant being an inside toilet, which bordered on the luxurious for the Farrars, who were accustomed to using an outdoor toilet in all weathers. The Farrars moved in during September 1954 and became *the first family to occupy 30 East Drive* (right).

At this juncture, it is interesting to ask why number *30 East Drive and the neighbouring house, 79 Chequerfield, were the last to be built* (left)? An obvious answer is that the estate planners were working in a logical order, with number 1 first, numbers 30/79 being last. A less obvious but more interesting potential explanation would be that the large stone well which lay at the precise location where the estate plans dictated the last semi-detached house was to be built, would be the most problematic of them all – in other words, they saved the worst until last. It wasn't possible to relocate the properties – the topography of the estate saw to that, so a specific solution needed to be found. As things turned out, the buttress of the houses ended up bridging the well, resulting in half of the well underlying number 79, and the other half lying beneath number 30.

The existence of the well has been witnessed by several people in living memory, most of whom saw it when the floor in number 79 Chequerfield was lifted in order for the well to be capped with concrete to end the damp problem that had long plagued both properties. Neighbour Darren Burke recalls:

"It was a large old stone well; I'd say medieval in construction. I was a lad, so after the council workers left for the day, my mate Phil dared me to go down it using the ladders that had been left there. So, I did. I remember it being very deep, and damp. It wasn't nice down there, I was frightened. I remember the workers finding a gold ring at the bottom somewhere."

Bill set about decorating and adding fitments, such as cupboards and cabinets, to the property, slowly transforming it into something more to his and Barbara's liking. At the time, council properties were presented very much as bare-bones shells. There were three shops in town that sold wallpaper, paint and so on, and timber could be purchased from a local wood merchant, yet what should have been straight forward for a handyman like Bill somehow managed to become anything but.

He clearly remembers perfectly squaring up two cupboards one day, only to return to fit doors a couple of days later and discover that the cupboards were somehow askew, with the doors now a far from perfect fit. The house refused to warm up, and getting hot water was also a real problem. Council workers would frequently come around to check the system but would simply scratch their heads and conclude that there was nothing more they could do – there appeared to be nothing wrong with it.

Then there was the wallpapering. Bill would put up a strip of paper, then start on a second; just as he was smoothing down that second strip, the first piece would, almost mockingly, peel itself off the wall and flutter to the ground. "I had sized the walls prior to applying the paper, so this should NOT have happened," Bill recalls. Over the next few weeks, he tried every different brand of wallpaper paste available, but had no success anywhere in the house.

On one occasion, Barbara's mum, Nancy, offered to baby sit at 30 East Drive to allow Bill (who was now a firefighter) and Barbara the opportunity to spend a rare, hard-earned night off at the Crescent Cinema or the playhouse in Gillygate, Pontefract. When they returned, Nancy was upset and was quick to point out that baby Jane was very unsettled. Nancy insisted that she herself be taken straight home. Nancy had looked after Jane many times at her own home with no problems, but whatever happened had really bothered her. Whatever it was, she would never speak of it.

Barbara was always accusing Bill of moving things, such as her vases and various knick-knacks from the mantelpiece that she had arranged in a very specific way.

For his part, Bill was absolutely certain that he hadn't touched the objects in question; in fact, he was often losing mugs of tea, or tools he knew for sure that he had placed conveniently to one side.

The effect that being in the new house seemed to have on *Jane, their two-year-old* (right), was of the greatest concern. Bill and Barbara would have to constantly pick up their daughter, because she would cry every night, yet when she stayed at Barbara's parent's house she would sleep like a – well, like a baby.

Naturally, a parent's concern for their child was such that a visit to the Doctor was inevitable. Doctor Young, the family physician who had delivered Jane, knew the entire family well. As soon as he walked through the door of number 30, his first words were, "It's like walking into a barn, coming into this house." This was a rather strange, off-the-cuff remark for a normally tight-lipped, old-fashioned doctor. He examined Jane thoroughly and said he couldn't find any medical reason for her distress; she showed no physical signs of being unwell. All that he was able to do was to recommend that Barbara take Jane out more.

"She didn't need much encouragement," Bill reflects. "Barbara was an outgoing, fun loving girl and used to love going with me on long bicycle rides into the country. Occasionally we'd go to the theatre to see Vaudeville and classical singers. When I was working, she would often get on a bus to Castleford and go shopping with Jane, or further afield to Leeds for adventures, but 30 East Drive seemed to change all that.

"I was spending a lot of time out of the house, doing part-time work when off duty from the Fire Service, which meant that

Barbara was often alone in the house. It was around this time that I noticed a marked change in my wife's normally sunny disposition – she seemed to be very unsettled and withdrawn. She would take Jane to her grandmother's more and more often, and usually wasn't home when I got back late. Sometimes, Barbara would simply stay over at her parents' place leaving me alone in the house. She kept on finding random excuses for her absence, she simply never seemed settled in at 30 East Drive."

Most worrying of all were the blood marks and scratches that started to appear on Jane's tiny face. Her parents were naturally concerned that Jane was accidentally scratching herself when she slept, so Barbara put cotton mittens on Jane's hands, but the scratches and blood kept appearing on her face regardless. There was no family pet to be held responsible, and neither Bill nor Barbara could figure out where they were coming from.

Gillian, Bill (left) and Barbara's second child, was conceived at 30 East Drive. Unlike with Jane, Barbara was troubled with medical issues which taken as a whole were serious enough to place the pregnancy at risk. Barbara became seriously unwell, needing weekly injections, which meant regular visits to Doctor Young's surgery – because after his first and only visit to 30 East Drive, he flatly refused to ever make a house call there again. Further proof of his refusal to return to number 30 was the fact that Barbara's pregnancy bridged the move to a new house, and Doctor

Young had no problem whatsoever going there in order to administer the injections.

Something about 30 East Drive apparently didn't agree with him... but what?

The house was full of strange noises. Voices echoed in the empty rooms from time to time. The coal house had such a strange and intimidating feeling about it that Barbara would never go in and get the coal.

There were occasions when milk spilt out of the bottle for no apparent reason. Rips and tears appeared spontaneously in the fabric of the settee. They looked alarmingly like cuts – the same cuts that now began appearing on the hood of Jane's toy pram when nobody was at home. The side gate would not stay shut, even with a brick placed behind it in a futile attempt to wedge it in place.

Another peculiar phenomenon was that nothing would grow in the back garden. "I tried flowers and vegetables," Bill explains, "and although I had been brought up helping my father from a very young age in his garden and allotment, and had more than sufficient knowledge of how to raise a garden, try as I might, I just could not get anything to grow on that god forsaken patch of ground..."

To this day, the garden of 30 East Drive is utterly barren.

Only now is Bill finally beginning to understand why Barbara would not go to sleep with the bedroom curtains closed, once the bedside light had been switched off. She would always make a point of either opening the curtains herself or asking Bill to open them before he switched the lights out. This continued for the rest of her life, long after she had left 30 East Drive behind.

Then there were the religious objects. Barbara wasn't a very religious person by nature, and certainly didn't believe in any kind of Hell, but Bill noticed that various religious items from her parent's house started to appear at 30 East Drive, as though somebody had snuck them in there after a visit.

"At the time, I always thought that there was a rational explanation for it all," Bill recalls, "but thinking back on it now, something very strange *definitely* happened to Barbara… something that she could never explain. She never once, in all our years together, revealed to me what had happened to her, yet I am certain that she experienced *something,* perhaps in the little bedroom. We never used it, even though initially we were going to put Jane's cot in there. It was a dark and gloomy room, and it had an unusual air, so we decided not to use it. The stairs had a similar feel to that room too; I often felt unsteady on them. Whatever happened to my wife in that house changed her for the rest of her life – and not for the better."

Then, one day, Barbara had the good fortune of bumping into Jean Pritchard at what was known as the 'Cir,' a half-ring of shops located right at the heart of the community. Jean and Barbara had a polite exchange, as one does, only to serendipitously discover that they both expressed a mutual unhappiness in their respective homes.

"We should do a swap!" suggested Barbara. It was a deal that was definitely more favourable for Jean than it was for Barbara. 30 East Drive was an end-of-road property, one with a large garden and three bedrooms that her growing family would make very good use of.

"It came to a head one morning in the spring of 1955," Bill recalls. "When I came off night duty. Barbara greeted me with the defiant words, '*We're moving house!*' As you can imagine, I was taken completely by surprise, but the look on Barbara's face told me it was something she just had to do. We sat down and talked it over, and for the first time she admitted that she didn't like the house, though she failed to tell me why exactly. She had been to the council with her mother and had arranged an exchange with the Pritchard family at 47 Chequerfield Road. She must have been so desperate to leave that house to have organised all of that without my involvement or say-so, so I agreed – knowing that by this time something was seriously affecting her.

"Hooky Walker loaned me the use of a removal van in exchange for my giving him some occasional help with moves, and my fireman colleague and friend Nobby Noble helped me move everything, including *Barbara, Jane and Gillian to be, to 47 Chequerfield Road* (above right), and the

Pritchard family moved into 30 East Drive. This would have been May of 1955."

[Authors' note: Bill Farrar also mentioned in passing that not only did Jean Pritchard want to move into number 30 because of the extra space it offered, but she may have also wanted to move to escape the ghost of a young girl residing at 47 Chequerfield Road – that the Farrars saw on a number of occasions. This is particularly interesting when added to the number of properties in that area that have claimed to be haunted by one entity or another; it's almost as if the whole area is paranormally active].

"I have to admit that throughout my life, I have had experiences that I cannot explain," Bill concludes, "things that I could feel, but not see. People talk of ghosts and spirits, and are often committed believers or resolute non-believers, but I think most people at some time in their life have walked into a building and felt something palpable; joy or gloom, pain or happiness, for no apparent reason. Historians, spiritualists, the clergy and many clever men for centuries have tried to explain these phenomena, but they never seem to be able to.

"After my experiences of being part of the first family to live at number 30 East Drive, I can honestly say that Barbara was affected by something very profound: a spirit, an aura, something mischievous at any rate, and – after what it did to my daughter –

I'd have to say that it was also something undoubtedly cruel. And that's a grounded, *very* grounded, matter-of-fact, no-time-for-fairytales, Yorkshireman talking."

Bill and Barbara were indeed the first to move into number 30 East Drive; *a local census proves the fact* (right). If the theory about poltergeists making use of adolescents as an energy source is in fact true, the things that the Farrar family experienced make little sense. Either number 30 is home to a poltergeist, and the theories about how poltergeists are energised are either incorrect or incomplete, or whatever is at number 30 is something other than a poltergeist: rather, it would have to be something completely different, perhaps something much darker and less pleasant.

The Farrar experiences also throw into question another theory: That someone in the Pritchard family inexpertly toyed with a Ouija board, failing to close it down correctly (Phillip would seem like the most likely candidate) at a time when the Ouija board offered a popular distraction for bored teenagers. But it is evident that mild paranormal activity was occurring there well before the Pritchards moved in, although there can be no question that the activity reached its zenith when both Phillip and Diane were in their adolescent and early teen years. We will discuss this in more depth later.

A final eyewitness memory from the Farrar's tenure comes from Sue Buttrick, Bill's niece:

"I reckon I was pre-school age, so maybe four or five. But I can remember the house. There were no PVC doors or windows at that time. The exterior at the front had a flat slab porch over the front door, and the side passage was open with the side kitchen door on the left.

"Opposite the side kitchen door was the door where the coal was kept. I remember the window and internal doors in horizontal panes of glass which were frosted inside.

"On one occasion, Auntie Babs was wearing a maternity smock and she was talking to my mum. She said that she'd gone upstairs because Jane was crying, and she had found her with a pillow over her face. She said that she was going to the council to ask if they could move to another house. I must have picked up on the fact that she was upset, and I can remember asking my mum what a poltergeist was. Mum just said 'It moved things…' Auntie Babs had heard her things being moved from the mantelpiece in her house, and the noises had frightened her."

As we can now see, the haunting of 30 East Drive predates the arrival of the Pritchard family by at least a decade. Yet it was not until they moved into the house that whatever it was that haunted the place finally showed the full extent of its power.

CHAPTER TWO

They've Got a Ghost

1966 was a tumultuous year for Britain. The Beatles were soaring in popularity, with John Lennon famously declaring that they were more popular than Jesus; they would go on to play their last ever concert together in San Francisco later that summer.

In the East End of London, the Kray Twins ruled a criminal empire with extreme violence and ruthlessness. Harold Wilson's Labour Party was in power. Myra Hindley and Ian Brady, the despicable Moors Murderers, were finally brought to justice and sentenced to two and three concurrent life sentences respectively. In July, the British people were glued to their television sets, riveted by the England football team's stunning 4-2 victory over West Germany at Wembley Stadium, taking home the World Cup.

To the eye, there was nothing special about the Chequerfield Estate at first glance. Perched high atop a hill, it looked like one of a thousand similar estates, scattered across the length and breadth of Great Britain. Yet going back in time to the summer of 1966, events were soon to take place in a small corner of East Drive that would be talked about passionately more than half a century later.

Many people were heading to seaside resorts in order to enjoy the August bank holiday. Among them was the majority of the Pritchard Family: Joe, Jean and their twelve-year-old daughter, Diane. Joe and Jean Pritchard also had a fifteen-year-old son named Phillip, who had chosen to stay at home with his maternal grandmother, Sarah.

The definitive written record of the initial outbreak of paranormal activity at 30 East Drive is surely Colin Wilson's book *Poltergeist! A Study in Destructive Haunting* (reprinted by Llewellyn Worldwide, 2009). In preparation for writing his own account of the case in 1980, Colin Wilson travelled to Pontefract and conducted a series of assessments and interviews; he has recorded the Pritchards' own eyewitness testimony for posterity, something that no future authors (ourselves included) are likely to be able to do. Joe Pritchard died inside the house itself. Many years after his death, Jean Pritchard finally sold 30 East Drive and moved to another private residence in the area. By all accounts she does not like to discuss either the haunting or the house, and out of respect for her privacy we have refrained from seeking her out. Diane and Phillip have long since grown up and have their own lives, having left 30 East Drive and the Black Monk far behind them when they moved away from Pontefract. The authors of this book would like to acknowledge the tremendous debt that they owe to Colin's work; we truly are standing upon his shoulders and encourage those who are interested in learning about the early stages of the hauntings to read Colin's superb book.

Another scholar of the 30 East Drive phenomena is Andy Evans, who spent many days and nights studying the house along with fellow paranormal investigator Steve Hemingway, each of whom have written their own books about the house: *Don't Look Back in Anger,* and *Living Next Door to Malice,* respectively. Both Andy and Steve graciously consented to be interviewed about their experiences during the writing of this book, something for which the authors are most grateful.

We have also drawn upon interviews that we have personally conducted with Carol Fieldhouse, a long-term neighbour who has extensive personal experience with the house itself and the family who once lived there. She still lives next door to number 30, helping to oversee the upkeep of the house and to supervise the steady flow of visitors that regularly cross over its threshold.

It is unknown whether the Pritchard family experienced any warning signs of what was about to descend upon them. Sometimes such things can be subtle, and easily mistaken for the mundane, such as the sounds of a house cooling down at night after a hot day. What we do know is that Phillip and his grandmother were the first to report a brush with the otherworldly on a lazy August holiday afternoon; a shower of fine, chalk-like powder was falling from the ceiling inside the living room. Except that it *wasn't* falling from the ceiling at all: On closer inspection, the layer of particulate matter had somehow formed and stratified a couple of feet below the ceiling, which effectively ruled out the possibility of it having originated from the ceiling itself.

Hardly the stuff of which great stories are made, we're sure you'll agree, and it would have been easy for the teenager and his grandmother to simply shrug it off as being 'just one of those things.'

In the annals of paranormal case lore, the appearance of objects from thin air is relatively common during poltergeist cases. Such objects are referred to as *apports*, and number 30 would see more than its fair share of them over the long course of the haunting. They still occur with some regularity to this day, with one of the more common types of apported objects being (rather disconcertingly) kitchen knives. It is impossible to say exactly where the powder appeared from – Phillip and his grandmother considered the rather dubious possibility that it had somehow wafted in from outside via a window – but when the particles continued to fall, leaving everything covered in a white residue not unlike volcanic ash or snowflakes, the theory seemed to hold less and less credence.

No sooner was the mess cleaned up than a second peculiarity was discovered, this time located next door in the kitchen/dining area. Pools of water were beginning to appear on the linoleum floor; each was relatively small with clearly delineated edges, as if each one had been poured with exacting care. This too is a common symptom of the poltergeist-type haunting, having been noted at Enfield and in numerous other cases from all around the world. One of the authors of this book encountered the phenomenon himself while investigating a private residence in the United States, and no satisfactory explanation was ever discovered.

At this early stage, neither Phillip nor his grandmother had the slightest inkling of what they were dealing with. Believing that the pipes might be to blame, they called in a professional plumber to assess the situation. After checking out the sewage and plumbing facilities, he was left scratching his head, unable to offer a convincing explanation for where the pools of water, which seemed to be multiplying, were coming from: they were definitely not coming from beneath the kitchen floor, as they discovered to their surprise after lifting up the linoleum to check – the floor was bone dry; the linoleum, soaking wet.

Could high levels of humidity have been to blame?

Possibly. Except for the fact that according to the records, August of 1966 was a very hot and dry month. Excess moisture was in short supply. Whatever the cause, the outbreak of watery spots appearing stopped just as quickly as it had begun.

Another characteristic of poltergeist hauntings is that the phenomena are often rather playful – at least, they are *at first*. Such was the case with 30 East Drive. Later that same day, the kitchen was somehow scattered with tea leaves and sugar grains, thanks to a mechanical dispenser whose button appeared to be operating itself. This happened in plain sight of both Phillip and his grandmother, which rules out human trickery – unless you believe that they themselves were complicit, something which seems extremely unlikely… especially given the independent witness, in the form of the plumber.

The source of a strange sound that emanated from the hallway turned out to be a potted plant that normally lived at the bottom of the stairs; it had been removed from its pot and was now halfway up the staircase. Its pot was sitting at the very top. It was now early evening, and the hallway was dark: Phillip and his grandmother were able to see because the light switch flipped itself on when neither of them were standing within arm's reach of it.

The doors to one of the kitchen cupboards were being shaken violently: When Phillip summoned up the courage to look inside, he found that the cupboard contained nothing beyond its normal articles.

Banging and thudding noises started up next, coming from somewhere upstairs. It is hard to blame Phillip and his grandmother for being unable to summon up the courage to go and investigate in person.

We can only imagine what they were both feeling, but it is reasonable to assume that there was no small amount of fear running through them both. Some people find it easy to brush off the possibility of the paranormal truly taking place, dismissing it with a sneer or a laugh. That is all well and good until it happens to you personally, staring you right in the face and refusing to be ignored. Both authors of this book have had such an experience, and it's fair to say that it changes one's way of looking at the world rather drastically. Unless there was a flesh and blood intruder running amok within the house, then that left only one inescapable conclusion: 30 East Drive was haunted.

Once the initial outbreak had kicked off, it didn't take long before the haunting shifted into high gear. Now at their wits' end, the stunned residents of the house felt that they had nowhere else to turn, and so called in the police. After a thorough inspection of the house in which it was searched high and low, the somewhat nonplussed police officers admitted that there were no signs of any physical intrusion. Whatever was tormenting the Pritchard family, it did not fall within the purview of the Pontefract police – after all, how did one go about trying to arrest a ghost?

The events that would now take place at 30 East Drive would check all of the boxes of a high-intensity poltergeist episode… and many more besides. Objects flew through the air, sometimes flying as though hurled with great force, whereas on other occasions they seemed to be under the control of invisible hands and guided with great precision. Knocks, thuds, and raps sounded throughout the house at all hours of the day and night, sometimes sounding in direct response to questions or requests. Lights would turn off and on, electrical devices went haywire, objects appeared and disappeared, family photographs were slashed and torn up, and on one particularly memorable occasion – a shower of keys rained down on Mrs. Pritchard while she was cleaning the chimney flue.

One day, a neighbour came to visit Jean Pritchard for an

afternoon cup of tea. The two ladies were standing at the foot of the staircase, idly chatting about nothing in particular. Suddenly the grandmother clock which stood on the upstairs landing began to sway from side to side, before falling forward down the stairs and breaking itself to pieces where the shocked women had been standing just seconds before – they had been forced to dodge out of the way in order to avoid getting seriously injured. The clock was heavy and full of cogs and other components which could have caused them harm.

On another occasion, Jean Pritchard heard a buzzing sound emanating from within her wardrobe inside the master bedroom. Puzzled, she opened the door, only to find a swarm of bees flooding out. She was stung quite badly on multiple parts of her body and maintained that the entity which haunted the house was responsible for putting them there.

A neighbour who lived across the street from number 30 knocked on the front door one day, a rather bemused expression on his face. When Jean asked what was wrong, he wordlessly indicated the front garden, which was strewn with the records, bedding, and clothes that belonged in Diane's bedroom. They looked up and found that the window was wide open. Somebody had taken all the contents of Diane's bedroom and tossed them out of the window. Such bizarre happenings were taking place at 30 East Drive with increasing frequency. Fortunately, the sympathetic neighbour was kind enough to help Jean carry everything back upstairs again and put them back where they belonged. According to next-door neighbour and spiritualist medium Carol Fieldhouse, the same would happen with the contents of Phillip's bedroom and the master bedroom, this time the event was noticed by the window cleaner.

In a very Hollywood-like twist, there was a period in which green slime would emerge from the taps whenever they were turned on. A similar viscous substance then began to appear inside the kitchen cupboards. Unfortunately, when a sample was taken and submitted for chemical analysis, the material could not be identified. This too would cease as quickly as it started, once again without apparent explanation, leaving the house slime-free once more.

Called in to consider the possibility of an exorcism, the local vicar solemnly declared that whatever the presence was which had taken up residence at 30 East Drive, it was both unholy and evil. This malevolence was further highlighted when the type of paranormal activity took a turn for the worse, becoming more violent and angry in nature after the clergyman had visited.

Joe Pritchard was by all accounts a rough, no-nonsense working man, not particularly imaginative and certainly not one who was given to flights of fancy. He was the last one to truly accept that 30 East Drive could be haunted and dismissed much of the early activity with a wave of the hand and a laugh. Things finally came to a head one day when Joe went into the coal house, a cupboard next to the downstairs toilet used for the storage of coal supplies.

What happened to Joe inside the coal house that fateful day remains unclear, but the few who heard him talk about it have said that he was attacked by some invisible force or malevolent entity. Those who knew him say that *Joe Pritchard* (right) emerged from the coal house a changed man, his will and spirit completely broken. Never again would he scoff at the possibility of his home being haunted.

Yet if 'Fred,' as he became known by the Pritchards (perhaps as a way of attempting to normalise the entity's presence) had an affinity for anybody in the family, it seemed to be Diane. In what can only be described as an ambush, the teenager was heading to bed one night when she suddenly found the hallway plunged into darkness. Colin Wilson reports that, in conjunction with the air suddenly turning ice cold, a looming dark shadow appeared in the hallway. Suddenly, an unseen force took hold of an extremely hefty wooden hall stand and used it to pin the terrified Diane down.

What is most remarkable about the nature of this particular occurrence is the sheer amount of *finesse* required on the part of 'Fred.' Consider just how difficult it would be for an extremely strong and fit man to lift such a heavy piece of furniture, manoeuvre it through the air and use it to pin down a young woman; he would have to use just enough force to keep the stand in place. It is a kind of 'Goldilocks effect.' Use too much force, and the stand could be lifted up and away from the trapped adolescent; use too little, and the sheer weight of the furniture would crush her. Wilson documents that while Diane was struggling, Phillip and Mrs. Pritchard were unable to pull the hall stand off her. Yet when she relaxed, at the suggestion of her mother, they were suddenly able to manoeuvre it free and clear.

In terms of both the amount of energy required to pull off such a feat and also the very precise way in which it would have had to have been employed, this particular episode was one which ought to baffle every single physicist alive today. It must also be pointed out that 'Fred' could easily have caused great physical harm to Diane, if it had chosen to do so – yet she escaped without a scratch from her ordeal. One is forced to conclude that 'Fred''s motivation must have been to instil as much fear in her as possible, for this went well beyond the practical jokes and pranking for which poltergeists are usually renowned.

The entity plainly wanted to scare her, but not harm her… for now, at least.

The first sighting of the infamous Black Monk was made by Joe and Jean as they lay in bed one night. Their bedroom door had just opened itself, and the astonished couple caught sight of a dark, robed figure standing in the doorway, its face obscured beneath a black hood. The apparition disappeared before Joe had a chance to get out of bed and investigate.

It was only after comparing notes with Elsie May Mountain next door that Jean learned her neighbour had seen the same figure, but this time standing behind her in the kitchen while she was engaged at the sink. 'Fred' would also be seen by a family friend, and by both of the Pritchard children.

The entity's interest in Diane reached a terrifying apogee when a hysterical Diane was dragged up the staircase by an unseen force, in full view of her mother and brother. The incident left noticeable bruising on the throat of its victim and sent notice to the Pritchard family that 'Fred' was capable of far more than simple mischief if he so chose.

There were a few more instances of poltergeist-like phenomena, though fortunately nothing that caused any physical harm to the family. And then, just like that, the phenomena stopped. Phillip claimed to have seen a black figure disappearing into the floor of the house one day, and suddenly peace and quiet returned to 30 East Drive.

After two years, the Pritchard family's nightmare was finally over.

Or so they thought.

After being *headline news* (right) during its peak, the Black Monk of Pontefract case once again gained prominence when Colin Wilson published his book. For the Pritchard family, some small degree of fame (and perhaps notoriety) came along with *Poltergeist!* and yet they did not benefit financially from their involvement with Mr. Wilson.

Diane and Phillip grew up and moved out, as children tend to do, going on to have lives of their own. Sadly, Joe Pritchard passed away inside the house on June 21st, 1986, dying on the floor of the upstairs bathroom. The coroner ruled that he had died of a heart attack.

Jean Pritchard continued to live at number 30 for the next 25 years (right), mostly alone with just a parrot for company. As we shall learn later, it appears that she had not seen the last of 'Fred.'

CHAPTER THREE

The Domino Effect

The director of the movie *When the Lights Went Out* (right), Pat Holden, had a very personal stake in the film. Jean Pritchard was the sister to one of Pat's Aunties, and his mother Irene Holden regularly visited the house during the hauntings and was very supportive of Jean throughout.

Though not a direct relative, Pat thought of Jean as an Aunty – in those days any adult close to the family was referred to as Aunty or Uncle as a matter of respect. Pat himself never had the opportunity to visit the house during the hauntings because he was too young. Never-the-less, he would listen to the stories his mother would tell the family with great interest, and excitedly share in the buzz that the events generated throughout the neighbourhood, which understandably led to a fascination with the place and to the eventual writing and directing of *When the Lights Went Out*.

However, despite popular belief, none of *When the Lights Went Out* was shot at 30 East Drive. Instead Pat had the house interiors re-created in superb detail in a large film studio in Huddersfield, a few miles from 30 East Drive, and *a location in Huddersfield was selected for the exteriors* (right). The reason for the build for the interiors was in part because of the convenience of manoeuvring a large film crew around a set, optimum camera angles and so on, but one would be forgiven for assuming that at least the exteriors were of the actual house? But at the time of filming it was assumed that Jean was still very much in residence, so both *Pat Holden, the director and Bil Bungay, the producer* (left) made a conscious decision to steer well clear of Jean for fear of creating undue stress for her in her old age.

It wasn't until the film was completely finished, and Bil began searching for innovative ways in which to promote the movie, that their assumption proved wildly incorrect and an incredible opportunity was missed.

With a background in advertising that went back for many years, Bil wanted to do something a little more memorable than the usual process of distributing trailers, posters, and press interviews – something truly unique. Something *newsworthy*.

Was it serendipity, or did the house somehow draw Bil to it? By an extraordinary coincidence, one of Bil's advertising clients at the time happened to be a confectionary producer in Pontefract: they were the makers of Pontefract cakes, a treat as black as the Black Monk of Pontefract himself, made from the liquorice root said to have been grown in monastic gardens back in the 16th century.

Bil suddenly found himself on the train to Pontefract for the first time. It was almost inevitable that he would make the short taxi ride to East Drive after his meeting had concluded. Suddenly, there it was: the infamous 30 East Drive – the house that, despite his scepticism, had held such great fascination for Bil for well over a decade, to the point of making a theatrical movie about it.

His first reaction to the house was one of truly mixed emotions. It looked like an ordinary ex-council semi-detach; modest, a little run-down, in need of some TLC. It felt rejected, friendless, alone but also strangely ominous and threatening. It was almost as if some kind of mist shielded the house.

"I felt that I couldn't really observe it properly," Bil recollects, "it definitely felt otherworldly. I was drawn to it, but at the same time had a strong sense that it was somehow warning me away.

"But what's that? A *For Sale sign* (right)? Don't tell me it's for sale?" It turned out that 30 East Drive had been on the market for nearly four years, after Jean had moved to a local retirement home. "We could have filmed with the actual house dammit!" What an opportunity missed!

On the other hand, it had somewhat unsurprisingly failed to sell, its reputation too legendary for any local to want to purchase it, which meant that it was cheap. Could it be the newsworthy idea that Bil was looking for? He could buy it, use it to promote *When the Lights Went Out*, then do it up and sell it? After all, there was "*no way* that the house was still haunted, not after all these years?" Bil reasoned "assuming, of course, that there had ever been any truth in the legend in the first place. And even if there was, poltergeists only stayed for a short while until their source of energy in the form of a pubescent teen has been exhausted… didn't they?"

Bil was a rational man, not one who *really* believed in ghosts and things that went bump in the night. Indeed, the only reason he had made *When the Lights Went Out* in the first place was because of the irresistible story line: 'Poltergeist moves into council house.' After all, they are traditionally associated with large dusty mansion houses, or dark dank castles. Who wouldn't want to watch that movie?

He would soon learn just how misguided his scepticism was.

The availability of 30 East Drive seemed like an unmissable opportunity, and it wasn't long before Bil had signed the necessary paperwork and had *the keys to one of the world's most haunted houses* (left). It was amusing to note that the *Sales Progression Team for the estate agent was ironically located in Goole* (right).

Some movies have their premiere screenings in London's Leicester Square, and whilst *When the Lights Went Out* did have a Leicester Square premiere, its actual premiere was somewhere entirely more appropriate: in the living room of the very same house in which the Black Monk was said to have terrorised the Pritchard family fifty years before. As marketing events went, it was unprecedented, and two lucky competition winners found themselves nervously walking along the tiny, footpath-wide red carpet up to the unassuming side door of number 30.

Standing just in front of the house, Paul and Chris, the two 'lucky' (if that's the right word) attendees were asked what on Earth they were thinking by stepping foot inside the house where 'Fred' was still supposed to be lurking. The lads replied that they were both sceptical but open-minded and hadn't wanted to pass up such a unique opportunity. With a knowing wink, radio chat show host, author and host for the evening, Sam Delaney provided them with a *box containing several crucifixes* (left) ("in case one or two didn't work"), communion wine, a Bible, and a small bottle of holy water... along with a clove of garlic, presumably in case some vampires wanted to crash the horror movie screening!

Paul and Chris enjoyed the film by all accounts but were not disturbed by anything ghostly, adding weight to Bil's firm belief that the house was void of anything paranormal. Publicity work on the film continued apace. Bil hosted a small get-together at the house, bringing together some of the stars of the film. The film was beginning to generate some PR buzz, and interest in 30 East Drive was on the rise evidenced by growing numbers of people turning up outside the house at all hours of the day and night.

It was at the first of the PR events that Bil was to meet next-door neighbour and medium Carol Fieldhouse. Before Bil had a chance to formally introduce himself, she warned Bil in a matter of fact way. "He's here right now and he's given you a year to get out."

"Erm, hi, I'm Bil… and *you are*?"

"Carol, I'm your neighbour, your tenant is over there."

"And who might that be?"

"The Black Monk."

"Right. And he's here right now, is he?"

"Yes, he's stood at the bottom of the stairs, watching."

Bil turned to look. He couldn't see anybody standing here, least of all a tall monk in a hooded black robe.

"Give over Carol! Do I look like I believe in ghosts? Erm… one year you say? Is that a year of ownership or a year of residency? As I've no intention of living here!"

"But I thought you didn't believe in ghosts?"

"I don't, it's my neighbour I'm worried about!"

Bil nevertheless found himself wondering whether Carol truly knew something he didn't. She seemed totally sincere, and unbeknownst to him, he would develop a healthy respect over the coming months for not only Carol, but also for 'Fred' himself.

Carol went on to explain that the resident ghost didn't allow himself to be limited by something as mundane as a brick wall. 'Fred' liked to make his presence known in Carol's own house, when he wasn't stomping around empty number 30. She would lay in bed at night and hear bangs, crashes, voices, and heavy footsteps coming from the house next door.

After discovering that Jean had moved out, and out of respect for what had been Jean's home for over half a century, Carol felt a responsibility to keep an eye on the place. At first, she has thought that the empty house was being broken into, but whenever she went to carefully inspect the front, side and back doors and all the windows – everything was always locked and secure; the lights were off, and no 'flesh and blood' visitors could be seen through the curtain-less windows.

Bil did his best to hide his innate scepticism when it came to the house being genuinely haunted. After all, you found ghosts in ancient castles and ramshackle old manor houses, not in the middle of busy 21st-century council estates... right?

Then things began to take a turn toward the strange.

At the first PR event and Bil's second visit to the house (the first being a quick viewing of the property *after* buying it), Bil handed his iPhone to a special guest named Lisa Manning, who coincidentally was living with her own violent poltergeist at the time (we will learn a little of Lisa's case soon). Lisa steadied herself to take a photo of Bil alongside two of the stars of *When the Lights Went Out*. "Oh, the phone has just died!" she exclaimed.

Bil was nonplussed to discover that his trusty iPhone died on the spot, going from a 75% charge to stone cold dead in the space of a few seconds. It had never behaved like that before and didn't ever do so afterward. Plugging the phone in, Bil allowed it to recharge for a couple of hours before switching it back on and skimming through the photo library. He was disappointed to find that the photograph of himself and stars Tasha Connor and Hannah Clifford hadn't been taken. Grumbling, he was still more willing to write off the loss as being the fault of Steve Jobs rather than the Black Monk of Pontefract.

Things looked a lot different several weeks later when a spookily *blurred image of Bil and the two actresses* (left) suddenly appeared on the home screen of his phone. He had carefully checked through the contents of his photo library several times and was absolutely certain that the picture hadn't been in his phone. The picture had never been taken.

It must be pointed out that such unexplained power drains are very common at haunted locations. Richard has experienced them on multiple occasions over the years, most recently at the historic Stanley Hotel in Estes Park, Colorado (inspiration for Stephen King's *The Shining)* and on the battlefield at Gettysburg.

Bil's disappearing and reappearing picture phenomenon, however, seems to be a little less common. It would be far from the last technical malfunction that took place within the walls of 30

East Drive.

Bil kept in contact with Carol over the following months, occasionally stopping by to look in on his purchase. Carol always had hair-raising new stories to tell. The loud noises coming from inside the empty house were getting more frequent and more intense; usually at around three or four o'clock in the morning – yet whenever she checked, the door and window locks were all secure: It seemed that 'Fred' was determined to continue to make his presence felt, perhaps out of frustration at not having Jean to pester anymore.

The paranormal activity still continued to bleed across the dividing wall into her own home next door. She reported seeing balls of blue light floating through the corridors. Perhaps even more alarming was the incident in which the duvet on her son's bed was discovered to have been moulded into a distinct human shape. This caused a significant amount of distress to Carol's son.

Despite the sheer volume of Carol's anecdotes, Bil was still determined to take the ghost stories with a hefty grain of salt. After all, with the exception of a questionable camera–phone power malfunction, which could quite easily be written off as a one-time anomaly, he hadn't personally experienced anything in the house that might be considered truly paranormal... yet.

The arrival of a documentary camera crew changed everything. They wanted to record a short film titled *Can You Brave a Haunted*

House (right) for Bing, the search engine. The crew interviewed a number of local people – including a police constable – who were all too happy to talk about 30 East Drive's ghostly reputation in front of the cameras. "Something doesn't feel right," one of the visitors claims while standing at the foot of the stairs.

"Would you like to follow me up?" Carol asks. "Whatever you do," she advises the obviously nervous visitor, "hold on, because his party piece is to push you downstairs if you don't."

Both guests are taken aback when Carol tells them that two spirit people are standing in the bedroom next to them, watching their every move. Finding the atmosphere just a little too heavy to cope with, a distressed Carol steps out onto the landing in order to compose herself. When she has, she tells the incredulous female visitor that the spirits "will probably have a bit of fun with you tonight."

Cue some scary music, some crystal divination, and the segment is over. No real evidence was shown, and yet when Bil turned up to visit the crew at the end of the shoot, he learned of some puzzling events that had taken place off-camera. For one thing, the kettle had taken to switching itself on despite nobody standing anywhere near it. Shrugging, they had written it off as a simple electrical glitch... the first few times, at least.

The small crew had slept in the house, and one of them had woken up in a state of fright, convinced that they were being held down on the mattress by some unseen force. This was in the smallest bedroom (Diane Pritchard's old room) located at the front of the house. Determined to find a rational explanation, the crew concluded that perhaps their colleague had simply suffered a night terror; after all, just stepping foot inside a house with a reputation like that of 30 East Drive makes one predisposed toward interpreting everyday experiences as being something ghostly. Maybe this was simply a nightmare, a trick of the mind, a sleepy central nervous system in the process of waking itself up? Plus, she confessed to having had night terrors before, when she was *three*.

But then, how to explain the fact that one of the producers had lost a bundle of keys, leaving them stranded in Pontefract unable to return to London? After searching the house high and low, the keys finally turned up in the belly of an old 1970s-era vacuum cleaner that Bil had bought at a charity shop in order to add a bit of ambience to the house. There was just the little detail that the vacuum cleaner didn't actually work, and therefore couldn't have sucked up the keys in the first place... and even had it been able to, how could it possibly have happened without everybody in the house hearing the vacuum cleaner (which wasn't plugged in at the wall anyway) start itself up – let alone having the power to suck up a heavy set of keys?

This harkens back to some of the original poltergeist activity at 30 East Drive, as documented by Colin Wilson and frequently recounted by Jean Pritchard. One morning, Jean was on her hands and knees cleaning out the kitchen flue, when some keys rained down on her from somewhere up above. A couple of the keys seemed to be much older than the others and hadn't originated from anywhere inside the house that the family knew of. Such appearances of everyday objects seemingly from thin air – known as *apports* or *apportations* – are a hallmark of the poltergeist-type case.

Although Bil was perfectly willing to write all of this off as just the latest in the string of bizarre occurrences that the house was reputed for, he was about to have his own brush with the spirits of 30 East Drive. It was getting on for two o'clock in the morning when the film crew finished packing and had left for London, leaving Bil and a couple of helpers in order to tidy the house a little and lock it up securely.

The night was cold, clear and completely still – no wind at all. Bil went outside and walked around to the side of the house, taking a moment to look up and down the length of East Drive.

The streets were empty, with most residents of the Chequerfield Estate having long since gone to bed.

Bil had taken on the glamorous task of litter patrol, wondering around the grounds looking for bits of rubbish that may have been inadvertently dropped by the visiting film crew. After dropping the last bits of rubbish into the dustbin, he went over to the concrete apron where cars were usually parked, with the intent of closing the double wrought-iron gates to the street, that had been left partially open in the wake of the film crew. Bil closed it and made sure to drop the locking bar into its small post-hole in the concrete. He made absolutely certain that both halves of the gate were firmly closed, going so far as to move a *heavy cement block up against them both* (left) to ensure that they were properly secured. Anybody wanting to gain entry to the driveway would have to give the gates one almighty shove in order to get them open.

"Right," Bil said to himself, heading back around to the front of the house, "it's time to lock the place up and get out of here."

Just then, his two helpers emerged from the front door. He couldn't help smiling at the slightly nervous spring in their step, at the body language which said that they were really looking forward to getting out of the house for the night. It was becoming an increasingly common reaction from visitors to 30 East Drive: an almost tangible sense of unease, the feeling of being watched by someone who most definitely didn't want any company, thank you very much.

"Ready to go?" Bil asked. The helpers both nodded, trying not to appear too eager. "Fair enough. I'll just lock the door and then we'll get out of—" He froze in mid-sentence, looking in the direction of the gate.

"It's open. It's completely open, I just shut it – the gate!" Without a sound, or catching Bil's eye, one half of the gate had swung wide open once again, a full 90 degrees. His mouth gaped open in shock and the hairs on the back of his neck jumped to attention. It had been a little over a minute since he had closed it and wedged the concrete block up against it. Now that same concrete block was sitting off to one side of the open gate, almost as though somebody had pushed it aside as an afterthought.

Bil was genuinely flummoxed. This didn't make any sense at all. He knew, with one hundred percent certainty, that he had closed and locked that gate. Yet there it was, swinging wide open, practically taunting him to come up with a rational explanation for how it could possibly have happened. "You are on high alert in that place, which means that you think very carefully about all of your actions" Bil comments. "I remember very clearly closing the gate and putting my back into pushing the concrete block into place, the gate was as secure as it could have been without a lock. I very deliberately and consciously closed and secured it!"

Could it possibly have been a prankster walking by – one who had seen Bil shutting the gate and was now trying to mess with him? Highly unlikely. The streets were deserted, and it was bitterly cold – cold enough to deter even the most determined prankster. Besides, there were no proper hiding places where any such practical joker could have hidden: Bil had specifically looked up and down the street when he was shutting the gate and had enjoyed a clear view of the gate the entire time. Neither was there a slope on the driveway, or any ice on the ground that day to have at least offered a possible explanation for how the block slid, thereby allowing the gate to silently pop back open (but that still wouldn't account for the iron locking rod popping out of its hole). Pushing the block into place had taken *a lot* of effort against the rough surface of the driveway.

Might it have been the wind then? Bil dismissed that idea straight away. Nothing short of a hurricane-force gale could have opened that gate, and the leaves were barely moving in the trees.

What about the helpers – could they be trying to spook him, having a little fun with Bil and his haunted house? Also highly unlikely. Both of them had been upstairs since the film crew had left, putting up a lampshade (in the dark, no less!). Neither of them could have gotten down and past Bil and the only unlocked door without his having seen them, and besides, why would they bother pulling such a stunt? They would also need to have done so in absolute silence, something almost impossible to pull off on a calm and quiet night when there is very little ambient sound to mask one's movements.

That was when pragmatic advertising executive and movie producer Bil Bungay truly came to believe that 30 East Drive was indeed haunted. It is an opinion that has only strengthened with time, thanks to the steady stream of eyewitness accounts from friends, acquaintances and strangers alike that poured in over the course of the next few years.

The next day, Bil was reluctantly forced to call in a locksmith in order to replace the entire front door lock, as the keys were nowhere to be found. As he watched the man work, Carol wandered over from next door to say hello. Bil told her about the gate. She nodded sagely as he spoke, and then nonchalantly explained that this sort of thing happened all the time where 'Fred' was concerned.

Bil was struggling to continue to deny the existence of... well, *something* uncanny inside his house, and 'Fred' seemed as good a name as any to call 'It' by. Somehow, putting a label on the unseen force made it a little less scary. But just a little.

Still, he desperately needed proof that he wasn't imagining things, that he wasn't simply losing his marbles – what he had already experienced was just so inexplicable, so ludicrous. Who better, then, to validate his experiences than Gordon Mac, famous founder of Kiss FM, and paranormal cynic Massimo? Who better than a grounded fella like Gordon to confirm that Bil was or was not just going around the bend?

Gordon enthusiastically agreed to run a Halloween promotion on his new radio station Mi-Soul, where the prize was for the winner to join Gordon and his wife Debra for a night at number 30. The draw was made and unsurprisingly, the winner failed to claim their prize, much to Gordon's chagrin. A second prize draw was made, and a more willing winner was selected.

After a lengthy drive from London up to Pontefract, with Gordon more or less committing himself to the 'Bil's a nutter' camp, they all arrived at the house.

The following is taken from an account of their visit, written by Gordon's wife, Debra:

If you are at all jumpy and have a weak tolerance for the paranormal, then you might want to look away now…

It all started at the London, Leicester Square film premiere of When the Lights Went Out. *The Producer, Bil Bungay, is a friend, and when we found out what the film was about, we just couldn't resist.*

Having a drink in the bar afterwards, I mentioned to Bil how cool it would be to stay in the house and experience it first-hand, only to get the reply "You CAN, I've bought it." It was at this point that I realised that my fly-away comment had to be executed through to the end.

The rest, as they say, is history…

Mi-Soul radio ran a competition for two 'lucky' winners to join us crazy cats in staying the night in the Pritchard's' home (names changed to Maynard in the film) where all the horrific happenings took place back in the 1970s.

George Kay pulled the winning name out of a hat during his Friday evening show, and we set a date to visit 30 East Drive in Pontefract, West Yorkshire.

Sadly, ten days before the trip, our winner vanished, never to be heard from again (can't see why!). We picked a runner-up called Delia, who brought along her friend Lucy for the ride.

The anticipation of what may unfold made for a nervous ride up the M1. We realised that we had all packed poltergeist-fighting equipment such as salt, sage, crucifixes and garlic. All the while my husband and our driver, Gordon, chuckled to himself in disbelief and slight embarrassment.

On arrival we met the lovely neighbours, Carol and Darren, who did a very good job of near enough freaking us out. Darren, who has lived next door all his life, and his partner Carol, a spiritualist medium, live on a daily basis with what we had come up to experience. They gave us a guided tour of 30 East Drive and told some of the history of the Black Monk of Pontefract, including some of the things that they had both personally witnessed.

We started the tour in the living room. The furniture and carpets were a moment frozen in time, adding to the authenticity of the whole experience.

Carol led us to the hall by torchlight, only to drop the bombshell that 'the monk was standing on the stairs, but it's OK.' I quickly asked if we could wait until he moved, but we didn't have a choice in the matter. Up the stairs we marched, straight to the bedroom of the young girl who was tormented by the spirit(s).

We huddled (embarrassingly) like sheep in one corner of Diane Pritchard's old bedroom, and as if that wasn't bad enough,

Carol showed us the dents in the ceiling where the bed had been flipped up vertically, throwing Diane off it.

We speedily moved on to the Joe and Jean's old bedroom, where we were introduced to a long light cord that allegedly strangles people – not to mention the wardrobe that has drawers that open and close of their own accord. We moved swiftly on...

The third bedroom, Phillip's old bedroom, was thankfully not as disturbing as the first two... but then we were led to the bathroom. Carol, who allegedly feels quite at ease with ghosts, wouldn't enter for all the money in the world. If anyone didn't feel uneasy before this, then they did now. It was explained to us that it's the most active room in the house as it's a portal to the spirit world (right).

After a blessing, only Gordon and I ventured in to have a look. We returned to the living room and while they were settling us in an inexplicable thing happened: a penny miraculously dropped from what seemed to be the window ledge, bounced off the radiator and rolled under a table. We all heard it and, out of the corner of our eyes – saw it!

Carol and Darren then left us to our own devices, and to watch the film When the Lights Went Out. *The film is true to actual events that happened in the house in the early 1970s. 'Are you crazy?' I hear you say, and at that point, yes, we thought we were!*

Even though Gordon and I had already seen the movie,

watching it in the house was a terrifying prospect that gave us more chills than we ever thought possible, but it was a once in a lifetime experience that we were determined not to miss!

Throughout the film and the night, we heard knocks, creeks and bangs – all the signs you'd expect from a haunted house – but Gordon always found a way of calming everyone down with rational explanations.

As the clock approached 2am, we were all ready to crash (left), *as it had been an exhausting adrenaline-fueled day. Bil had gone all-out to try and make us feel comfortable, putting beds in each of the bedrooms – but we soon realised that no-one was prepared to risk going upstairs, let alone sleeping up there! Instead, the winners huddled on the sofa while we slept on the original 1970s carpet (three layers of clothes, shoes on – no, we weren't scared!)*

That was the beginning of a VERY *long night…*

Lucy, who had been fearlessly telling us how she was into the paranormal and not to be scared, ended up keeping poor, frightened (very polite) Delia awake all night and was adamant that we had to stay awake too!

I woke feeling stiff, but surprisingly fresh, considering the circumstances. We broke open the croissants, brewed mugs of tea and caught up on the events of the night.

Delia began by revealing that she had heard numerous knocks and noises coming from a wall separating the kitchen from the living room – but we were the only people in the house! Gordon's theory was that the likely culprit was the central heating system that hadn't been turned on in a while.

Then Lucy nervously revealed that she had seen a dark mist cross the living room, followed by a 6ft tall shadow of a man, disappearing into the wall. Gordon put this down to self-induced sleep deprivation, although Bil has subsequently confirmed that Carol has witnessed the monk passing back and forth between number 30 and her house next door.

I then had the courage to disclose something that had freaked me out. While I was dropping off to sleep laying on my side, hood up, duvet over my head and in the foetal position, I felt what I truly believe to be a finger draw a circle in the middle of my back.

Yes, I KNOW I sound crazy, but there is no rational explanation for it. I said nothing and tried to sleep as I thought no one would believe me, and besides, I didn't want to cause a stampede to the comfy and safe SUV parked outside!

After sharing everything, including Delia revealing that I had had a kicking, screaming night terror "That was no normal nightmare." Gordon remarked how our experiences were all witnessed by individuals and not by the group as a whole. Literally ten seconds later, the TV turned itself off. Silence.

Gordon ('Mr. I have a rational explanation for everything') impatiently asked who had the remote, only to discover that it was on the mantelpiece behind him. He tried to turn the TV back on with the remote, only to find that it wasn't on standby or on a timer – it had been turned off AT THE WALL.

We decided it was time leave, as we felt we'd overstayed our welcome! The TV switching off and the penny falling from the window ledge, things that we all experienced together, were enough to prove that there really is either a poltergeist or some inexplicable form of energy in that house to this day.

When I say 'We,' the penny dropped for Gordon too!

Debra Mac

When Gordon got back home on the Sunday evening, he spent a good hour on the phone to Bil, regaling him with his experiences, "If Gordon can come back 'a believer,' thought Bil, perhaps I am not going crazy after all!"

Most of the people that live on East Drive are friendly folk, and all seem to have their opinions about the infamous haunted house. These range from 'It's all made up.' to 'That house is evil.' and everything in between. Occasionally a local resident will make a request in relation to the house, such as using it to host a charity fundraiser (Bil loves the paradox of such a dark force doing so much positive for local causes), or to pop in with their wide-eyed children for a quick visit to say they have been in the infamous house 'around the corner,' often getting given a marble 'thrown by a poltergeist' as a souvenir. Perhaps one of the strangest requests came from a local who complained that 'It' would run along the back gardens behind the houses of East Drive and Chequerfield Road and 'could Bil keep a tighter rein on the ghost' – as if he somehow could. The request is intriguing as it is local knowledge that an ancient water course, presumably the one that feeds the well under 30 East Drive, runs off the hill, under the back gardens towards the valley below, making one wonder if this somehow supports the theory that poltergeists aren't purely reliant on the energy coursing through adolescents for their power source, but can extract energy from flowing water too. Based on this powerful out-of-the-blue eyewitness account, one could hypothesise that 'Fred' can move wherever there is a flowing water source, a little like a Scalextric car following the source of electricity beneath its contacts.

It also raises another interesting point: If the haunting is not entirely confined to 30 East Drive, but rather extends across the entire Chequerfield Estate, possibly due to the water course running its length, could it be possible that multiple entities are at work – possibly the remnants of the bloody battle which took place there during the Civil War? The possibility is an intriguing one. Although some residents of the estate like to remain tight-lipped when it comes to ghost stories, particularly if outsiders are the ones asking the questions, others will freely and frankly admit to having ghost stories of their own. Could 'Fred' really be responsible for it *all?* Or is there a bigger force at work here? It is our view that the jury is still out.

To this day, Bil takes great care to show 'Fred' respect and due deference. He is very open about the fact that he wants the spirit to leave him well alone, and at the time of writing Bil has never spent the night at 30 East Drive. An uneasy detente seems to exist between Bil and 'Fred,' a case of 'let's leave one another well alone, shall we?' It is a policy that Bil has no intention of changing in the foreseeable future, because he has no desire whatsoever to antagonise his ghostly tenant: it is for this reason that Bil has flatly banned the use of Ouija boards on the premises, and promptly throws out on the spot any visitor who breaks the rule. Even Richard and his team were not permitted to use a spirit board of any kind during their stay, a rule which they respected without question – and yet still somehow managed to get on 'Fred''s bad side.

As time went on, the stories and *emails continued to come in* (right). It became almost a rite of passage for Bil's circle of friends and acquaintances to spend the night at 30 East Drive, and while some had quiet nights, many had new accounts of inexplicable occurrences to add to the growing list. Perhaps the most common happening was the appearance of icy cold spots inside the house, seemingly at random times and places. This would happen on the hottest summer days and the coldest winter nights, when the central heating system was working at full capacity.

It seemed that whatever was in the house enjoyed playing with the central heating system, and with just about the only item in the house from the 21st century apart from the fridge – the portable thermostat. The first film crew to stay there for a week reported the thermostat going missing constantly. Bil himself unwittingly photographed the *errant thermostat on Diane's bed* (left) one time; it had somehow made its way upstairs from its usual location on the kitchen mantelpiece.

Determined to get to the bottom of this, Bil invited another group of close friends to spend the night in the house: *Gary, Jane, Suzi, and Bil's wife Nelly* (right). Gary, among other things, is a trained heating engineer. He quickly noticed that the central heating was on full, so he turned all the radiators down physically, one by one.

The following morning, after what seemed to be a quiet night – indeed Nelly described sleeping there as "One of the best night's sleep I've had in ages," (though she puts that down to the protection spell she kindly received from Sue, a local healer, before entering the house) – *all* of the radiators had been manually cranked up to their maximum setting. The control knobs had each been physically turned, something which requires no small amount of twisting force.

Gary was baffled – unless somebody had been inside the house that night, there was no rational explanation for what had happened... and yet, there it was for all to see; a ghost that was trying to warm itself up, or a paranormal prankster showing off for an audience? Either way, there was no denying the reality of what happened.

Crossing over the threshold of 30 East Drive is like going back in time, setting foot in the 1960s and 1970s. The TV screen is covered with a printed cloth showing the infamous young *girl with a chalkboard* (right) that used to grace the BBC2 airwaves back then, something that every British child of that era will remember. A row of Betamax video tapes lines one of the living room shelves, which are also crammed with children's toys and boxed games. 'Fred' seems to delight in playing with them, and if visitors are lucky enough to catch him in the right mood, they may even get to catch him in the act... or at the very least, witness the after-effects.

One day, Bil walked into the house unannounced to find Darren from the house next door kneeling on the living room floor, swearing and grumbling under his breath. Scattered around him all across the carpet were pieces of a jigsaw puzzle that Bil had purchased at a local charity shop. The rub was that the puzzle box had been sealed with Sellotape when he had bought it and was still sealed now – it appeared that 'Fred' had somehow managed to transport the pieces out of the box without actually opening it. We will consider how this might have happened in the final chapter of this book. The tape running around the rim of the box was undisturbed, which was more than could be said for Bil and Darren. A frustrated Darren ripped the side of the box away in Bil's presence and returned the missing pieces. He didn't bother sealing the box again... after all, what would have been the point?

Even had Bil been tempted to dismiss the incident with the gate opening by itself as being non-paranormal in nature (something of which he has never quite managed to convince himself) then what happened next would have settled the issue once and for all. It was Valentine's Day 2016. Bil was visiting the house for one of his periodic inspections. Having first greeted 'Fred' in his usual manner ("Hi 'Fred,' it's only me, I hope you are OK? Please don't freak me out – I am not sure your landlord's heart can take it!") he then greeted the *East Drive Paranormal* team and caretakers busying away tidying the house for the evening's guests, did his usual scan of the house to check all was in order then went to the kitchen sink to wash up some cups and dishes that had been left behind by some recent visitors.

While the crockery clattered in the sink, he was thinking about the last time that he had stood at the same sink alone in the kitchen (indeed, alone in the entire house on this particular occasion) performing the same mundane task, when he had suddenly heard footsteps upstairs, followed by the sound of knocking coming from the kitchen cabinet to his lower left – as if someone or something was inside the cupboard. The knocking began mere seconds after the footsteps had abated.

After a few moments had passed, Bil suddenly got the strangest sensation that he wasn't alone in the room, that there was actually somebody behind him. Perhaps Carol, Darren or one of her team had snuck into the kitchen, but then again – perhaps not? In a scene that wouldn't have been out of place in a horror movie, he turned his head slowly, his imagination half-expecting to see the Black Monk standing there, as once experienced by Jean Pritchard on exactly the same spot four decades earlier. But instead of a dreamt-up, fictional Hollywood moment, something truly extraordinary and real happened instead. A small object popped into existence in mid-air to the left of the folded dining room table and came flying through the air in a ballistic arc, heading directly toward Bil's face.

He flinched, certain that the object, whatever it was, was going to smack him right between the eyes, but it veered off slightly at the last moment, changing course fractionally in mid-air and caroming off the kitchen window before bouncing off the draining board and clattering onto the kitchen floor.

Shocked by his close call, Bil uttered a few choice (but unprintable) words and bent down to examine the projectile. It was a small wooden domino.

Carol and her team came running into the kitchen, alarmed by Bil's reaction. Could it have been any of them, he wondered? But he had literally *seen* the bloody thing materialise with his own two eyes. He was completely alone in the kitchen when it happened. He wasn't hallucinating, as the small rectangle in the palm of his hand definitively proved. He had witnessed something undeniably paranormal: the materialisation of a solid object in thin air, and he was one hundred percent sure about what he had witnessed.

Bil kept the domino as a memento (left), and still has it to this day. It's a mundane object with an extraordinary story that became the catalyst for this book; because as Bil says, *"When an object materialises out of thin air before your very eyes – you write a book."*

Although he didn't know it at the time, Bil's experience of narrowly avoiding being hit by a flying projectile is a common occurrence in poltergeist cases. Quite often observers will catch an object mid-flight, become totally convinced that it is going to hit them in the face, only to have it change its trajectory at the very last second.

"Thanks, 'Fred.' I've always wanted to see that," he exclaimed, "now, how the hell did you do that?!" Bil was still coming to terms with the worldview-changing personal experience. He had finally been offered something that none of the countless second-hand eyewitness reports could have given him;

incontrovertible proof that 30 East Drive was home to something truly and extraordinarily paranormal. But *what* exactly?

He soon came to regret having expressed his gratitude. For the next two hours, Bil was greeted with more projectiles of all shapes and sizes. Sticking with the toy theme that the invisible entity had now established, the next object was a marble, which passed through the kitchen ceiling without leaving a trace and smacked into the piano fallboard with such force that it chipped the heavily-varnished surface, exposing the bare wood underneath. Bil cared less about the minor damage to the old piano than the fact that the marble had come within a whisker of hitting his ear.

"I felt it breeze past my right ear," he remembers "it was as close as it could have gotten without hitting me, and at the speed it was travelling, it would most certainly have smarted."

'Fred' then graduated from throwing marbles to chucking screws, and in a prank that didn't seem particularly funny to Bil, three large screws shot down from the ceiling in Diane's bedroom, passing on either side of his head. Once again, their sharpened tips missed Bil's ears by millimetres.

A little later, he was in the kitchen, engaged in face to face conversation with Carol, when he suddenly watched a red plastic ball materialise in the air just over her right shoulder. As before, he barely had time to try and duck away, before the ball came flying through the air, directly at his face. Fortunately, it missed by a narrow margin just like all of the other objects had – only, unlike the other objects, it occurred to Bil that it would have been highly amusing, rather than painful, had this lightweight trigger object struck Bil right between the eyes!

Perhaps the creepiest incident took place when Bil, Carol, and her team of caretakers were sitting in the living room chatting before Bil's return to London. The mood was light, and there was a lot of laughter as they discussed 'Fred''s various pranks and tricks that afternoon, with everyone enjoying the fact that Bil had been the target of all of the activity – activity that was all too familiar to Carol and her group. Bil was blown away by what he had witnessed.

"Perhaps it's love?" one of the team remarked, it *was* Valentine's Day after all. Suddenly there was a little 'pop!' followed by the sound of something light and plastic hitting the floor through the open doorway that led into the kitchen, "What was that?" came a chorus from the front room.

Carol climbed out of her favourite seat (the armchair in the corner of the front room) to go and investigate and found that her young grand-daughter had just wandered in through the front door in search of her grandmother, and was stood *sinking her teeth into a brightly-coloured polystyrene orange* (right).

"Don't bite that, sweetheart," Carol said, gently taking the fake piece of fruit from her grand-daughter's hand, "it's not a real orange. Where did you get it from?"

"The man in black gave it to me, Nana."

The man in black. Everyone present heard what she had said, and they all knew exactly who would fit that description. There was a bowl of faux fruit, and other objects (including the red plastic ball Bil had placed back there after it had been thrown at him earlier) sitting on top of the kitchen counter now missing its single fake orange. It seemed that the entity had taken a liking to the young girl and had offered her a gift – note that 'It' was not so ill-behaved as to throw it at her – and had made no effort to hide his appearance from her when he did so.

It may be of interest to note that it later occurred to Bil that *all* of the objects he had thrown at him he had somehow connected with that day prior to them being thrown: Bil had noticed the Domino sat on the leather-bound bible on the cabinet in the front room when he did his initial tour of the house, the marble was thrown at Bil at the *precise* moment he was dropping a marble into a bowl of other trigger objects – to the point where Bil seriously thought the marble he dropped had somehow been the same marble thrown at him, the red plastic ball and orange were almost the only brightly coloured objects in the kitchen, so always caught the eye when you arrived in the house, Bil had personally removed eighteen screws from a bin bag after wrongly binning them, placing them carefully to one side – several of them were missing after the event – and Bil's hat was thrown off his overnight case onto the sofa. It was *his* phone that died during the PR event to promote the movie, and Bil that had firmly closed the gate before the film crew had left for London… There was also an incident with a large balloon and his mobile phone that we will return to. None of the events that have occurred to Bil have been completely random and disconnected – they have all been 'pre-registered' as such.

After Bil had owned 30 East Drive for just a few months, he soon reached a point where the reports of bizarre activity were coming in so thick and fast that he felt the urge to record them for posterity. Thus was born the 30 East Drive guestbook, in which he invited any and all visitors to write down their experiences and impressions of the house.

The book itself is fascinating. On review, it transpires that roughly half of the guests report nothing odd happening at all ('we had a very quiet night, where was 'Fred?') whereas the other half encountered activity that may well have been paranormal in nature. What follows are some highlights from the guestbook, along with experiences that visitors have emailed in to Bil or related to him in person.

This is by no means an exhaustive list and readers are encouraged to visit the website at 30EastDrive.com for more reported events, and also to join the 30EastDrive Owners Facebook page to both hear and share experiences.

CHAPTER FOUR

I Know What I Saw

Bil maintains a written archive of the paranormal experiences that are reported to him by visitors to 30 East Drive. While they record a very diverse spectrum of phenomena that range from strange noises all the way up to sightings of full-bodied apparitions, if you should sit down and sift through them, one thing becomes clear: there are patterns and commonalities to the experiences too.

One of the things that makes the house so fascinating is the fact that hundreds of people from a multitude of backgrounds (from ghost hunters to brick layers and everything in between) seem to be having the same sorts of experiences over and over again. Most of them have never met one another, and some didn't believe in the paranormal at all until they first set foot inside 30 East Drive.

APPORTS and MOVING OBJECTS:

Six people sitting in the living room witnessed a penny dropping from somewhere up above, hitting the carpet and then rolling to a halt.

Keys appear and disappear at seemingly random intervals, as do knives.

A candle pot set down in the kitchen somehow managed to work its way on top of a beer tankard without anybody touching it.

Phillip's bed was moved (the sound was heard by the visiting investigators) when the bedroom had nobody in it.

Doors and kitchen cabinets regularly open and close themselves, sometimes gently and sometimes violently as though they were slammed by someone who is very angry. Likewise, in some instances they are seen to move by observers, but in other instances 'Fred' seems subtler, acting when there are no witnesses (and usually no cameras) around to catch him in the act.

While doors opening and closing of their own accord is one thing, the flip side of the coin also seems to be true. The cupboard underneath the stairs opens very easily when pulled... except when it doesn't. Some visitors have found themselves tugging in vain at the handle, pulling as hard as they can in a desperate attempt to heave it open. The vast majority of the time, the door opens smoothly on its hinges, so there is no good reason for it to stick like that.

The cupboard under the stairs refusing to open is more of a curiosity than a cause for concern. The same cannot be said of the door to the coal house. It is here that Joe Pritchard had his terrifying encounter with 'Fred' at the height of the original phase of the haunting: it was said that when he could finally escape after all but battering down the jammed wooden door, he was a changed man forever afterward, haunted in both the literal and figurative senses of the term.

The coal house is extremely confined and unlit, with the

special kind of darkness that comes from the complete absence of light. The door itself opens easily, except of course on those occasions when it *doesn't,* and such incidents are usually attributed to 'Fred.' Fortunately, recent visitors to the coal house don't seem to suffer quite the same intensity of assault as was inflicted upon Joe Pritchard; although that doesn't make the experience any less frightening when 'Fred' does make his presence felt.

Several visitors have witnessed one of the glass doors that separate the living room from the kitchen open itself. This happened several times during Richard's stay at the house (Chapter Thirteen). A little in-depth investigation revealed that standing on a certain part of the living room floor seems to act as a trigger, sending just the right amount of vibratory force running through the floorboards and popping the door open. While this mundane explanation works for a number of cases in which the door appears to have opened itself, there are exceptions. For example, Nick Groff was sleeping soundly on the couch when the door opened itself in the middle of the night, an incident which was captured on one of his static cameras (Chapter Fifteen) . The video footage proves that nobody was walking around in either room, so we are forced to ask what made the door spontaneously open itself? Something/someone heavy stood on the dodgy floorboard, perhaps, or something/someone opening the door on purpose?

In a similar vein, an intriguing piece of apparently paranormal activity was captured by a visiting team when they were sitting in the living room. After a surge of K2-registered EMF activity, the front door of a furniture cabinet swung itself open without anybody touching it. Although the K2 activity is impossible to validate without knowing whether anybody present had their mobile phone switched on, the footage of *the cabinet door opening* (right) is more impressive. Although the effect could possibly have been faked using a piece of thin monofilament wire, as one particularly cynical commenter has pointed out, there is no evidence to suggest that is what happened, and the reactions of the onlookers couldn't be more genuine. Doors and gates opening either on request or of their own volition are nothing unusual at 30 East Drive.

'Fred' seems to have a penchant for throwing things, particularly small objects such as marbles, screws, and dominoes. Bil was the target of several such projectiles on Valentine's Day 2016 inside the house. Numerous others have been hit with marbles, such as the police officers who paid a very short flying visit in the company of Phil Bates (Chapter Fourteen).

On one of several visits to 30 East Drive, Carrie and Cam from *Pitch Black Investigations* were upstairs having a look around the house. As they reached the top of the stairs, a sudden whizzing sound took them both by surprise. They were amazed to see a domino zip through the air at high speed, hit the bathroom door, and drop to the floor. The upper floor was empty at the time, and the phantom domino-flinger was never identified.

30 East Drive's decor is heavy on the religious iconography, which definitely adds to the creepiness factor of the house (something about which Bil remains cheerfully unrepentant). 'Fred' was believed to be a monk, after all, and so wouldn't a man of the cloth appreciate a few crucifixes and saintly figurines as part of the decor?

They certainly seem to attract his attention, or that of some other entity inside the house. For example, on one occasion the sturdy wooden cross which usually resides in the master bedroom was relocated from the dressing table onto the windowsill by unseen hands. During a controversial visit from *Most Haunted* (Chapter Twelve), the *same cross was seen to land on the bed as though it had been thrown* (left), although due to the way in which the shot was framed it is hard to tell if this was a paranormal event or was thrown from off-camera by a human being. The framing was as close to as wide as it could go for the room however, so hiding an adult 'in on the game' would have been tricky at best.

There are a number of dolls of various sizes scattered around the house. It is not unusual for Carol or one of her colleagues to enter the house in order to give it a bit of a clean, only to find that the dolls have been moved or turned to face the wall. The most obvious explanation would be that the visitors have moved them themselves, but whenever Bil has asked them about it, they always deny it.

On a number of occasions, the movement of these dolls has taken place during a paranormal investigation and has been noted down by the visiting team and on at least two occasions a doll has been filmed, once during the *Most Haunted* initial investigation where a doll was filmed being thrown at the presenter's feet during a solo visit to the top floor, that sadly must be discounted due to questionable practices during their 'Halloween special' at the house. More recently, *a doll was filmed leaning over and falling onto a lit candle* (left): Of course, it may have been poorly balanced and have just fallen, but the video creates the distinct impression that the doll was firmly upright and that it was nudged in the direction of the lit candle, not least as the cameraman was cajoling the entity into moving it. Fortunately, the visitor was present when this happened avoiding a potential fire.

AUDITORY PHENOMENA:

A team using a *Spirit Box* ask the question "Who's there?" and are rewarded with the word "Monk." When asked if the entity wanted the investigators to leave, it replies "Yes." Later during the same session, the words "December 1974" came through the box.

At the end when the investigators stand up, one finds an old piece of newspaper under their seat with '1974' written on it.

Bangs, thuds, knocks and raps sound from the upper floor, usually heard by witnesses who are downstairs or by Carol next door when the house is empty. Some investigators have had success with getting knocking sounds on request, as Pete Barry once did (Chapter Seventeen), whereas others hear strange noises when they are least expecting them.

In what could be a classic ghostly example of British toilet humour, a female guest was engaged inside the bathroom. When she was asked whether she was alright (having presumably been in there for quite some time) she replied, "Yes thank you." Nothing too unusual about that, one might think, but in the split-second that the lady had spoken, the entire team exclaimed, "Did you hear *that!?*" All had heard the sound of a man's voice saying, *"Mmm-hmmm,"* as though in mocking agreement with the lady's reply. Possibly another example of 'Fred''s questionable sense of humour at work.

Claire Cowell's recording from the master bedroom must also be added to this list. The disembodied voice of a young girl answering the question "How old are you?" with the word "Seven," is a prime example of an interactive EVP. It's particularly interesting to note that nobody heard the word spoken at the time; it only showed up during Claire's evidence review the following day.

Unexplained knocking sounds are also fairly common, going back all the way to 1966 and the earliest stages of the haunting. Richard and his team heard some banging on the wall of Phillip's bedroom on their first day in the house. This wouldn't usually raise an eyebrow, but in this case the wall in question was an exterior wall, and the knocks would therefore have to have been delivered some fifteen to twenty feet up in the air, which is difficult without a ladder or throwing objects. When the American investigators looked outside, nobody was within a hundred feet of the house. The source of the brief series of knocks was never satisfactorily explained.

They would go on to get their own EVP when Richard, Jason, and Andrew were upstairs conducting a session in Phillip's bedroom. All was quiet, and nothing odd was heard at the time. Jason was asking questions about the identity of whichever spirits haunted the house and asked whether they had an occupation. The answer comes in the form of a sigh, one which sounds distinctly female in nature. It certainly didn't come from one of the male investigators. No words can be heard even after audio enhancement by computer software, but it remains an intriguing bit of evidence nonetheless.

LIGHT ANOMALIES:

A glowing ball of blue light has been seen floating in the corridor at the foot of the stairs by passers-by on multiple occasions.

PHYSICAL CONTACT:

As already mentioned, a member of a visiting film crew reported being pinned down by an invisible force while sleeping in Diane's old bedroom. It was theorised that this was nothing more than a night terror, although the witness hadn't experienced one since she was a young girl.

Another visiting investigator claims to have been pinned in the coal house and to have glimpsed a shadowy figure between them and the door. Very similar to what happened to Joe Pritchard.

TEMPERATURE:

Bil's wife Nelly experienced a localised column of icy cold air in the corridor leading to the stairs, as have many others.

MECHANICAL AND ELECTRICAL:

Long before a television set was brought back into the house (in the early days, when Bil had just taken over) the sound of one blaring at high volume was heard coming from the empty house by Carol Fieldhouse and her family.

Radiators have been switched up to full blast when the empty house was locked up overnight, after a qualified heating professional turned them all down to low the night before.

Many people have reported malfunctions with their phones

and cameras inside 30 East Drive. Bil experienced this at first hand when a photograph of himself and two of the actresses from the film *When the Lights Went Out* disappeared from his phone for several weeks after the phone's charge dropped from 75% to zero in the blink of an eye.

The house has several clocks in it, some of which no longer work but have been left there because they add a 1970s-style flavour to the place. One of the clocks sits on the windowsill near the piano in the kitchen, and a number of visitors have reported seeing the clock either having been moved (turning to face a different direction when nobody was looking) or firing itself up and beginning to tell the time again.

A number of people walking past the house when it happened to be empty and locked up have witnessed lights turning themselves off and on in different rooms. They also see curtains twitching as though an unseen observer is looking back out of the window at them.

MEDICAL AND PHYSICAL PHENOMENA:

Many visitors to 30 East Drive report feeling a sense of deep oppression and heaviness, almost as though the barometric pressure is increasing. This might be explainable if a thunderstorm was building, but it has been documented in all types of weather. On Richard's second visit to the house, his colleague Lesley, who had never stepped foot inside the place before, immediately remarked upon how heavy and close the atmosphere felt. Ten minutes later she was vomiting into the downstairs toilet.

We have to accept that the sense of impending dread which often permeates the house is a completely subjective phenomenon, one which we would have to dismiss as evidence if it weren't for the fact that so many visitors have reported it independently of one another.

The physical phenomena experienced by numerous people inside the house over the years, on the other hand, can be a different matter entirely. Some can still be filed under 'potentially subjective,' such as author Richard Estep's colleague Charlie's disturbing experience at the sink, when his feet were pinned to the floor. But others are undeniable: Consider the *scratches many visitors have sustained* (left) inside 30 East Drive, including poor Charlie (see Chapter Thirteen for Charlie's experiences).

One must conclude either all of the many various marks, blemishes, and sometimes outright wounds are faked (in which case there is a *lot* of fraud and self-harm being perpetrated in this case, often by multiple people who have never met one another) or that something truly uncanny is going on. Even though some of the accounts should be taken with a grain of salt, such as the man whose leg allegedly suffered a spontaneous fracture during a particularly active night at the house (Chapter Seven), there are still a great many cases in which physical phenomena have been seen to take place by a wide range of trustworthy and reliable eyewitness, such as both authors of this book. We may doubt the *why,* but there is no doubting the fact that it does take place.

APPARITIONS AND SHADOW FIGURES:

The original 30 East Drive apparition is one that needs no introduction – the famed Black Monk of Pontefract himself: A tall, hooded figure that has been seen both inside the house itself and in Carol's home next door. This dark, hooded figure lies at the very heart of the furore that has engulfed an otherwise anonymous-looking council house for the better part of half a century. Although the identity of this mysterious figure remains unproven, one thing can be said for certain: it is not the only ghost to have been seen at 30 East Drive.

It has also been claimed that the house is haunted by one or more children; two little girls named Emma and Emily according to one psychic. It must be pointed out that there is no record of two such girls ever having lived at 30 East Drive, so quite why they would haunt the place is open to question. Some have speculated that these may be two of the victims who were supposedly assaulted and murdered by the Black Monk, but that only works as an explanation if one buys into the Black Monk's origin story being true – something for which there is little to no evidence at all.

On the night that Claire Cowell and her colleagues at *East Drive Paranormal* recorded an EVP in the master bedroom which sounded like a little girl's voice, Claire decided to sit on her own in the master bedroom with the lights out to ask a few impromptu questions.

Glancing over at the wall which separated Jean and Joe's old room from Phillip's, Claire saw what looked like the shadow figure of a young girl come walking towards her, as though passing from the next-door room into the one she now sat in before disappearing.

Wondering whether her eyes or her mind could be playing tricks, she got up and stuck her head around the door of Phillip's bedroom to compare notes with the members of the other team. When asked whether anything unusual had just happened to them, they replied that they too had seen what looked like a little shadow form that disappeared through the wall separating the two bedrooms.

No sooner had Claire gone back to sit on the big double bed than she heard somebody call out from next door, "Did you see that? I could have sworn I just saw a little girl run across the landing!"

This understandably caused a bit of excitement. The same investigator asked, "Have I just seen you out there on the landing? If that was you, how old are you?" It was only upon playing back her audio file the next day that Claire realised she had caught a child-like voice giving the answer – "*Seven.*"

Residents of East Drive have reported seeing a shadowy figure running past their back windows on occasion. Many blame this on a spirit from number 30, which may or may not be true. It would be tempting to dismiss these sightings as being nothing more than local kids up to mischief, except for one small detail: the phantom runner goes straight *through* the garden fences.

PHOTOGRAPHY:

Sceptics often cite lack of photographic or video evidence as proof of the non-existence of paranormal phenomena, often leaving believers to frustratingly point at the expense of equipment required to capture proof, but that has all changed. We now live in an age in which practically everybody has a camera and a video about their person at all times, usually integrated with their phone, and access to sophisticated affordable technology that allows investigators to 'look beyond' is prevalent.

The result is that there is a growing body of evidence to support the existence of the paranormal. Much of that evidence has been captured by visitors to 30 East Drive, who often come very well equipped. Indeed, until comparatively recently, some of the technology now implemented on 'ghost hunts' would have been available only to the military: heat-sensing thermal cameras, infra-red cameras, laser grids, motion sensing equipment of a large and often creative variety, Microsoft Kinect cameras, radio scanners etc. added to the plethora of video and stills cameras of all shapes, sizes and capabilities – have all been used inside the house with varying degrees of success.

As the editor of the official 30 East Drive website, Bil receives a regular influx of images from those who have spent time inside the house and has the unenviable task of trying to determine which might be genuinely paranormal in nature and separating them from those which are not. Most of the latter are well-intentioned accidents. Some are nothing more than *pareidolia, for example* (right). The human brain is predisposed to want to see either a human face or body when it looks at an incomprehensible object – in other words, we are wired to take random shapes and attempt to impose some kind of meaningful pattern on them. Perhaps the best example of this, the one that we can all relate to, is the Man in the Moon: Of course, we all know that there isn't *actually* a face looking back at us when we stare up into the night sky, but once you see the Man in the Moon for the first time, it's practically impossible to *un*see it – This is pareidolia at its finest.

For some, visiting a location such as 30 East Drive is a once-in-a-lifetime experience, so considering the sheer sense of anticipation and high expectations that build up before crossing the threshold of number 30, it's easy to see why a few visitors want desperately for their visit not to have been in vain, and will grasp at straws in an attempt to produce some 'evidence.' Many photos inside the house are taken in conditions of near-total darkness, when it is all too easy to interpret any patch of shadow as being a ghost, or with the use of a flash, which reflects from nearby specks of dust, pollen, natural fibres, and other particulate matter and creates the all too explainable 'orb effect' which most serious researchers will freely admit is the bane of modern paranormal photography.

Sadly, the prevalence of Photoshop and easy-to-use apps that insert ghostly figures into photographs also make even the best so-called ghost photograph questionable, even if the reputation and character of the photographer is beyond repute. Just fifteen years ago, most of those images would have had photographic negatives which could have been submitted to the laboratory for professional analysis. Now that the vast majority of photography is done digitally, investigators no longer have that luxury, and are reduced to examining the metadata of computer files in an attempt to root out trickery.

And yet, of the tens of thousands of photographs that have been taken inside 30 East Drive, there are a number that simply defy easy explanation. It must also be pointed out that most of those who visit the house are honest people who are simply insatiably curious about one of Britain's most haunted locations: they don't come to fake, but rather to try and gather genuine evidence in an attempt to shed light on some of the many mysteries that surround the place.

Having worked in image creation businesses for many years, Bil casts an objective and critical eye over each image that comes his way. As the owner, he knows every square inch of the house, and recognises the natural patterns of light and shadow throughout. When something is captured on camera that doesn't appear to be quite right, Bil's eye is naturally drawn to it. He then attempts to find a conventional explanation, something which isn't always possible.

One of them is an extraordinary picture taken by Craig Longson of *Ghost Hunters of Stoke on Trent (G.H.O.S.T)*, who had set up a Canon 5D camera on a tripod mount at the top of the staircase looking down toward the downstairs hallway. Although the field of vision appeared to be empty at the time the camera was remotely triggered, the photograph clearly shows a *sinister black mass floating at the top of the staircase* (right). It looks very much like a blobby humanoid form and for all the world seems to be staring into the camera lens, almost as if it has been caught off-guard by the automatic camera.

While it is theoretically possible that this image has been digitally enhanced (i.e. faked) just as any of the photographs under discussion could have been, the authors consider it to be highly unlikely. Bil, an art director by trade and trained image specialist, believes that the dimensions of the figure, its position within the frame in relation to the stairs, and its overall posture have more than a whiff of authenticity about them. Indeed, in the process of establishing the authenticity of this image, Bil tried (and failed) to recreate it in Photoshop, noting that the subtle but specific characteristics present would require a professional degree of photographic and compositional know-how, combined with skilful illustrative and retouching skills, to create the original. The scale (something tall), the perspective in relation to the camera (the head is bigger, as you would expect it to be if it were nearer camera), what would seem like the tilt of the head in the direction of the camera, the overall humanoid shape (head, body, two arms, two legs – all as you would expect them to be were the subject of human form), the subtle transparent edges of the shadow, and the ominous, light-trapping, seemingly solid-black interior, and the way that the shadow hovers perfectly over a step rather than making contact with it.

Bil is keen to emphasise that there are definitely image specialists more skilled than he who *are* capable of faking such an image, given time and inclination. This process would involve: a human subject standing on the step, staging the concept of having the subject 'caught by the camera,' a photo with and without the subject, some skilful retouching following the subject's form (including careful shadow considerations), finally outputted to a 'snapped' camera file, rather than a post-retouch Photoshop file. Given that such artisans are few and far between, and probably working for visual effects houses, it would be an extraordinary thing indeed if Craig himself turned out to be just such a specialist. But, even if so – why cheat? Not only would he be cheating us, but he would be cheating himself out of effort, expense and reputation, a ridiculous and frankly pathetic notion, all for no apparent gain.

[Author's note: Bil would like to emphatically add that whilst he himself is an image specialist, possessing both the knowledge and the contacts required to ultimately execute such a pointless fraud, he has never and will NEVER FAKE ANYTHING in relation to 30 East Drive. He recognises the significance of the secrets it holds, and to this day Bil is quick to bar and blacklist anyone suspected of behaving fraudulently or indeed, disrespectfully toward the house (or its neighbours). As a result, he regularly challenges questionable claims *(right) of having captured images of a paranormal nature. Think about it, if Bil was to ban a fraudulent story, one that could potentially enhance the reputation of the house and may in turn ultimately benefit its owner, it would be in his best interests to keep his mouth shut wouldn't it? And what's more Bil is 100% willing to take a lie-detector test to support his personal claims and experiences!]*

Another interesting facet of this particular image is the fact that there was reportedly a sudden sharp temperature drop immediately prior to the camera being remotely fired. Cold spots are a common finding throughout the annals of paranormal research, and some have theorised that they either presage or accompany the manifestation of paranormal phenomena: It may be that the thermal energy is somehow leeched out of the air and converted into another form of energy, thus resulting in the sudden onset of a cold spot or draught, or is perhaps the result of an as-yet unknown phenomenon associated with the opening of a 'portal' to another dimension; a theme we will come back to later on. In any case, the coldness that came just a short time before the appearance of this photographic anomaly seems to the authors to be more than mere coincidence.

As the old saying goes in the world of real estate, 'Location, location, location!' The staircase has been the scene of multiple apparition sightings, usually of the black and shadowy variety.

'Fred' (or something that meets his description) has been encountered by many witnesses on the staircase over the years. Poor Diane was dragged up them by an invisible force, and quite a few visitors have been shoved in the back while descending them. If the theories about there being spirit portals inside the house are correct, then some part of the staircase would be a good location for one of them to be found.

Odd shadows quite often appear in photographs taken on the staircase and are usually there in one frame and gone the next, as though the shadowy masses are moving fairly quickly. It is easy for the sceptical to dismiss them as simple variations in light and shade, perhaps a cloud passing over the sun or some other natural condition. Yet there are those images which defy such simple explanation and are worth discussing in greater detail here.

One such picture was taken by Claire Cowell, a member of *East Drive Paranormal*, on the night of November 22, 2015. She and a few of her colleagues had been inside the house for several hours. It had been a very active night so far, with 'Fred' and company being on fine rambunctious form. Marbles had been thrown at team members: a loud growl had been heard, along with an assortment of taps, bangs, and raps – and several people had felt themselves being touched by something unseen. In other words, 30 East Drive was in full swing.

It was getting late, and many of the investigators and their guests had left for the night. Only Claire, Carol Fieldhouse, and three others remained, one being an investigator and two being guests. Two of them were upstairs taking photos in Phillip's bedroom, and then getting down to the business of packing away their equipment. Claire, Carol and one of the guests were taking a quick break, having a bit of a chat in the living room.

Feeling a little thirsty, Claire got up to fetch herself a glass of water from the kitchen. She switched on the kitchen light and made her way over to the sink. Every door in the house was open. She could still hear Carol and her guest chatting away through the French doors. Filling a glass from the cold tap, Claire suddenly heard a knock coming from the foot of the stairs.

"What was that?" Carol had obviously heard it too. "While you're up, will you go and have a look?"

Claire obliged, moving to the kitchen doorway and taking some photographs of the bottom of the staircase. She couldn't see anything amiss and wondered whether yet another marble had been chucked down the stairs; if so, it certainly wouldn't have been the first one of the evening. The kitchen and living room lights were throwing some ambient light out into the darkened hallway. She could see quite clearly that there was nobody standing at the foot of the staircase, and there had been no staircase creaks to announce someone's descent; only the clicking of an SLR camera upstairs could be heard.

Looking down at her phone, Claire brought up the photo she had just taken. Nothing unusual had appeared on it, so she switched over to camera mode and snapped a second picture.

A chorus of shouting and swearing suddenly came from upstairs.

"What's going on?" Claire hollered.

"Have any of you just been on the staircase?" the investigator who had been taking pictures in Phillip's bedroom called back, obviously quite excited. When Claire replied that no, nobody had just climbed the stairs, the two of them came downstairs and told her that a marble had just been thrown at them with some force.

Claire now checked her second photograph, and what she saw there made her blood run cold. "I think we need to get out of here," she told the others. "Now!"

When the group of five had left the house and Carol had locked it up securely, they asked why exactly it was that she had felt compelled to leave in such a hurry. By way of explanation, Claire held up her phone to show them the second photograph. None of them could believe what it contained.

There, draped over the edge of the staircase bannister, was a hand, extending from the end of a black sleeve. Looking at one another in shock, the five investigators wondered aloud whether this was the *forearm and hand of the Black Monk* (left).

Closer inspection of the photograph reveals some other interesting features. Firstly, something long and cordlike seems to be dangling from the wrist and swinging from side to side, much as some people might wear a rosary. Something else of key importance relates to the angle of the shot: The mirror mounted on the wall at the foot of the stairs (the same one which would mysteriously break during Richard's first day at the house, as discussed in Chapter Thirteen) is visible, and the arm's owner is not reflected in it; in fact, neither is the arm itself.

Keen to try and get to the bottom of the mystery, Claire showed the photograph to Bil the next time he visited the house. Agreeing that it looked extremely strange and given Bil's determination to verify the authenticity of every single image and video that he is sent, he suggested that they try to *recreate the image* (left) themselves. Acting as a guinea pig, Bil took up a position partway up the staircase and stuck out his right arm in an attempt to mimic the position of the arm in the picture.

Using the same automatic camera settings as before (the only difference being that the flash didn't trigger because of the daylight flooding through the front door windows), Claire framed the shot with her camera phone and took several photographs of Bil stood there patiently. No matter how hard they tried, the pair of them were unable to replicate the effect of the first photo; each time, a vaguely bemused-looking Bil was visible in the mirror.

[Author's note: In order to circumvent the inevitable sceptical accusation of Claire's capture being a camera/photographic anomaly, I wish to emphasise that I have worked with professional photographers, and as a photographer, for over 35 years; using practically every format of camera, lighting set-up, subject, angle, film, film size, film brand and so on. During that time I have rarely, if ever, observed any 'pareidolic' anomalies that I could have claimed to have been paranormal in nature – save for some very early random stains caused by chemical processing. When I switched to the digital format (well before it was available to the general public, and years before it was available on our phones) I did so reluctantly, because I felt that the format 'lacked soul' - that it was too cold, clinical, precise. But it is precisely because of

this 'digital precision' that I can confidently assert that digital photography is an absolute blessing for paranormal investigation, because it is highly unlikely that something captured that claims to be paranormal in nature is an error from the digital camera itself: A digital camera captures what is available for it to see. Bil]

The picture remains unexplained at the time of writing. It wasn't long before the photo went viral. *GHOST HUNTER CAPTURES 'CLEAREST IMAGE YET OF NOTORIOUS POLTERGEIST' DUBBED THE BLACK MONK OF PONTEFRACT,* screamed the headline on the *Daily Mirror.*

One year later, the media would latch onto another strange occurrence on the 30 East Drive staircase. A paranormal events organisation named *Pitch Black Investigations* had already been to 30 East Drive on several occasions and knew the place well. They had gotten results before, but the night of October 1, 2016 would take things to a whole new level.

The team assembled at around 8.45 in the evening. As with all of their events, things kicked off with introductions, a safety briefing, and the establishment of some basic ground rules.

"Although every night is different, with some nights being quieter and less active than other nights we have hosted there, we feel that every time you leave the house the unexplainable activity experienced would draw you straight back," the team's spokesman told the authors of this book.

They headed upstairs and began a lights-out session with their guests, calling out and running an EVP session. Things began quietly enough but after a while, as tends to be the way with 30 East Drive, odd things started to happen. It began with strange noises coming from the empty downstairs, which soon progressed to disembodied footsteps. The *Pitch Black Investigations* hosts knew that they were locked inside the house, and whenever one of them went downstairs to check out the footsteps, nobody was ever found. It was classic 'Fred,' stalking the people who had shown the temerity to trespass inside his home.

Things began to calm down after midnight. By 1.50 in the morning, everybody was starting to think about getting ready to go home. A clattering noise sounded from the direction of the staircase. Everybody came running, only to find that a toy push-chair had just been pitched down the stairs, which had been sitting on the upstairs landing for the entire evening.

The most obvious explanation was that one of the guests had given it a nudge, perhaps inadvertently, perhaps not – yet when the footage from the team's locked-off video camera was reviewed, the truth turned out to be far stranger: The film shows that nobody was within touching distance of the *push-chair when it took its lemming-like nose-dive down the stairs* (left). Although it might be possible to fake this effect with a very thin piece of monofilament wire, this ignores the fact that not only the *Pitch*

Black Investigations team members but also their guests would *all* have to be in on the fraud in order to make it work, something that the authors do not believe to be remotely likely, nor is there any reason to doubt the integrity of *Pitch Black Investigations*. The incident seems to show 'Fred' (or perhaps the young girl reportedly residing at the house; it is said that she likes to play with the pram, and the dolls for that matter) at his volatile best, performing physical phenomena at one of his favourite parts of the house.

PUSH SCARE, was *The Sun*'s take on events. HAS FILM OF BUGGY FALLING DOWN STAIRS FINALLY CAPTURED NOTORIOUS POLTERGEIST KNOWN AS THE BLACK MONK IN ACTION?

The article went on to claim that some members of the team were so scared that they refused to spend the night in the house, instead choosing to check into a nearby hotel. Team member Steve Archibald is quoted as saying, "But there is lots of poltergeist activity there. I have seen marbles thrown through closed doors in the house before. I don't think most of [the activity] is threatening, but on the stairs it does feel threatening."

With the exception of Carol Fieldhouse, few people have spent as much time investigating 30 East Drive as Andy Evans has. Choosing the locations for his cameras with great care, Andy often sited them on the staircase in the full knowledge that it was a hotspot. He also liked to take manual photographs, and on one occasion took two images in rapid succession.

The first showed nothing unusual, just the stairs, bannister, and upstairs landing, which was completely bare. The grandmother clock which now occupies it hadn't been placed there yet. On the second photograph, however, a black shape appeared, one which looks remarkably like that captured by Craig, and it is fair to say that the resemblance between the two anomalies is quite uncanny. The angle of Andy's photograph allows us to clearly see that the *black mass at the top of the stairs is floating* (left).

Not content with just one, Andy also managed to capture a second, this time at the very bottom of the staircase. Whereas the dimension of the first anomaly had been somewhat human-like, the one that appeared at the base of the stairs during broad daylight is a much more amorphous and *blob-like shadow figure* (right). Assuming that both are the same entity, could one perhaps show an earlier stage of the manifestation process than the other?

The French doors which separate the living room from the kitchen were at one time covered with lace curtains. This is unfortunate because in another of Andy's photographs, the *shadowy figure of a man apparently reading a newspaper* (left) or a book, mysteriously appeared behind the curtain – offering us a tantalising glimpse of what may have been one of 30 East Drive's resident entities. A comfortable leather chair had always been positioned in that spot, making it a natural place for somebody to sit and lose themselves in a good book or the day's paper for a while. The unusual thing is that nobody was present in the kitchen at all when Andy took the photograph, and he didn't notice anybody there at the time. Yet another photo that raises more questions than it answers...

On Andy's first visit to the house, he and his friend Steve were allowed to have a look around by Carol. It appeared that 'Fred' wanted to make his presence known, albeit in a fairly playful way. On the kitchen countertop was a leather-bound Bible, which was sitting in direct contact with the large guest book that Bil had started up. Carol told Andy that the Bible hadn't been there yesterday when she had last been inside. Dutifully taking reference pictures of everything, he recorded the original position of both books quite clearly.

It was fortunate that he did. After taking a whistle stop tour of the house with Carol as their guide, during which she maintained that 'Fred' was currently right there in the house watching their every move, Andy and Steve came back downstairs to find that the *Bible had been moved a significant distance* (right).

He also reported all of the chairs at the dining table having been pulled out a short distance, after having seen Carol push them in beneath the table with his own eyes. No living human being had been present in the house other than the three of them, all of whom were within plain sight of one another throughout, and so the two comparison photos Andy took – his 'before' and 'after' pictures showing the Bible's original and finishing position – make for a fascinating piece of evidence.

Andy and Steve visited the house many times after that and experienced a range of phenomena, which are recounted in their books *Don't Look Back in Anger* and *Living Next Door to Malice*. Perhaps the most shocking photograph they took was snapped by Steve, who was in Phillip's bedroom at the time. He took a series of photographs of the landing through the open doorway. One of the images picked up a *bizarre-looking figure, standing in profile and framed by the doorway itself* (left).

Although roughly humanoid, there is something innately *wrong* about the form: there appear to be legs, a torso, a head, and a neck. There is spinal curvature similar to that of a person, and there even appear to be knees; yet that is where the similarity ends. The lower legs taper down to a point where the ankles should be, and there are no feet to be seen; instead, the skirting board is plainly visible where the figure's feet ought to be. It appears to be leaning forward somewhat at the waist, with head bowed and hands clasped in what might be prayer or benediction. Extending beyond the figure's clearly-delineated lines can be seen several lighter shadowy layers which look like a long robe of some sort.

Although Steve and Andy had some companions with them on the night that the photograph was taken, and one has to consider the possibility that is was perhaps one of the team, both Andy and Steve were genuinely perplexed by whatever it was that they had captured, significant given their years of experience in the paranormal field. They are particularly intrigued by the subject seemingly floating several inches above the ground.

The word 'demonic' is one that is often bandied about among some members of the paranormal research community. It has distinct religious connotations (as, of course, does the idea of a monk haunting the house) and while not every investigator believes in the existence of demons, most are open to the possibility of non-human entities. A number of those who were interviewed for this book have expressed the opinion that the main entity which haunts 30 East Drive isn't a monk at all, or indeed anything that has ever walked the Earth as a human being – in other words, something inhuman.

There is no shortage of supporting evidence for this theory. A number of animalistic growls have been recorded during EVP sessions inside the house (particularly in the area of the coal house) and scratches have appeared on the bodies of several visitors, including Charlie, a member of Richard's team.

Could the photograph have captured this inhuman entity somehow 'phasing' into our plane of existence, caught for just a split-second by the lens of Steve's camera? It must be pointed out that he saw nothing with his naked eye when he was taking the picture, which implies that the dark figure appeared beyond that portion of the visible light spectrum that we are capable of perceiving. If such is the case, then this picture is a smoking gun. Steve submitted it for review to a priest in the United States who was well-versed in the field of demonology. The priest had no hesitation in proclaiming it to be both authentic and proof positive of there being a demonic infestation at 30 East Drive. As with so much about this incredible house, in the end it all comes down to a matter of individual belief.

[Author's note: Whilst I have no reason to doubt Andy and Steve's integrity, they are paranormal investigators of high repute and I have absolutely no doubt that they believe this image to be genuine (they definitely haven't faked it): the low-light, long-exposure, back-lit nature of the photograph and presence of other team members makes for the reasonable possibility that this is a passing team member captured in a way that would all but eliminate the fast moving parts of the subject (the arms and legs) creating the sensation that the subject was floating, but the thickness of the girth would cut out the background light for longer creating a solid black core. Likely taken on a camera with a

sensor: a team member, perhaps unwittingly even Andy or Steve, would trigger the camera at precisely the right moment, an event forgotten when reviewing post-visit images. Compare this to the static silhouette floating over the stairs in broad daylight, taken by Craig (page 95): a perfect silhouette floating off the ground, with NO movement from the subject – the subject's feet are missing because they are simply not there and not because they are moving too fast for the camera. Bil]

Perhaps the most incredible photo of all was captured by Amanda McIntyre who visited 30 East Drive shortly after Bil opened the house up to the public. She was visiting with her friend Gemma and her small dog 'Missy'. Their intention wasn't to investigate, per se, but rather to just experience this most infamous of haunted houses. That said, they did bring one item regularly found in the paranormal investigator's arsenal: the full spectrum camera, a type of camera that captures all available light, including infrared, allowing it to see in near-complete darkness.

At around 3am they found themselves sitting in Diane's bedroom in total darkness (a room that still retains the same wallpaper, carpet and scarred roof tiles from when Diane slept there), taking intermittent infrared photos down the corridor leading directly to the upstairs bathroom, its door wide open.

It wasn't until they looked through their images in the safety and comfort of their own home, that they discovered a truly incredible image on their camera. A *ghostly human form just standing there* (right), looking directly back at them from the bathroom doorway.

After making contact with Bil in an email which had distinct overtones of disbelief that they had captured such a thing, Bil immediately set about trying to establish the authenticity of the image.

Bil recognised the precise location of the picture as the bathroom doorway and upstairs wall by the stairwell, clearly highlighted in the infrared spectrum. But there was also what appeared to be the figure of a young girl, her diminutive height being determined in contrast with the full height of the door. She appeared to be somewhere around ten to twelve years of age.

What's more, she seemed to be wearing a ragged, worn-out gown or dress, which could be the basic working clothes of a farm girl; but then again, it could also be a once-fine dress that is now tattered by some event. (Why, we ask, do clothes appear to make their way into the spirit world too? Or is this peculiarity perhaps a clue to another altogether different explanation for the phenomena? More on this later).

Bil set to work, importing the image into Photoshop (an application that is simultaneously the paranormal world's nemesis and blessing) and meticulously examined it, observing that the shadows that gave form and shape to the girlish figure were sufficiently well-defined to be picked out with a pen line. Drawing what was there, rather than what he expected or wanted to see, Bil carefully followed all the dark lines, a bit like brass rubbing a faded tomb stone to reveal its hidden message.

What revealed itself to Bil was nothing less than horrifying.

It did indeed appear to be a girl, but one that wore *a ghastly, demon-like face, with wide eyes piercing through the darkness* (right). Tufts of hair sprouted from her head.

Despite the terrifying nature of the image, Bil couldn't help but feel that this was somehow a lost child, someone that had suffered a terrible ordeal and had appeared that night because of the warmth and welcoming energy that Amanda and Gemma had exuded.

One awful and tragic detail that is *clearly visible is the mouth of the figure* (left). It is as if it has suffered a terrible trauma and has somehow been brutally cut open. Those readers who have watched *When the Lights Went Out* will know that the concept of a monk raping and murdering young girls is part of the 30 East Drive legend. Could this be one of his victims, supposedly thrown down the well by the Cluniac killer, who, having already poisoned it with the bodies of the girls he killed, was later forced to suffer the same ignominious fate? Legend has it that the monk cut the tongues out of his victims in order to silence them – if so, what would the traumatic injury inflicted upon their mouths look like…?

It isn't the only amazing experience Amanda and Gemma have had at 30 East Drive. They also captured a video of light anomalies appearing at the same time as the curtain at the foot of the stairs move and *as a shadow sweeps across in the foreground* (right). And if that wasn't remarkable enough: one of the ladies filled up a small jug with water to pour into a bowl for 'Missy' (a rare breed, in that it's one of the few dogs to have successfully made it into the house!). The women sat on the floor of the kitchen and continued with their chat as 'Missy' lapped gratefully at the water beside them. A little later, they looked to see if she had drunk enough water, only to notice, to their utter bewilderment, that *the jug had filled itself back up again, right to the very brim!* (right). It would seem that at least one of the entities that resides at 30 East Drive had taken a shine to the guests: it's an act of kindness (providing more water for the dog) that sits in stark contrast to the dog-hater that resided in Lisa Manning's house in Coventry (more on this later). That's not to assume that it was a poltergeist that filled the jug, of course. So, for the comfort of our sceptical readers – we offer a more plausible explanation for the jug mysteriously filling itself back up: Perhaps 'Missy' was not only thirsty – but desperately needed to pop outside too? But not wishing to interrupt the conversation, the clever little pooch managed to strategically, and skilfully urinate in the jug.

We're being ridiculous. The house is old, there was a leaky pipe that dripped through the ceiling and filled the jug…? Condensation? It's obvious, Amanda and Gemma must be lying. The picture of the demonic girl is a clever fake. One of the women dressed in Hollywood standard prosthetics and wardrobe and they spent the entire night trying to get the lighting, composition and effect exactly right, so as to shimmy past Bil's eagle eye? And they then paid £1000 an hour to access to a world-class special effects suite, probably in London, and took time away from their jobs to creative direct the orbs and randomness of the shadow passing in front of camera to make fools of us all? *Look* – there must be a logical reason for the jug filling itself back up, because poltergeists don't exist… do they?

CHAPTER FIVE

The Whole House Shook

No Ouija boards.

No sage burning.

No exorcisms.

As long as visitors to 30 East Drive are respectful of these and a few slightly more common-sense rules, both believers *and* sceptics are welcomed. Indeed, co-author and house owner Bil Bungay stood very firmly in the sceptical camp before his not so much camp-changing as *life-changing* experiences, and as a result is adamant that all visitors should visit as sceptics and let the house do the talking.

Both authors also know that no matter how many incredible stories are presented in this book – a sceptic will always remain a sceptic, hence our objective being to convey what is happening at 30 East Drive as honestly and accurately as possible, rather than being on a mission to convert sceptics into believers.

And sceptics don't come much harder than Dale Makin. Dale, in his mid-thirties, has been into paranormal investigating for twenty years, forming his group, *Paranormal Truths*, in 2016. Dale willingly admits that his objective has essentially been to disprove the nonsense of the paranormal from day one.

His modus operandi had always been to travel light. He is

always wary of getting distracted by technologies that are at risk of being misread and convincing the uninitiated that they are communicating with a ghost, when the explanation could easily be more mundane, such as the passing lights of a car, random coincidence, a misinterpreted infra-red shadow, or something of a similar ilk.

Dale has always preferred to wait for something physical and real to occur to him personally but has recently made a slight concession to a sound recorder, EVP meter and temperature gauge – all equipment that has come to be regarded as standard but essential components of every ghost hunter's arsenal.

One other characteristic he adheres to is persistence. As a sceptic, Dale knows that visiting a location several times reduces the potential for paranormal believers to wheel out the usual litany of clichés in defence of a location's supposed 'hauntedness.'

'It's the luck of the draw,' 'You were there on the wrong night,' 'Some you win, some you lose,' 'The atmospherics just weren't right,' and so on, and so forth.

Visiting a location multiple times reduces the validity of at least some of those typical excuses and strengthens Dale's claim that the location in question is, on balance, a dud.

One such location that risked Dale's wrath was 30 East Drive. Indeed, were it not for his persistence, 30 East Drive would have been veritably annihilated by Dale and his ghost hunting partner, Justin Cowell, some time ago. You can still visit their YouTube channel to see a fairly uncompromising view of 30 East Drive that was uploaded in 2017. Dale and Justin had visited several times and found little to prove that the location was what it claimed to be, but just enough to inject at least a little hesitation in their delivery and spice to their strategy of persistence – a strategy that finally paid off in spades.

Paranormal Truths decided that one final push, a couple of full nights at this legendary house, would seal their opinions once and for all. With Dale and Justin on their own for the first night, the house almost seemed to mock their efforts, delivering little to nothing, as is often the case.

But the second night changed everything.

Perhaps it was the change in energies brought about by the addition of some female guests that fundamentally altered the dynamic, but very soon they were getting what they could only describe as "crazy EVPs."

The investigators heard a young girl most definitely asking for "Mummy," and in Phillip's bedroom, light anomalies were seen, along with a measurable 10-degree drop in temperature.

These were all great things to have captured, admittedly, but for hardened sceptics, they were nothing to get excited about. What Dale and Justin really wanted to experience was something definite, something beyond debate, something that the whole group experienced, so as to eliminate the prospect of them leaving and questioning their experiences later 'with hindsight,' as so often happens with some of the more subtle events.

It was only when they were all gathered downstairs that something began to build, something that truly captivated the whole group. The very clear sound of footsteps could be heard upstairs. Then came the whistling. Possibly because of the commonly-held assumption that the primary entity in the house is male, Dale suggested that perhaps 'It' was trying to attract the attention of the females: so, the women decided to go upstairs alone to see if they could communicate with whatever was making the racket up there.

But as is very often the case at 30 East Drive, 'It' became shy in the presence of the living and abruptly ceased its disruptive behaviour. Disappointed, the ladies traipsed back downstairs.

Just as they got back to the lads in the kitchen, the noises started up again. Only this time, they were louder. Bangs, footsteps, whistling. The whole gamut.

Yet again, the female investigators mounted the stairs in an attempt to see whether the entity would communicate with them directly, perhaps even reveal itself, but to no avail. Again, the women descended back to the kitchen, feeling let down and perhaps even a little contemptuous of the attention-seeking phantom failing to capitalise on its captive female audience; like a teenager at a night club imploding after being called out by the girls for his cocksure bravado.

This back and forth continued a little longer, until the women finally decided that enough was enough and called out that they weren't going to play the game any longer.

It was 3.30 in the morning and they were "fed up with the entity and its showboating," adding that they were going to ignore it from now on.

With that there was an enormous bang, one so loud and heavy that it shook the structure of the entire house and left the lampshade in the kitchen swinging wildly to and fro.

Nine people witnessed this incredible event, and it's hard to imagine a scenario in which nine people could have incorrectly witnessed what had happened.

The sounds were also recorded by Dale and the group, and subsequently analysed by Doctor Barry Colvin. A commonly-used technical term for the sounds that poltergeists make is 'poltergeist rapping'. The sounds are very distinct from the rapping sounds that we would make, in that a human-made sound starts sharply, is very loud in volume, and subsequently diminishes. This is clearly visible when viewed as a sound wave on an electronic display. When a poltergeist raps, the sound starts silently then ramps up to a peak before diminishing. It's how Dr. Colvin can determine the paranormal nature of the sounds, or not, as the case may be. The knocking coming from upstairs at 30 East Drive most definitely conforms to Dr. Colvin's amazing discovery – whatever was making the knocking sounds that day was not human.

Shortly after the bang, a voice was recorded from a remote

recorder upstairs. It sounds like 'Mattis gratis,' a seemingly Latin term which roughly translates as 'Thankful footing,' perhaps a sign that the bangs weren't aggression, but rather 'It' signalling its gratitude at the presence of some female visitors?

"That house does not conform to our assumptions of a haunted location," explains Dale. "For starters, when we last visited it was a mild dry August day, and whilst the most impressive activity happened during the so-called 'witching hours' of between 3 to 5 am, it would seem that activity can happen there at any time, even in broad daylight.

"Nor is this an example of the 'Stone Tape theory,' the repetition of a ghostly event somehow recorded in the minerals in surrounding stone, like magnetic tape – because whatever is in that house seems to respond to questions and requests, often on command. One thing's for sure, the house isn't rigged – I mean, to get an entire house to move, you'd need to put the whole house on a massive rig that was riding on powerful hydraulics – or use explosives! A ridiculous notion, and besides, I'm fairly sure Bil has better things to be doing with his time and money."

One thing is for sure, Dale and Justin, two former rabidly sceptical paranormal investigators, have now switched from one end of the opinion spectrum to the other and are now committed believers in there being something real, powerful and profound at 30 East Drive…

At the time of writing, *Paranormal Truths* are planning a

week's stay at 30 East Drive, with the ambition of establishing just what might be creating the intelligent knocks and voices. What invisible something can possibly have the power to shake an entire house?

The authors wish them well on their investigation and look forward to their report. Let's hope that 'It' is in a playful mood. We'd also recommend that they ask some female investigators to accompany them again!

But before they go back to the house, a word of caution, by way of a reminder: Dale, when you asked what the spirit would have you do – didn't you record a threatening response telling you to "*GET OUT!*"?

CHAPTER SIX

Tidy-Geist

Bil's phone rang. It was Carol, the neighbour and key-holder for 30 East Drive, and she sounded pretty miffed.

"Bil, under no circumstances let them lot that were in last night, back in the house," she insisted, "them four big lads clattered about the whole bloody night, screaming and shouting, I barely slept a wink!"

"Oh, dear. I am so sorry to hear that Carol," Bil said apologetically, "I'll confirm who they were and blacklist them – we can't have your life disturbed by idiots."

Barely fifteen minutes after Carol put the phone down, Bil's phone rang again.

"Bil, it's Steve. We were in last night. When can we come back?"

"Erm, Steve? Steve Richards? I was going to call you. How did your night go?"

Bil braced himself for the 'party line,' which usually went something like this: 'We turned up, got the beers in, had a right laugh,' and so on. He already knew that the conversation would end with Steve being banned from the property. But it was only fair to let him have his say first.

"It wasn't quite what we expected…"

"Ah, well, yes – it is very much feast and famine in that place.

I take it that you had a *quiet night??"*

"No, I mean, we were expecting bangs, knocks and so on, but we got *so* much more."

"Huh?"

"Bil, it started the moment we walked into the place. It was pitch black and we couldn't find the light switch, which given the reputation of the place, was already an ominous start. But the thing that immediately struck us all was a horrible, crushing feeling in our chests, all of us. It felt like our ribs were closing in. You could feel there was something in that house, and almost immediately something *growled*."

"Seriously? Growled?"

"We finally found the light switch," Steve went on, "and immediately noticed that one of the kitchen drawers (we assumed it was the knife drawer) was taped up. Even though we were all believers in the paranormal, we did think that that was a bit of a gimmick, a scene-setter so to speak, so we removed the tape and saw that it was indeed where the knives were kept. There were five knives in there, all of them sharp – we counted them carefully.

"My brother Dave suggested that we re-seal the drawer, but my view was that they were never going to move, and if they do – amazing! So, for a bit of a laugh we left the tape off."

Not a very bright idea, Bil thought to himself, but didn't interrupt.

"My brother and I decided to go straight into the coal house.

Almost immediately, something growled between us. We both reacted at exactly the same time – so neither of us was winding the other up.

"Then we did a little tour of the house on our own whilst Griff went out to collect a few things from the car, and Griff's dad Peter took to the comfy arm-chair to read the visitors' book (he doesn't like to move very much).

"We were upstairs for less than five minutes before we came back down again. That's when we came across two sharp kitchen knives, one on the third step, and the other on the fourth from bottom step of the staircase. Our first response was to suggest that the knives were there when we came into the house, a previous visitor having placed them there for a laugh, but a) why didn't we notice them when we went up the stairs? They would have been pretty obvious. And b) when we went back to the knife drawer – there were two knives missing."

"You're kidding me, right?" Bil said, already knowing that Steve wasn't.

"No Bil, I swear to you I am not."

Caught wrong-footed, and quite frankly gobsmacked, Bil listened intently for the next hour as Steve passionately recounted the almost unbelievable experiences at 30 East Drive that he and his guests had undergone.

"It's important to add that my mate Griff and his dad Peter, the two that in this specific instance, could potentially be accused of cheating – never saw any of the *Most Haunted* episodes, and so knew nothing at all about its reputation with the knives (see Chapter Twelve): They both swore blind, Griff swearing on his daughter's life, that they had nothing to do with it.

"Also, Griff is a whopping 6 feet 5 inches tall [1.98m]. His dad is 6 feet [1.82m], and they both come in at around the 22 stone mark [300lbs/138kg], you can hear them walking around from the *next* house, as Carol will willingly testify. To expect them to hold their heavy breathing and float like ballerinas and butterflies to get the knives to where they ended up, and not have us hear them inside that quiet little house – *is a very big ask*.

"Also bear in mind that you are attuned to hearing the smallest of footsteps, bumps, creaks in there. We'd likely even have heard the tight-fitting knife drawer opening up in the first instance. It's been three years and I still ask them to this day if they did it – and they continue to swear blind that they had absolutely nothing to do with it."

Subsequent to his first visit to 30 East Drive, and indeed his first ever ghost hunt, Steve has established his own private little enterprise called the *Ouija Bros*. But back in 2015, Steve, like a lot of visitors to 30 East Drive, was visiting purely out of curiosity. He and his guests (all close friends and family) were most certainly not there to cheat or to frighten each other, because they were believers in the paranormal that had no one to impress or to entertain.

They arrived with no equipment (a fact that Carol disdainfully observed), no psychic medium, no experience… in other words, without a clue. This for them was simply a private adventure, and a chance to see and experience this infamous house at first hand.

"So, we made a cuppa and tried to gather ourselves," continued Steve. "I had a laugh with Peter, discussing the prospect of him sleeping alone in the house were someone to give him fifteen thousand pounds – to which, with a noticeable air of nonchalance, he had no hesitation in agreeing to, in principle at least… despite the things that we had already experienced. He was in his own words, 'No big girl's blouse,' and with his large stature and gruff, no-nonsense demeanour, his bravado seemed well-founded."

For now.

"We noticed that there was a TV in the corner of the front room. It was covered by a small blanket, so while the kettle was boiling, we took the blanket off to reveal a nice plasma telly. We folded the blanket and placed it on the little wooden foot-rest next to the TV, planning on watching a bit of telly later."

Dave went upstairs again to check if anything had moved. Peter took to the armchair in the corner of the dining room once more, whilst Griff prepared the tea, and Steve went back into the *coal house* (right).

As Dave came down from upstairs, he went via the front room and noticed the uncovered TV and folded blanket again, before heading back out to Griff and Pete in the kitchen. With that, Griff almost immediately made his way into the front room to take a good look at things, as one often does in a new environment.

"Erm, who put the blanket back over the telly?" asked Griff.

"Huh? But I've literally just walked out of the front room, and I know for sure it was off," responded Dave.

"But… how did it get back on the telly?!" exclaimed Griff.

The blanket was indeed back over the television set, and what's more was perfectly positioned.

"And by perfect, we really do mean *perfect*," continues Steve – not something easily done in a hurry, or in complete silence. It was then that another round of loud accusations and emphatic denials began.

"We had only been in the house for something like forty minutes, and now *this* had happened. It was total disbelief from us all, a case of *what the hell has just happened?* I'd trust my brother Dave with my life – he would never cheat; he definitely didn't put the blanket back."

It is interesting to observe that more or less all of the events that occur at 30 East Drive can be slotted into one of two camps, broadly speaking; the terrifying and the playful.

Strangely, it's the playful events that can mess with the visitor's mind the most because, thanks to the media, our basic assumption of a poltergeist is that everything it does is violent, hurtful and evil: so, placing the blanket back over the TV is all the more extraordinary because it defies our conventional expectations of poltergeist activity. Tear the blanket off – but not put it back on, and *tidily* at that! Who wouldn't want a poltergeist that tidied up all the time?

But as if to remind Steve and his guests of what they were truly dealing with, *this* happened – in Steve's own words:

"Over the red armchair that was in the corner of the dining area at the time, hung an ornamental frying pan with a brass lid. The lid was suddenly positioned up instead of being down, as it had been before. Peter, who had spent more or less all of his time in the armchair, suddenly felt very cold all down his right-hand side, then said that he felt as if something was crawling down his body.

"Peter yelled, 'What the hell is this? Oh my god!' then he lifted up his trouser leg and we saw that he had three clear scratches on his ankle. You could see them getting redder and redder as we watched. He jumped out of that chair like a gazelle – it looked like he was going to have a heart attack! He never sat back down in it again after that!"

But it didn't end there. At the time, a previous visitor had brought a large white polystyrene ball into the house as a trigger object. It was impossible to miss, what with its brilliant white colour being in complete contrast to the muted, earthy tones of the house. Steve picks up the story again:

"The white polystyrene ball was at the centre of the front room. Suddenly, it was by the TV. None of us saw it move. But it's a ball – so you naturally assume it could have rolled – a breeze, a kick, something like that. So, we placed it back at the middle of the room and continued with our investigation upstairs. When we all returned to the front room together, the ball had gone. Straight away we started to accuse each other again, just as we had before. There was too much happening in this house, one of us had to be messing around, we thought.

"So, we all patted each other down. It was a big ball. You simply couldn't have hidden it anywhere on your person. And none of us had even tried. So, we turned the entire house upside down. *Countless times.* We even checked the toilet cistern. If it was there to be found, we would have found it – it had literally vanished into thin air.

"We then went lights-out and started calling out in the front room for a few minutes. When we turned the lights back on, we went to the coal house to see if anything had moved, and would you believe it – a doll we had placed on the top shelf earlier, and a bracelet we had placed on the shelf underneath – was now on the bottom shelf, and was *holding the bloody bracelet*!

"Yes, it was unbelievable, but we found it more shocking than incredible. We immediately went back out to the kitchen to collect our thoughts, and I glanced, just out of curiosity, into the front room – and guess what? The big white polystyrene ball was back, sitting in the centre of the floor in the front room!

"Needless to say, the swearing and ranting kicked in yet again. But this was beyond any accusation. I was the last to leave the front room, the ball was definitely *not* there when I left. And I most definitely did not put it there, even though the lads quite understandably tried to accuse me this time. But I had an energy drink in one hand and a torch in the other, and the ball was impossible to hide! As far as the doll was concerned, it was in the coal house on its own, which meant that it was impossible that one of us could have got to it without being noticed.

"We had been in the house for less than an hour and it was already blatantly clear to us all that this house was legitimate, it's paranormally active – without a shadow of a doubt."

Whatever was there must have been closely observing the activities of the group, particularly their whereabouts, and seemed hell-bent on messing with their minds. This was most definitely not the behaviour of something intent on simply throwing objects or breaking things, some random spirit, breeze or energy – this was something altogether different, something that was creatively interacting with Steve and his guests... like a stand-up performer on a stage goading his audience. It seemed apparent that this particular something was evidently enjoying watching their reactions to its actions.

Whatever 'It' was, it seemed intent on creating fear. It was demonstrably provocative, invisible, intelligent, and, presumably – *dead,* or at the very least, not human.

The night had only just begun, and already Steve and his guests' first ghost hunt had delivered far more than they could ever have imagined possible. But there was plenty more to come.

"This time, I was the one that made for the top floor to see if anything had moved," Steve went on, "and there it was, the wardrobe door in the master bedroom – standing wide open, for all to see. All of the doors were definitely closed on our earlier visits. I called for the lads to come upstairs and see.

"Just as Dave arrived, Pete was rounding the top of the stairs, and Griff was about half way up, when all of a sudden something blew past us all like a passing truck. First it passed Griff, then Pete, breezed past me outside the master bedroom, and finally shot by Dave, who was standing in the doorway of Diane's bedroom… where it flipped the quilt!

"There is simply no way that quilt could have flipped itself. Almost straight away, Peter began feeling faint. He said that he felt as if he was going to have a heart attack, and then, unbelievably, scratches appeared on his ankle *again*, but it was his *left* ankle this time.

"The rush of wind, passing force, quilt flipping, feeling of having a heart attack and more scratches, all happened in less than twenty terrifying seconds."

Steve paused to catch his breath. Bil waited patiently, letting the man tell his story in his own time. Based on countless other eyewitness accounts, it had a ring of truth to it, as far as Bil was concerned.

"There are those who say that the house is rigged," Steve continued, "that there are speakers in the walls and devices under the floorboards that are creating knocks and bangs. All I can say is that these people are deluding themselves! They don't want to admit that things like this can exist, or worse still, are armchair critics – but more pertinently, this sequence alone would have literally been impossible to fake, even if we were all in on it! The breeze, the passing force, the flipping of the quilt, the scratches – any one of those things would require an incredibly complex set-up to achieve, about the only accusation a sceptic could level at us would be that we are *all* lying, and that wouldn't be an accusation I would take at all lightly. Speak to us all independently and you will discover that we all tell exactly the same story of what happened to us that night, we are not lying and will never lie about this."

The house seemed to calm down after the quilt-flipping episode. Fearless Peter, in his mid-sixties, was exhausted, so he said that he would go and hit the sack. "We said that it was a good idea and wished him a good night's rest," continues Steve. "Peter climbed the stairs alone, whilst we continued our vigil in the front room. It wasn't 5 minutes before Peter came thundering back down the stairs. Almost as soon as his head hit the pillow, he heard walking on the landing, talking, knocks and so on. There was no way he was staying upstairs on his own."

Steve reminded him that he thought he said he'd stay in the house on his own for £15k, "No bloody way!" came the reply, "not in a million years!"

Peter stayed awake with the group for another four hours, well past his body's pleas for rest. Eventually the group got their heads down, four big brave lads huddled together for safety in the same bedroom upstairs; Peter sharing a bed with his son Griff and David and Steve crashing on mattresses on the floor. Just as soon as the lights went out, they could hear the dragging of chairs downstairs in the kitchen/dining area.

Dave suggested going to see what was creating the commotion. Pete was at his limit, "Let 'em effing drag – I'm sleeping!"

But Griff showed slightly more courtesy, throwing a child's football down the stairs and saying, "Here, play with this!"

The lads tried to settle down once again, trying to ignore the troublesome, attention-getting sounds of the presence downstairs. But as if to show its contempt for their having ignored it, it decided to up the ante, a whole new level of activity that blew them all away. Steve takes up the story again…

"After Pete's declaration that he would definitely now not spend the night in the house alone, I wanted to understand if anything would get him out of the house right now, and if so – what would it take?" "If a big black monk appears and tells me to leave, yeah, that'd do it!" he clarified.

"We all laughed nervously, not least because the activity we had experienced definitively proved that we were not alone: There was something profoundly intelligent in that house, and it seemed entirely plausible that we could potentially see something physical – an actual manifestation.

"It wasn't long before our expectations were realised. Dave was the first to hear it (he is something of an insomniac). It sounded very much like a car's spark plug firing. Then, out of nowhere, right next to Dave's head, a bright orange ball of light appeared with a loud bang, jolting us all completely awake.

"Peter shouted, 'What the hell!' as the tennis ball-sized fiery orange sphere flew in a curve, like a David Beckham-style free kick, and shot straight out of the closed window!

"It was real, it was visible, it was incredible, and it was utterly unbelievable. We all heard it, and Dave and Pete both saw it with their own eyes."

After a restless night, the group awoke feeling utterly drained. "It was like we were hung over," Steve said, "the drain on us must have been huge."

The first thing the lads did, when heading for a reviving cuppa, was to look for the ball that Griff had jokingly thrown downstairs. It was gone. Yet again, the object was too big to hide, and the lads knew with absolutely certainty that they had all spent the night together upstairs – no one had been brave enough to venture downstairs on their own to check out whatever it was that they could hear dragging the chairs around.

They had enough strength left to check the whole house again, to no avail. The colourful plastic football, twice the size of the polystyrene ball, had simply vanished.

"An exhausted Dave made us all some teas," continued Steve, "whilst the others and I packed our belongings upstairs, ready for the long drive home. Even though we could have stayed until lunchtime, we were all more than ready to call it quits.

"Dave left the teas brewing in mugs before going upstairs to pack his bag. He finished and we all descended to drink the teas before leaving, only to discover all the teas overflowing like waterfalls. The whole kitchen surface was *soaked* with tea. I asked Dave what the hell he had been thinking – who makes tea like that?? But then I remembered that my brother was one of those annoying people that only fills the cup 60% of the way. It would have been completely unlike him to fill the cup, let alone fill it all the way up to the brim. It was obvious to us that 'It,' 'Fred,' the 'Black Monk,' whatever you want to call him, was playing one last mind game with us. The very thing that would have revived us before our departure, that would have given us a little solace after such an exhausting night, was a heart-warming cuppa – and '*It*' knew it."

Steve, his brother Dave, and Pete's son 'Big Griff,' all have 30

East Drive to thank for their passionate interest in ghost hunts (they now travel the length and breadth of the UK in search of spooks), but they will all willingly declare that their first explosive ghost hunt at 30 East Drive blows everything they have experienced since completely out of the water. They still visit the house, and have had many more incredible experiences (too numerous to mention on this occasion) and firmly declare 30 East Drive to be the most haunted house in Britain bar none, if not *the most haunted house in the world.*

Pete, on the other hand, now refuses to "ever set foot in that house ever again," and was so affected by his experiences that he has never been on a ghost hunt since, nor has he any intention of doing so in the future.

After taking a few moments to collect his thoughts, Bil picked up the phone again.

"Carol, it's Bil."

"Ey up. Did you ban Steve yet?"

"Erm, not exactly. But I *did* find out why they were making a racket. Those four big, burly lads were frankly crapping themselves, and spent the entire evening screaming and hollering – which is totally understandable. Just wait 'til I tell you what happened to them…"

Carol and Steve have since made up, and Carol's respect for Steve went up when she heard that he had finally purchased some ghost-hunting equipment.

CHAPTER SEVEN
Break a Leg

Hazel Ford ought to know something about haunted houses: after all, she runs the United Kingdom's biggest paranormal events company.

Paranormal tourism may have started out as a cottage industry, but at the time of writing (early 2019) business is booming. Thousands of people are willing to hand over their hard-earned money in exchange for the privilege of spending a night in a haunted location. While it isn't accurate to call these events 'investigations' – they are primarily intended to be entertainment, rather than a controlled and objective study – they do put a steady stream of witnesses into those haunted locations, each one of whom may or may not have their own encounter with something otherworldly.

A quick search of the Internet will produce plenty of business organisations that cater to those who would like to have such an experience. The biggest and most well-known is *Haunted Happenings.* Thanks to her interest in all things ghostly, Hazel started out working for a paranormal events company. She soon struck out on her own, wanting to do things her own way. *Haunted Happenings* put on more than two hundred events in the year of its inception, all run by Hazel and fifteen of her team members. At the time of writing, this number has exploded to over eight hundred events each year, and the ranks of her team have swollen to more than fifty.

"I'm by no means an expert in the paranormal," Hazel likes to point out, "just somebody who enjoys finding out as much as I can about it, and also someone who wants to provide that experience for others."

One day, Hazel happened to be running an event at a haunted location that was owned by a friend of hers. When he asked her whether she had heard of the infamous 'Black Monk House,' she shook her head. The friend excitedly showed her an article that had been cut out of a newspaper.

Her attention was well and truly piqued. If the story was to be believed, the house on East Drive was a true paranormal hot spot. Although number 30 had recently been investigated by a few individuals and teams, it wasn't nearly as famous (or should that be infamous) as it would soon become.

Hazel contacted owner Bil Bungay and asked whether she could spend a night in the house with a small team. If the evening was successful, she reasoned, then it could be the ideal place to hold future *Haunted Happenings* events.

Bil readily agreed, and so having secured permission, Hazel made the drive to Pontefract with a handful of trusted colleagues in order to experience the house for themselves. Given number 30's fearsome reputation, hopes were understandably high among the team. They chatted excitedly with one another, optimistic that the house wouldn't disappoint them.

To say that their hopes were fulfilled would be an understatement.

"The level of activity we got was amazing and also terrifying," Hazel recalls. "Doors would open and close all by themselves. While I was setting up cameras, I personally saw light anomalies fly out of the cupboard in Phillip's bedroom, then turn around and dart back inside again. We heard disembodied voices and a host of other phenomena that we just couldn't debunk or explain away rationally."

Over the space of three years, Hazel spent over one hundred nights at 30 East Drive. Other *Haunted Happenings* team members have spent almost five hundred nights there in total. Some of those nights have been relatively quiet and uneventful; others have been every bit as spectacular as Hazel's first time in the house was. When it comes to paranormal activity, events at the house tend to be either 'feast or famine', with no way to tell in advance just what is going to happen on any given night. This adds a certain spice to the experience for the event guides, who can never be entirely sure what the coming evening will hold.

After looking at her own personal experiences and listening to the accounts of her team members, Hazel has noticed a certain similarity to the activity that takes place there, with the same phenomena being reported over and over again:

- Disembodied footsteps heard upstairs, sometimes

- seeming to come from the attic space.
- Cupboards, closets, and doors opening and closing themselves.
- Light anomalies that are seen with the naked eye and are also caught on camera.
- Visitors becoming unaccountably sad, tearful and/or hysterical, particularly younger females, who seem to be the most common target.

[Author's note: Bil has just returned from one of his regular visits to 30 East Drive. A young female producer working with a film crew at the house exited the toilet looking unwell. Bil naturally asked if she was OK, and she confessed to feeling nauseous and that she had been throwing up since she arrived. Later, after being dropped off at the station, Bil asked the producer how she was feeling now, "Much better," came the reply.]

The most remarkable experience that has happened to Hazel at number 30 took place in the kitchen. She was standing in front of the worktop, watching the monitor feeds as her customers conducted a series of lone vigils throughout the house.

At the beginning of the evening, Hazel had taken all of the chairs from the dining room and placed them in the living room prior to conducting an EVP session. The team member who was standing watch alongside her happened to have a bad back, so

Hazel offered to pop through into the room next door and fetch one for him to sit on.

Making her way through the double doors into the living room, she felt something slam into her knees. Looking down, she saw that she had collided with a chair.

"Hazel, you're never going to believe this," her colleague called out from behind her, "that chair just moved across the room all by itself!"

He had been watching the camera and had seen it happen with his own eyes. The chair had been sitting next to the sofa when Hazel had left the kitchen. As soon as she had set foot in the living room, it had slid across the carpet to intercept her.

"Nobody's ever going to believe this," was Hazel's first thought, but then she realised that if her companion had seen it on the camera feed, then it must have been recorded.

She asked him to spool the video footage back to the point in time where the incident had taken place. When the video was cued up, they could see both the sofa and the chair standing next to it. Unfortunately, the camera angle was such that only the upper third of the chair was visible.

Both of them watched with mounting anticipation as the playback approached that point. First Hazel's head and shoulders entered the frame, then the chair itself began to move – almost as if it was pushed by a pair of unseen hands. The chair disappeared at the bottom of the screen at the exact same moment that it had crashed into Hazel's knees. They still hurt.

Hazel and her colleague couldn't help but feel a little disappointed. *They* knew exactly what had happened – the living room was completely empty, as a thorough search quickly verified. But thanks to the fact that the bottom section of the chair wasn't visible on the playback, nobody was ever going to believe that they hadn't faked it. There is a prevailing attitude among members of the paranormal research community that if something looks too good to be true, then it probably *is*… a point of view that, in all fairness, isn't entirely undeserved. In an age of Photoshop, cheap special effects and other even simpler visual shenanigans, most of the so-called 'ghost videos' that go viral turn out to be nothing more than smoke and mirrors. No wonder Hazel didn't want the ridicule that would almost certainly come with releasing the video onto a disbelieving Internet.

Yet the incident left her in absolutely no doubt that 30 East Drive was haunted and based upon the pain that the fast-moving chair had inflicted upon her, the entity in question probably wasn't very friendly.

During another *Haunted Happenings* event, a small group of visitors were sitting with Hazel in Phillip's bedroom. One of the guests happened to be sitting on the floor. He had chosen a spot in one of the corners, which gave him a good view of the door and the closet that contained the water heater.

The guest suddenly yelped, grabbing at his leg. When Hazel asked him what was wrong, he replied that his ankle was on fire. "It feels like a Chinese burn!" he said, reaching for the top of his sock.

"See if you can walk it off," Hazel suggested. Gingerly, he tried climbing to his feet, but the leg simply refused to bear weight. Each time the guest attempted to stand, he claimed that waves of agony would shoot out from his ankle. He sat back down once more, allowing the others to inspect the limb.

A huge red ring completely encircled the man's ankle, the skin swollen and inflamed. The sight of it drew gasps from the other visitors, and even Hazel had to stop herself from showing her surprise. His leg had been just fine when he first arrived at the house, and he had been walking around at the start of the evening without any complaints at all.

Most *Haunted Happenings* events at 30 East Drive finish up in the early hours of the morning, allowing the guides and the customers to make it home at a reasonable time. This particular guest and his friends had arranged to spend the entire night at the house, sleeping over in whichever bedroom took their fancy.

"If that ankle gets any worse, *please* promise me that you'll go to the hospital," Hazel pleaded with the injured guest. Seeming a little nervous but still willing to spend the night, he agreed that he would see a doctor if it didn't get better very quickly. Bidding them a good night, Hazel stepped outside and locked the front door, trapping the small group inside for the rest of the night.

Hazel was so tired she fell asleep the minute her head hit the pillow. Waking up the next morning, the first thing she did was reach for her phone. Her eyes widened in surprise. Blinking the sleep from her eyes, she saw that there was a big stack of missed calls from the night before. She immediately recognised the phone number of the injured guest.

"What's wrong?" she asked after phoning the guest back. The man sounded absolutely terrified and went on to tell her that after she had left for the night and locked them inside, 30 East Drive had practically exploded with paranormal activity. Most of it was physical phenomena. For example, plastic dominoes and playing cards were hurled through the air at the disbelieving visitors, who quickly realised that although they had come to East Drive with high hopes of experiencing something ghostly, they were now getting far more than they had bargained for.

"We just couldn't take it anymore," the guest concluded, his voice still shaking. "But we couldn't get out through that locked front door, so we ended up climbing out of a window."

It is tempting to dismiss the guest's story as being nothing more than a tall tale, except for one thing: the same man turned up at a different *Haunted Happenings* event the following week, with his foot in a cast and hobbling along on a pair of crutches.

"I went to the hospital and they X-rayed my ankle," he

explained. "Don't ask me how, but it was fractured... just from sitting there on the floor in Phillip's bedroom..."

Either the man was telling the truth, or he was taking fakery to the extreme. If Hazel had woken up during the night and answered her phone, she would have been able to check on the guests, verify their story – and let them out. The repeated phone calls certainly implied that they wanted her to do just that.

"Like most people, I need to see the evidence for myself before I am willing to make any judgment about whether a place is or isn't haunted," Hazel explains. "There are many things that can be debunked at 30 East Drive, I'm sure, but that chair was a truly personal experience that showed me beyond a shadow of a doubt that someone – or some*thing* – is creating some form of energy inside that house, that is not easy to either debunk or dismiss.

"I have absolute respect for 30 East Drive, and always recommend that those who choose to visit should keep an open mind and trust their own experiences."

CHAPTER EIGHT
Shadow Figure

In his capacity as a tour guide for *Haunted Happenings*, Phil Barron is starting to lose track of the number of nights he has spent inside the walls of 30 East Drive: At our request, he checked his records and found that at the time of writing, he has investigated there on no less than 42 occasions.

His passion for all things ghostly began back when he was a child glued to the TV set. "I was addicted to a TV show called *Arthur C. Clarke's Mysterious World*," Phil laughs, looking back nostalgically. "That led me to a magazine called *The Unexplained,* which was always chock full of ghost stories."

Phil's first foray into the world of field investigation took place in 2002, when he was looking to do something "a little different" for his wife's birthday. That 'something different' involved a ghost hunt at a haunted hotel in Ludlow, Shropshire, named *The Feathers.* Both he and his wife experienced things at that overnight ghost hunt that neither of them could satisfactorily explain, and Phil has spent the last fifteen years trying to find answers to exactly those kinds of questions.

His first visit to 30 East Drive was on April 10, 2015. It was an active night, and would be just the first of many, which continue to this day.

Early one night, a few minutes before the vigil was scheduled to begin, Phil gathered his guests together in the kitchen. He took up a position in the doorway that leads from the kitchen to the downstairs toilet, coal house, and the front door. Leaning casually against the door frame and facing the small group of guests, he began to lay out the plan for the evening ahead, talking about which equipment would be used and which rooms they would begin to rotate through.

The guests nodded their understanding. When Phil paused for a breath, somewhere behind him a female voice said, "Excuse me."

Everybody looked at one another in confusion. Who had just spoken? All of the guests were in the kitchen and accounted for. Other than that, the house was completely empty: Phil had gone from room to room when he first arrived, making sure of exactly that.

Yet the voice had been loud and as clear as a bell. What's more, it had definitely come from somewhere behind Phil. Assuming that it hadn't been somebody shouting outside – unlikely, as the voice wasn't muffled, which it would have been if it had been heard through the door – then the only places it could possibly have come from would be the toilet, coal house, and the rear scullery which was now used as an sort of museum, full of photos and curios related to 30 East Drive.

With no time to lose, Phil and his companions quickly checked each of the back rooms together, making sure that there were no uninvited guests; and as he suspected, they were completely empty. Not one to give up so easily, his next attempt at debunking involved his going outside onto the front garden path, closing the door behind him, then calling "Excuse me!" as loud as he could. After several attempts, everybody agreed that this wasn't how the female voice had sounded at all – Phil's voice was not nearly as clear when it was coming through the closed front door.

Not only had the front door been closed, but the windows in the kitchen and the bathroom had been closed too. The voice had to have come from inside one of those rooms, but who – or *what* – was responsible?

Phil's experience, which was shared with eight other witnesses (all of whom were in complete agreement on what was heard) seems at first glance to be a residual auditory phenomenon. This type of event has been theorised by some to be a form of natural recording mechanism, a means by which sounds are somehow imprinted on the environment when they first take place, only to be 'played back' at a future date, when those who are sensitive enough can sometimes hear them. This type of haunting is by no means confined to just sounds – there are similar types of visual apparitions (phantoms that, when seen, seem totally oblivious of their surroundings and of the living observer) and olfactory phenomena, such as the smell of flowers or cigar smoke, to name just two.

Could it possibly have been the voice of Jean or Diane Pritchard, speaking to him from years past? Although both women were still alive and well at the time of Phil's visit to 30 East Drive, contrary to popular belief, it is apparently unnecessary for a person to be dead in order for their apparition to be seen or heard: There are numerous recorded instances of what are commonly called 'phantasms of the living.'

When we delve a little deeper, however, there is an equally strong argument to be made *against* this being a residual phenomenon. Phil just so happened to be blocking the kitchen doorway at the time the voice was heard: the words, '*Excuse me,*' imply that somebody wanted to go into the kitchen, which meant that they would have to get past him to do so and had therefore asked him to move. Such behaviour implies a form of intelligence on the part of the speaker. Assuming that it was indeed a disembodied entity of some sort, it would have been necessary for it to see the obstruction (Phil) standing between it and its intended destination, processed that information, made a decision to act (politely asking him to move) and then to physically form those words so that the whole room could hear them.

That all requires some degree of cognitive processing, which in turn requires a form of *consciousness.* At the time of writing, the identity of the mysterious female speaker remains just that – a mystery.

Perhaps the most common example of paranormal phenomena that Phil has experienced at 30 East Drive is that of disembodied footsteps. "I've heard them so many times when I was all alone in that house," he says, "and they almost always come from somewhere upstairs. Usually I'll be sitting in the lounge or in the kitchen and hear the sound of footsteps on the floorboards above my head, which means they would have to be coming from either Phillip's room or the master bedroom."

Showing a level of bravery that few possess, Phil once spent a night all alone in 30 East Drive. He arrived shortly before nightfall and made it his first order of business to walk around the house in order to ensure that it was both empty and secure, checking all of the windows and doors. He left the master key in the front door lock, making sure that nobody could get in from the outside.

The building was both empty and quiet when Phil settled in for the evening, wondering whether it would be a peaceful night or not. 30 East Drive tends to be very much a 'feast or famine' haunted location – sometimes the inexplicable phenomena come thick and fast, while at other times nothing noteworthy happens. This maddening unpredictability is part of the house's charm and appeal but has led some frustrated visitors to mistakenly conclude that it isn't haunted at all. The truth is that paranormal phenomena seldom take place on demand. Investigating such a place is a little bit like fishing: it takes a lot of downtime and boredom in order to get a bite, but the payoff is usually well worth the investment.

He began by sitting quietly in Phillip's room for a while. Nothing noteworthy happened. The occasional noise could most likely be put down to the house settling down. Most structures expand slightly during the relative warmth of the day and contract when the air cools down at night, leading to slight shifting and creaking in the walls and roof. Phil was very familiar with the rhythms and eccentricities of the house after so many visits, and none of the noises sent his hackles up.

Getting up to stretch, he made his way out onto the landing and sat down at the top of the stairs. Phil began to call out to any spirit entities that might be around, inviting them to come forward and make their presence known.

The sudden sound took him completely by surprise. It seemed to be coming from somewhere off to his right, from beyond the open doorway to Jean and Joe Pritchard's bedroom. At first Phil couldn't identify the noise, but as it went on for a few seconds more he became convinced that it was the sound of something being dragged across the carpet between the double bed and the fitted wardrobe.

Phil crept forward and stuck his head around the bedroom door. A dim glow seeping through the drawn curtains was all that lit the room, meaning that all he could see was the grey and black shadows. If this was a scene from a horror movie, this would be the point at which Phil came face to face with the terrifying apparition of 'Fred,' the Black Monk of Pontefract. Instead, the master bedroom appeared to be deserted. Nothing was moving.

A loud, throaty growl made him take a step back. For a split second, his brain wondered how the hell a dog had managed to get inside the house. Then his rational mind caught up with him. The growl had been too loud and coarse to have come from a canine. This was something different.

Something *unnatural.*

Reaching out a hand, Phil flipped on the light switch and looked around the room. Bed. Wardrobe. Dressing table. But no animal.

He waited for a few minutes longer, too stubborn to cut and run, but there were no more growls. Closing the door behind him, Phil went back downstairs, shaking his head at what had just happened. It was one of the most unnerving things that he had experienced at 30 East Drive so far, but he wasn't going to let whatever it was drive him away.

Phil sat down in a chair in the living room and tried to find a rational explanation for what had just happened to him up there. Try as he might, he just couldn't come up with anything plausible. Although a sceptic would probably say that he had either hallucinated or imagined the growl, the fact of the matter was that he wasn't the first person to report hearing such a noise inside 30 East Drive. A group of visiting paranormal investigators had recorded the sound of growling and scratching coming from inside the coal house, for example.

One term that is thrown around too readily when it comes to the haunting of 30 East Drive is 'demonic.' It's a word that carries heavily religious connotations. Those investigators of a more secular leaning may prefer the term 'inhuman' to describe it. Either way, the meaning is the same: Rather than being the spirit of a dead person, such an entity is believed to have never walked the earth in human form at all. Such a being would be no more human than a shark or a tiger, and many believe that they are every bit as predatory.

While we are (yet again) on the subject of the coal house, it is one of the rooms in the house that has been responsible for changing the core psychology of many individuals that have had the misfortune (in the case of Joe Pritchard), the courage or most often, the *bravado* to spend time in there.

One such incident involved a team member of Merseyside Paranormal. A 'team member' is someone that is considered to be an experienced ghost hunter, someone that is capable of taking care of others on a ghost hunt, and most certainly capable of taking care of himself. Steve White, the team leader, closed the coal house door behind his friend and colleague, and continued with making a cup of tea for everyone. In Steve's words, here's what happened next:

"After only a couple of minutes I called to him asking if he was OK... His response didn't sound good, so I decided to open the door to check on him. As I opened the door, what stood before me didn't even look like my friend and team member. One of his arms was sort of twisted and his face looked very strange, he couldn't move his arm. He was totally incapable of getting himself out of the cupboard – I had to drag him out of there.

"I took him outside away from whatever had hold of him, he was shaking and crying and couldn't control his emotions. This is a large man who has been on a lot of ghost hunts with me and shows no fear, in fact he's usually the first to volunteer to go into unknown territory alone, yet here he was shaking and crying in front of me...

"I knew then that there was a very powerful demonic spirit in that house. After my friend had had a strong cup of sweet coffee, he insisted that he was going home and could not stay in the house another minute, that proves just how scared he was."

Going on to confront the spirit using the *SB11 Spirit Box,* Steve was told in no uncertain terms that 'It' had hurt his friend, and it *now wanted Steve to 'F#*# OFF!'* (left). The last the authors heard – Steve's friend has given up ghost hunting altogether after his traumatic experience.

Perhaps it's why the *playful little girl's voice recently captured on a remote camera* (right) positioned in the kitchen adjacent to the coal hole – warns, "Don't go in there"?

Some types of phenomena are more common at 30 East Drive than others. One of the more frequent occurrences is that of thrown objects, particularly marbles.

Early in the evening before Phil's lone vigil fully began, he was upstairs setting up some infrared cameras. Engrossed in his work, he was suddenly distracted by a sound that came from somewhere downstairs.

Though relatively experienced with 30 East Drive, it didn't cross his mind that the occurrence might be paranormal. He simply assumed that something had fallen over. Slightly annoyed, Phil went downstairs to check it out. Just as he reached the bottom of the staircase and turned toward the kitchen, he felt something hit him high on the ankle.

Looking down, he was surprised to see a small blue-green marble rolling along the floor next to him. Stooping to pick it up, he examined it. The marble wasn't noticeably hot or cold to the touch, the marble had bounced from the bottom of his trousers, dropped onto the floor, and bled out the last of its momentum in the space of a second or two.

He was completely alone in the house. Exactly who might have thrown the marble, or where it may have come from in the first place, was never determined.

Another frequently-reported phenomenon at 30 East Drive is the feeling of being watched, the sensation that one is not alone even when the house is empty. Both of the authors of this book have experienced the same sensation, as have many other visitors.

"When I move around the house I always feel as if I'm not alone, that I'm being watched," he says. "Of course, I know that can be my mind playing tricks with my brain because of where I am…"

Phil is absolutely right. Tell somebody that a house is haunted – particularly one with the fearsome reputation of 30 East Drive – and it won't be long before even the most hard-nosed of sceptic begins to look sidelong at every creaking floorboard and gurgle of water through pipes, particularly when it gets dark outside. It is a well-documented psychological phenomenon, born out of the many ghost stories and scary movies that most of us are exposed to during our formative years, and nobody is completely immune to its effects.

"The feeling of being watched has also been described by a number of people I trust and has been documented by countless guests during our ghost hunts, all without anyone pre-empting them," Phil goes on. "Each room has a slightly different feeling to it, with the atmosphere in Jean and Joe Pritchard's room always feeling the most oppressive and thick."

Speaking of ghost hunts, we asked Phil what else he and his companions have experienced on some of their more active nights at 30 East Drive.

On one such evening, he and his group had congregated on the landing and inside Diane's bedroom. After settling in, they began calling out to any entities that might be present, inviting those spirits to come forward and communicate with them.

A device known as a *Cat Ball*, which could be triggered by vibration was placed in the upstairs bathroom, while the handful of people gathered in the small bedroom were using what is known as an *Alice Box* – a software application which some members of the paranormal research community (though by no means all of them) believe may allow communication with spirit entities. Quite how it is supposed to do so is unclear, and the program has both fierce defenders and vociferous detractors.

"Joe... Joe Pritchard. Are you there?" asked one of the male visitors. "If you're here, please let us know. Give us some kind of sign."

Almost immediately the *Cat Ball* began to flash in the bathroom; a room directly visible from the smallest bedroom.

It had been placed carefully on the floor in front of the toilet, exactly the same location in which Joe Pritchard was said to have died...

Nobody was moving at the time, and nobody was within touching distance of it. Just as the team was excitedly discussing the flashing lights, the *Alice Box* in Diane's bedroom suddenly piped up with the word 'Jo.'

Coincidence... or something more?

Phil is a big fan of using the *Spirit Box* device in an attempt to communicate with the spirits of 30 East Drive. One night, he and his companions were conducting a vigil in Jean and Joe's room with one. If the box is to be believed, they appeared to make contact with a male spirit, who they asked to talk to them and impart any relevant information that it felt like sharing.

One of the highlights of the session took place when they asked the spirit who he was, and were immediately told, "This is *my* house." Another member of the group asked where they were currently sitting. The voice promptly replied, "Mum and Dad's bedroom."

This intriguing response may support one of the theories regarding the identity of the ghosts of 30 East Drive. Numerous visitors have interacted with an entity claiming to be Joe Pritchard. Whether this is truly the case, or whether something within the house is misrepresenting itself *as* Joe, nobody can say for sure:

[Authors' note: We certainly mean no disrespect to Mr. Pritchard's memory – or to any members of his family, who at the time of writing are thankfully alive and well, yet we would be remiss to omit this information, or other stories we have received verbatim in relation to their old home, throughout this book – particularly in this instance where paranormal investigators bringing Spirit Boxes into number 30 regularly present similar information. We sincerely apologise if the following, or indeed any

comment and speculation about the Pritchard family in this book, in any way offends any of them; it is absolutely NOT our intent to do so and they have our deepest respect.]

Sometimes Phil finds himself all alone inside the house, either prior to or immediately after a vigil. On one such occasion, whilst sitting on his own in the lounge, he had made sure to lock the front door and leave the key in it so that nobody could get in to disturb him. He had also closed both sets of doors that led into the lounge.

Phil called out for a while and suddenly saw a shadow figure walk directly past the living room door towards the bottom of the stairs. It was both the size and shape of a fully-grown adult and moved just like it was walking. After a few seconds, Phil recovered from his sense of shock and went to investigate.

He searched the house from top to bottom and confirmed that he was the only living person inside it. To this day, he still has no good explanation for what it was that he saw that night, but one thing is very clear – he wasn't the first to see a shadow figure (indeed some *incredibly clear and sharp transparent shadow figures have even been captured on video*) (left) and he is unlikely to be the last to see such a thing inside 30 East Drive.

CHAPTER NINE

Right. Behind. Me.

After watching the movie *When the Lights Went Out,* Matt Penzer found himself fascinated with the Black Monk case. Although he had no real experience in the field of paranormal investigation, the story of the Pontefract poltergeist intrigued him so much that he began to research the facts of the actual case itself.

When he learned that it was possible to visit the house upon which the film was based, Matt arranged for himself, his partner, his mother, and his brother to spend the night there. They would be the only residents of 30 East Drive for an evening which none of them would ever forget.

"As soon as we stepped in the house, you could feel the oppression," he explains. "The whole time we were there, it felt as if someone was constantly watching you. We started exploring the house. I personally couldn't go upstairs on my own, even with all the lights on. I stood there, looking up the staircase and it felt like someone was at the top of the stairs just looking down at me."

About an hour after they had arrived, Matt's mother and brother both went out to fetch some Chinese food, leaving Matt and his partner all alone inside the house.

That's when the banging started.

Matt and his partner looked at each other, confirming that they were both hearing the same thing. They were standing on the boundary between the kitchen/dining area and the living room, next to the double doors which separated both rooms. Neither said a word, choosing simply to stand still and listen to what was quite plainly a banging sound coming from directly above.

"Maybe it's coming from next door," Matt said doubtfully, trying to find a rational explanation for the thudding sound which appeared to be coming from the floor of either Phillip's room or the master bedroom. They moved throughout the house in a vain attempt to pin down the exact location of the noise, putting their ears to the walls and also feeling for vibrations. The source of the banging remained maddeningly elusive.

Once his mum and brother returned, the four settled down to enjoy their dinner, fortifying themselves for what had the potential to be a long and active night ahead of them.

They had no idea of just *how* active it was going to be…

With night having fallen outside, Matt and his three companions decided to immediately go lights-out for the beginning of their stay. At first, the tentative would-be investigators all stuck together, electing to explore the house room by room.

From the outset, the downstairs floor seemed to be quiet and peaceful. Moving upstairs, the four went into what had once been Diane's bedroom. The atmosphere felt almost calm in there, so relaxed that it would have been easy to lay down on the bed and drift right off to sleep on the single bed which occupied the room.

Then the team moved next door into the master bedroom,

which had once belonged to Mr. and Mrs. Pritchard. The energy immediately changed, seeming to turn toward the dark and negative. Matt and his companions sat on the bed for a while, soaking up the atmosphere and acclimatising to the feel of the room.

After about 10 minutes, Matt's mother quickly jerked her leg. "Something just touched me!" she explained, looking around to make sure that it hadn't been one of her companions… which of course, it wasn't. It had felt exactly like a hand closing around her ankle, she explained, unable to find a rational explanation for what had just happened to her.

Something in the house was beginning to stir.

Deciding that it was time to move on, the four went into Phillip's bedroom. That, too, felt peaceful and calm… not quite to the same extent that Diane's bedroom had, but still significantly lighter and more welcoming than the master bedroom had seemed. They spent a quarter of an hour sitting in there, without any tangible results to show for it.

Matt's mother bravely volunteered to stay in the master bedroom on her own, while the remaining three went downstairs. She would be the only living occupant of the upper floor: perhaps that fact alone would entice something to come out and interact with her.

Once his mother was settled in the master bedroom, Matt, his partner, and his brother trooped downstairs to wait in the living room. They were far enough away to leave their mother in an isolated position, but close enough to come running if she happened to need assistance.

All four were using a software app to stay in contact with one another. SOMEBODY'S STANDING IN THE DOORWAY, their mother messaged them from upstairs. WHOEVER IT IS, THEY'RE STARING AT ME. I CAN *FEEL* IT.

Sitting in the living room, Matt and his two companions looked at one another with raised eyebrows. Then their phones all chimed again.

I'VE HAD ENOUGH!

COME GET ME!

Matt raced upstairs, down the short landing and into the master bedroom. More than a little startled at what she had just experienced, his mother revealed that after seeing a shadow in the doorway, she had felt the mattress sink as if someone had sat next to her. Remarkably, she had kept her nerve, continuing to sit there. She could see absolutely nothing in the darkness of the bedroom, and when she groped blindly in the direction of the invisible visitor, her had hand passed through empty air.

Yet again, she felt a hand on her ankle… an extremely *cold* hand. Matt looked around; there definitely wasn't anybody else in the room other than the four of them.

The upper floor, more specifically the master bedroom, was beginning to look like the epicentre for paranormal activity so far.

Matt's brother offered to stay on his own downstairs whilst the remaining three stayed up in the middle bedroom in order to investigate it further. He went downstairs and sat down on the couch, which sits behind the door leading out into the hallway. He had only been down there for five minutes before he yelled that the other three needed to come downstairs straight away.

When they arrived in the living room, he reported that whilst he was sitting on the sofa quietly minding his own business, he could suddenly hear the sound of male voices. It sounded as if a conversation was taking place, over in the corner by the French double doors that separated the living room from the kitchen. While he couldn't make out any specific words, Matt's brother was absolutely convinced that he had also heard the sound of grunting. He maintained that there was somebody else in that room with him, sitting in the corner watching him… the very same sensation that his mother had described just a few minutes before, while sitting all alone in the master bedroom.

It appeared that whichever entity or entities were present at 30 East Drive that night, it or they much preferred to target single individuals rather than larger groups.

Working on the premise that it might be better to leave nobody alone for the time being, Matt and his guests decided to split up, pairing off into two groups. While his mum and his partner went upstairs to investigate the master bedroom once more, Matt and his brother remained downstairs: his brother remained in the same spot on the couch, and Matt sat at the dining table. The double doors which separated the two rooms were left open.

The two men took turns calling out, asking questions into thin air and then waiting patiently for a response. For the next half-hour, all was calm and uneventful. The same was true upstairs, where the two occupants of the master bedroom remained undisturbed by the phantom ankle grabber. More than a little disappointed, the two teams swapped locations.

Matt took up a position in the master bedroom, while his brother sat at the top of the stairs. For the next fifteen minutes, 30 East Drive was calm and peaceful. The boys decided to switch positions, with Matt heading out onto the landing this time while his brother stretched out on the big double bed.

After roughly five minutes had passed, they both began to hear the definite creaking of floor boards. The sounds seemed to be coming from inside the master bedroom, close to the bed.

Footsteps…

Telling his brother to lie as still as he possibly could on the bed (just in case it was the bed creaking) Matt was soon convinced that the creaking wasn't coming from there. Nevertheless, he asked his brother to get off the bed and sit on the floor, just to be absolutely certain.

The sound didn't abate. In fact, the creaking intensified, passing through the open bedroom doorway and coming out onto the landing. The atmosphere was now so thick that you could have cut it with a knife.

"Sod this. I'm going back downstairs!" exclaimed Matt. There was no way that he was staying in that bedroom for even a minute longer.

30 East Drive remained calm and quiet for the rest of the night. Because they had a fair drive home ahead of them in the morning, the four visitors decided that a safety nap was in order before the sun started to come up. The group all stayed together in the living room, snatching a few precious winks of sleep before daybreak.

Matt's partner, however, just wouldn't go to sleep. He also made sure that Matt stayed awake with him.

"What's going on?" Matt whispered, trying not to wake up either his mum or his brother, both of whom were now well out of it, snoring gently across the room. "Why can't you sleep?"

"I've had enough," his partner admitted, "I want to get out of this house." Matt knew his partner well enough by now to tell that he was very apprehensive.

The two men slipped quietly out of the house, standing in the front yard and breathing the cold early morning air. "Why don't you come back inside for a bit?" Matt asked, trying to convince his frightened partner to stick it out for what was left of the night. "We've only got a couple of hours left."

Despite Matt's very best efforts at persuasion, his partner

wasn't having any of it. With a sigh, Matt suggested that he sleep in the car until it was time for the group to hit the road, a suggestion that his partner accepted gratefully.

"I stayed in the car with him, to keep him company and hopefully make him feel a little better. After about an hour and a half, I went back into the house again.

"As I was standing there in the kitchen, writing my name in the guest book and signing some paperwork, I suddenly felt heavy breathing in my ear. There was someone behind me… *Right. Behind. Me.*

"I didn't want to turn around, for fear that I would see someone – or worse, some*thing* – standing right there, looking back at me. So, I just closed my eyes and stood there. The breathing intensified, so I plucked up the courage to turn around as quickly as I could manage.

"There was nothing there…"

Matt finished writing as fast as he possibly could, and then went straight back out to the car. The experience had truly terrified him, particularly as he had been the only one awake in the darkened house when it had taken place. Once again, the inhabitants of 30 East Drive had struck when their intended target was all alone and vulnerable.

"There is something strange in that house," Matt says today, looking back. "I don't know exactly what, but there is something in that house and it is *not* positive. I honestly take my hat off to the Pritchard family for living in that house as long as they did. We were only there for twelve hours and we heard and felt so much. The atmosphere was depressing and oppressive, but I would like to return to the house again to do another investigation. The spirits don't just reside there, they haunt that house – they *haunt* it, and as soon as you walk through the front door, you can feel that they are there."

What about Matt's partner, his mother, and his brother?

"Everyone refuses to go back."

CHAPTER TEN

You Whore

Freaky Happenings is a paranormal events company, one which has hosted public investigations at many locations around the United Kingdom. The nights that they have spent at 30 East Drive have resulted in a wealth of reported paranormal activity. When we asked them to share some of their more memorable ones, the team was only too happy to oblige.

It always adds entertainment value to a public event when a guest attends who is openly and unabashedly sceptical. One such young lady signed up with *Freaky Happenings* and bravely decided to spend some time in the coal house, the scene of Joe Pritchard's life-changing encounter with an unknown thing which some have theorised to have been the Black Monk himself.

The young lady went into the coal house quite happily, settling herself down on the wooden chair that has been in there for the last few years. After ten minutes had passed, she suddenly began to scream hysterically, shoving the door open and running out into the hallway.

After she had calmed down a little, the young lady told us that she had felt something grab her ankles – exactly what had happened to Matt Penzer's mother upstairs in the master bedroom, and exactly what would later happen to Richard Estep's fellow investigator, Charlie, when he was standing in front of the kitchen sink (see Chapter Thirteen).

When team members from *Freaky Happenings* took a closer look at her legs, they discovered that she did indeed have red marks encircling her ankles, along with some faint scratches. Not too long afterward, a similar experience would be had by the crew from the TV show *Paranormal Lockdown* (see Chapter Fifteen). Plainly, something inside the coal house had wanted to make its presence known. After so many decades, could this have been the same entity that had so frightened Joe Pritchard?

During one of their experimental sessions, the team had an open phone connection running continuously; one phone was located upstairs, and the other was downstairs. The *Freaky Happenings* team members and their guests were engaged in a little glass divination in the living room, when they suddenly heard a voice come over the phone saying, "GET OUT!"

"Who are you?" the investigators asked, nonplussed.

"YOU WHORE!" came the reply. This was said in a very threatening manner, making it all too clear that the speaker – whoever it was – did not think too highly of the visitors that night.

A guest named Hayley, also an avowed sceptic, had her own personal experience – one that she would never forget. She was coming downstairs, stepping into the hallway, and suddenly let out a piercing scream. The team members rushed to her side and asked what was wrong.

Hayley explained that she had heard a very loud whisper in

her ear – the voice said quite distinctly, "F#%K OFF! F#%K OFF!"

On another occasion, the team was table tipping in the master bedroom. They were asking for simple *yes* or *no* answers. One of the guests said that she could feel a cold breeze swirling around her legs. In an attempt to gather some objective evidence, the investigators began to take photographs of the woman. On viewing the photos afterward, one can clearly see a grey mist underneath the table, close to the woman's legs.

Trigger objects are all part and parcel of the paranormal investigator's tool kit. The idea is to place an item that may have some sort of significance or attraction to spirit entities and see if they are willing to take the bait by picking it up and moving it.

One night, the team left a ball at the top of the stairs (spherical objects such as marbles and balls have been used as control objects with some success at 30 East Drive over the years). Every one of the *Freaky Happenings* staff and their guests were in the front room, fully accounted for.

When it was time to go back upstairs to investigate the bedrooms, the ball was found at the very bottom of the stairs. There was no possibility of the ball simply being caught by a draught and rolling down the stairs on its own: The team debunked this theory, as they discovered that if the ball rolled down the stairs, the people in the living room could easily hear the ball bounce.

Following another successful night of investigating, the team set about packing up all of their things. After putting their equipment away and getting ready to leave at three o'clock in the morning, they all heard the tread of heavy footsteps walking along the landing, before descending the stairs.

Thinking that perhaps a guest had gone back up there without them noticing, the team called upstairs and asked them to come down as they were about to lock up the house. There was no answer. When the investigators checked, they found the upper floor completely deserted. All of the guests were long gone.

CHAPTER ELEVEN
It Wasn't Me!

Alison Newell had developed a lifelong interest in the paranormal, reading books and watching the wide variety of television shows that covered the subject, but had never actually visited a haunted location… until she stepped over the threshold of 30 East Drive.

Along with her friend Julie, Alison signed up to spend a night at the house with *Haunted Happenings,* one of the UK's most respected and trustworthy paranormal event organisers. Julie and Alison joined the founder of *Haunted Happenings,* Hazel Ford, and nine other guests for an evening that none of them would ever forget.

On the long drive to Pontefract, Alison could feel her sense of anticipation steadily building. She was intrigued as to what the coming evening would have in store. Finally, once she had driven around the roundabout and parked her car, she looked up at the infamous house that she had read about and seen on television so many times over the space of a year. As she opened the gate and walked up the path to the front door, the whole thing felt surreal. The feeling intensified when she stepped inside the house itself. She had a hard time believing that she was actually there, standing inside what some claimed to be one of the world's most haunted houses.

As she stood in the kitchen and looked around the room, the

1970s-style décor transported Alison all the way back to her childhood, a time of flared trousers and disco music ruling the airwaves. She found her first reaction to be rather puzzling – after all, wasn't she meant to feel afraid inside this house, or at the very least just a little bit apprehensive? Yet instead, she was struck by an overwhelming sense of nostalgia.

That would soon change.

After the initial introductions had been made, Hazel kicked the night off with a group vigil held in Phillip's bedroom. So far as Alison was concerned, the warm feeling she had felt upon first entering the house was suddenly gone; she found the atmosphere upstairs to be both heavy and oppressive.

The visitors all spoke their names and declared their respect for whatever entities might be resident inside the house. They then began to call out, with people taking turns to ask if any spirit wanted to communicate with the group tonight.

Hazel had the guests use flashlights as an extra tool in their attempts to communicate with the spirits of 30 East Drive. As with most things in the controversial field of paranormal research, the 'flashlight technique,' which typically involves unscrewing the head of a Mag-lite to the point where it is barely in contact with the battery section, has both its supporters and its detractors. Advocates of the technique believe that this allows discarnate entities to make the light flicker in response to specific questions. Sceptics, on the other hand, maintain that the on-off activity of the flashlight is caused by thermal changes within the light itself; when the light is on, it heats the surrounding metal, causing it to expand slightly and increases the degree of contact it has with the battery section. As sections of the metal cool, they subsequently contract, breaking the contact and dimming or turning out the light.

It is the view of the authors of this book that both explanations have some validity, and there are cases in which we have seen the flashlight deliver answers to direct questioning that are almost uncanny in both their timing and accuracy.

During Alison's session at 30 East Drive, the torches obligingly lit up and darkened down on demand a few times. Two flashlights were used, and both behaved in an identical fashion. When some of the guests began to hear creaking noises out on the landing, Alison tried to think sceptically: many visitors to 30 East Drive have experienced what they are fully convinced are the tread of phantom footsteps, especially on the upper floor and staircase. Were they now hearing the sound of something unseen walking around on the landing outside Phillip's bedroom, or was it simply the house itself settling down for the night, its structure contracting as it began to cool?

The group had gone lights-out. Although it was completely dark in Phillip's room, apart from the small amount of outside light that filtered in through the curtains, their eyes were now properly adapted to working in the low-light conditions. Alison's friend Julie began to suddenly feel very hot, so much so that the top of her arms felt as though they were burning. Julie couldn't shake the feeling that someone or something was holding onto her, grabbing her by each bicep, and she firmly asked whoever it was to let go and leave her alone. It was only later on that the group looked at Julie's arms a little more closely and discovered that a band of angry red skin had appeared at the top of each arm.

After a short break, Hazel split her guests up into smaller groups, with the idea of covering more rooms at the same time. Alison and Julie paired off and elected to remain in Phillip's bedroom. Their mood was one of excitement and eager anticipation. The two women chose to sit just outside the closet, which is located next to the door and backs on to the upstairs bathroom.

After ten minutes had passed, Alison suddenly noticed a foul, pungent odour permeating the air all around her. Even today with the benefit of hindsight, she is unable to describe it precisely. Whatever the rank smell was, Julie was also experiencing it herself, much to Alison's relief.

There was no obvious explanation for the stink. Nobody was cooking inside the house. There had been no problems with the drains or sewers. As tempting as it might be to make a joke about flatulence, this definitely didn't smell like that, and nobody had used the upstairs toilet yet.

Whatever the smell was, it managed to follow Alison and Julie around the house for the rest of the evening. The ladies are neither the first nor the last visitors to experience this horrible smell, and its root cause remains unexplained at the time of writing – just one of the many as-yet unexplained mysteries surrounding 30 East Drive.

Various trigger objects had been set out in an attempt to entice the resident spirits to move them, but they didn't seem willing to oblige on this particular Sunday night. Hazel called upon the groups to switch location, sending Alison and Julie next door to the master bedroom – arguably one of the most paranormally active rooms in the entire house.

Sitting down carefully in the darkness, the guests made themselves as comfortable as they could manage and settled in to wait. Unlike with Phillip's bedroom, the atmosphere in Joe and Jean's old bedroom was calm and peaceful. Once again, they called out in an effort to communicate with any entities which might be around, but if there were any spirits present in the bedroom with them, they weren't feeling particularly talkative.

They both kept a wary eye on the porcelain doll named Victoria, which lives permanently in the corner of the room next to the dresser. Although undeniably creepy, the child's toy did little more than stare at them out of the darkness, bearing silent witness to their vigil. When Hazel called for them to rotate once again, the women reluctantly admitted defeat so far as the master bedroom was concerned and trooped next door to the smallest bedroom, which had once belonged to Diane Pritchard.

Unfortunately, Diane's bedroom didn't yield any results either: both Alison and Julie felt that it was so calm and peaceful, in fact, that they could simply have drifted off to sleep in there if they had been so inclined. They were now feeling undeniably disappointed, but when their session came to a close, they had high hopes for the next session, which would take place in the sitting room downstairs.

Hazel split her guests into two groups based on gender, sending the men upstairs to attempt a little glass divination, whereas the females were going to try out some table-tipping downstairs. This technique harkens back to the Victorian era of séances and involves placing the fingertips on top of a wooden table and attempting to get it to move via some type of unknown energy.

After opening up the table as a means of spirit communication, the group started out by asking questions of whatever spirits might be present. It wasn't long before they were hearing answers, the definite sound of tapping on the table in response to their queries. All of the women present looked at one another, carefully scrutinising the table top and making sure that the taps were not coming from one of their own number. No apparent fakery was detected; they could all plainly see one another's hands resting lightly on top of the table, their fingers all still and relaxed.

It wasn't long before a narrative began to form. Whoever or whatever it was that the ladies were communicating with via the table top, claimed to be the spirit of a young girl who had been murdered in the vicinity of 30 East Drive. Hazel and Alison both simultaneously felt suddenly sea-sick, feeling slightly off-balance, light-headed, and becoming nauseous.

Although the table did move a little, it was hardly substantial enough to be called paranormal at that point. Trying to boost things a little, the women clustered around the wooden table and collectively gave permission for the spirit to use their energies as a source of power.

Julie was sitting to Alison's right, and a lady named Emily was seated to her left. From out of the blue, Emily suddenly pointed to Julie and said, "What is *that?*" Afterward, Emily would describe having seen a flash of light very close to Julie. As soon as those words were out of Emily's mouth, Alison felt a burst of what she can only describe as electricity enter her body; it ran from the top of her right arm, shot straight through her upper chest, and then exited through her left arm at the same height.

"Oh my God, what just happened?" she gasped, shuddering. It had happened so quickly, but happen it most certainly had. Questioning the nature of the jolt she had experienced, Alison tried to compare it to other things she had felt during the course of her life, hoping to identify it. It wasn't the shivery sensation everybody sometimes experiences and usually writes off with a simple,

"Somebody just walked over my grave." Nor was it an *actual* burst of static electricity, the type you might get after walking on a carpet and touching a metal surface. This was something entirely different, and to this day Alison firmly believes it to have been paranormal in nature.

"Believe what you will, but I was there, and this *really* happened to me. Having since discussed this with a medium, she believes that perhaps it may have been a spirit passing through me. It's certainly a plausible explanation, and it's one that I will certainly take."

The group took a well-deserved break. Afterward, they took it in turns to sit on the stairs. Julie took up position at the top and Alison sat at the bottom: Hazel and one of the other guests were monitoring the live camera feed in the kitchen, keeping an eye on the activity throughout the house. Other than a few orbs caught on the monitor, something which most investigators tend to write off as being dust or other particulate matter, nothing happened to disturb their vigil.

One thing that seems to coax out the spirits of 30 East Drive is using a single individual as bait. Alison volunteered to carry out a lone vigil in the living room, while Hazel and Julie were next door in the kitchen monitoring the live feed. In order to keep Alison as isolated as possible, they closed the doors that led into the hallway and the kitchen area, shutting her in the living room.

Alison made herself comfortable on the sofa, sitting in silence. She made full use of the quiet time to process and absorb the events of the night so far.

"I didn't feel frightened," she explains, "and that initial burst of excitement was still there, but as time moved on, I have to admit that I was beginning to feel slightly jaded. I called out a few times, with no response. I think I was just beginning to relax, and that's when it happened…"

The loud *slam* made her sit bolt upright with a start, her heart racing at the sudden surprise. One of the glass doors leading into the kitchen suddenly burst open, as though it had been deliberately pushed with great force.

"Julie! Hazel!" Alison called out, fully expecting them both to appear in the doorway. There was no answer. Poking her head around the door, she found that the kitchen was completely empty: as it turned out, Julie and Hazel had previously left the kitchen via the open door that leads from the kitchen into the hallway. They were nowhere near the door when it had been shoved open.

Nonetheless, when she finally found them both, Alison immediately asked whether they had pushed open the door. The answer was a categorical "No!" *Haunted Happenings* is not in the business of pranking their guests: leaving aside the fact that such practical jokes on an investigation are simply the wrong thing to do, it would also be an extremely poor business practice, and one that the customers would most certainly not appreciate. Not only does Hazel have a great deal of personal integrity, but she is also far too savvy a business professional to put her entire livelihood at risk for a simple practical joke.

As mentioned earlier, the authors of this book are both aware that one of the glass partition doors can sometimes pop open of its own accord; this usually happens when somebody happens to be walking across the floor of the living room. However, it must be pointed out that the door only swings open a couple of inches each time this happens; it most certainly does *not* slam backward forcefully as though shoved, which is what happened to Alison. During her return trip, Alison encountered this lacklustre 'popping open' effect herself and confirms that this is definitely not what she experienced on that first Sunday night vigil.

The evening concluded with everyone getting back together in Phillip's room for a wrap-up. Alison was surprised to learn that in Hazel's opinion, it had actually been a relatively quiet night at 30 East Drive. She could only wonder what a *busy* night would have looked like!

"What I experienced in that house on that night will stay with me for the rest of my life," Alison explains, looking back on what would be her first but definitely not her last paranormal investigation. "On leaving the house I gave it a quick once over. I knew before I even got back in the car to head home that 30 East Drive was already calling me back…"

When Alison left 30 East Drive in September of 2016, she felt as though she still had unfinished business there. This is not an uncommon occurrence among those who visit the house – an indefinable hankering that just sits in the back of the mind, a siren song that draws certain people back. Something about the house exerts a powerful attraction on them.

Alison also thinks it is possible that she was simply trying to find answers and gain some greater understanding of what had happened to her on her first visit.

No matter the reason, she and her friend Julie once again found themselves standing outside the house on the night before their second vigil with *Haunted Happenings*. It was a seasonally warm May evening without any trace of a chill in the air. There was no real need to shiver, but both women found themselves trembling a little anyway. Each of them felt uneasy in their own way. Julie's discomfort may have stemmed from a dream she had had the night before, warning her to be wary of the stairs at 30 East Drive.

The two women simply stood there quietly, watching the house and wondering about the secrets it might hold.

The evening couldn't come around quick enough, so far as

they were concerned. Trepidation largely gave way to excitement. Alison and Julie were joined by three of their friends, Emily, Sarah and Hayley, all of whom they had met on their previous visit.

Five newcomers would also be joining them. Alison couldn't help but notice that one particular lady was apparently so nervous that she was quite literally shaking.

"Everything's going to be fine," Alison told the lady, resting a reassuring hand on her shoulder. While she wasn't entirely sure that she was telling the entire truth – 30 East Drive can be an unpredictable place at best, after all – her comforting words nevertheless seemed to calm the lady down a little.

Beneath her confident exterior, Alison was still feeling ever so slightly uneasy. As a form of spiritual defence, she and Julie read out a prayer of protection, something that they had agreed upon in advance. Both of them instinctively felt that it would be prudent after what happened to them the last time.

Walking back into the house, it felt as though no time at all had passed since last September. Very little had changed, right down to the oppressive atmosphere that was very much still in effect.

Alison headed straight for the double doors that separate the kitchen/dining area from the lounge. Her intention was to debunk what had happened the last time, when the door had apparently opened itself. She closed the door firmly at first, and then much more lightly, in order to try and make the door pop open. While it did exactly that, this time the door only moved a few inches – nothing like the wide and aggressive swing that she had experienced on her last visit.

So much for debunking the door...

Her next stop was the room that she felt most drawn to: Phillip's. Alison felt the oppression hit her with great force from the very first instant she stepped through the doorway.

Looking back on the experience later, she would describe it as feeling like walking into a brick wall. Although the entire house had a heavy and oppressive atmosphere, Alison felt it more strongly in this room than in any of the others. She was unable to shake the strong conviction that some kind of entity resided in this room.

The night's investigation started with the *Alice Box*; software that, according to the manufacturer, 'invites external influence by spirit entities.' The app is said to have an internal database of up to 10,000 words, which some believe can be carefully selected by disembodied entities and used as a means of communication with the living.

While participating in the *Alice Box* session, footsteps were clearly heard by some of the group. The footsteps sounded as if they were coming up the main staircase. No flesh and blood person was climbing the stairs at the time.

The larger group now split themselves up into smaller teams. Alison and Julie found themselves alone in Phillip's bedroom once more. Both women could hear tapping on the walls at one point, whose source of origin proved impossible to pin down. They respectfully asked if any spirits that might be present could repeat that noise again for them, but unfortunately their request was not granted.

Suddenly Natalie, the guide from *Haunted Happenings*, shouted up from the bottom of the staircase in order to inform them that while monitoring each room with remote cameras, she had just seen the immersion heater cupboard door open itself. Julie and Alison hadn't seen it happen, as they were sitting in the dark and didn't have any night vision equipment on hand. They were sitting on the floor at the opposite end of the room from the heater closet. Neither of them had heard the door opening, but it was entirely possible that this was what accounted for the tapping sound that they had heard.

Both women eagerly went to the door and verified that it did indeed appear to have moved by a few inches. When Alison moved the door back so that it was only slightly ajar, it obligingly creaked and groaned just as any old wooden door would be expected to do.

Their time in Phillip's room was up. They moved on to the master bedroom, once shared by Jean and Joe Pritchard, taking the *Alice Box* along with them. A *few interesting words came through* (left), the most relevant ones being *parents* and *stairs*. While it's possible that these words had come up purely at random – after all, even a stopped clock tells the correct time twice a day – it is also entirely possible that the words are not coincidental.

The remainder of the time they spent in the master bedroom was uneventful. After a short break, the two ladies took up new positions on the stairs, with Alison at the top and Julie sitting down at the bottom.

It didn't take long for Alison to feel increasingly uncomfortable. A very definite cold draught seemed to spring up all around her, coming out of nowhere. Before then, the house had felt a little on the warm side. None of the windows were open and there was no air-conditioning to account for the draught.

Julie suddenly called out that she had just seen a shadow pass quickly in front of the downstairs hallway mirror. Whether this was a genuine shadow figure, or a trick of the light, is impossible to say: but if the former turned out to be the case, Julie would have been only the latest in a long line of visitors to see a shadow figure in that very same location.

Both Diane's bedroom and the lounge were equally quiet, apart from a reference to Victoria, the name of the doll in the master bedroom, appearing on the *Alice Box* when in Diane's bedroom, and an odd scratching sound that seemed to originate from somewhere in the corner of the lounge. The scratching went on for roughly five minutes. One possible explanation is that the next-door neighbour has a parrot; the bird's sounds may simply have bled through the common wall that both houses share: noting that the parrot is housed in Carol's kitchen, and not in the front room; the room immediately adjacent to 30 East Drive.

One of the more interesting occurrences of the night took place during a glass divination session in Phillip's bedroom. The glass began to move almost instantly, and whatever it was that the sitters were communicating with claimed to be the spirit of Joe Pritchard.

When asked whether the spirit liked to drink alcohol, the glass moved straight to YES. The same answer was given to the questions, "Did you like going to the pub?" and more disconcertingly, "Were you a violent man?"

Somewhat nervously, the sitters asked the spirit whether he had died in the house, which was also answered in the affirmative. The glass went on to proclaim that it was protecting a young girl in the house from something evil. The sitters asked the age of the child, and the *Alice Box* instantly spoke the number 'twelve.'

Alison tentatively asked if the spirit remembered her from her last visit to 30 East Drive. The glass moved to *YES*. She then enquired whether she needed some form of protection after what had happened to her the year before.

YES

Was the thing that she needed protection from evil?

YES

Alison found herself wondering whether this really was the spirit of Joe Pritchard: could it possibly have been something else, either a trickster entity or something darker and more malevolent, simply playing with her for its own amusement?

It was a question that she was wise to ask. It is never safe to assume that whoever (or whatever) is communicating via means such as this, are who they claim to be. It could be a discarnate entity whose true identity is in fact very different from that of the spirit that it is claiming to be, or perhaps even the sitter's own subconsciousness doing the talking.

A number of visitors to 30 East Drive have claimed to encounter the ghost of Joe Pritchard. One of the more recent is Katrina Weidman, star of the TV show *Paranormal Lockdown*, who said that she caught a glimpse of a male apparition that matched Joe's description in the upstairs bathroom… the same room in which he died.

Alison's friends were beginning to grow a little uncomfortable with her line of questioning, so out of deference to them she let the matter drop. Although she wasn't unwilling to push boundaries a little, Alison had to admit that even she was starting to feel a little bit apprehensive at the thought of just who their invisible communicator might be.

Three o'clock in the morning soon rolled around, and while Alison was still keen to keep going, her friends and companions were eager for a little sleep before the long journey home. After one last glass divination session proved to be fruitless, she reluctantly called it quits and admitted defeat.

Like so many visitors before her had done, Alison bedded down on the lumpy living room couch. Three of her friends elected to bunk down in Diane's bedroom – Hayley and Emily lay side by side on the single bed, each zipped up inside their own sleeping bags, while Sarah had drawn the short straw and slept on the floor beside the bed.

Downstairs, Julie and Alison tried to get comfortable, but it was easier said than done.

They finally dozed off. Alison found herself being awoken gradually by the same rancid, pungent stench that she had experienced on her first visit to East Drive. At first, she thought that she must be dreaming, but as she regained full alertness, she realised that the smell was definitely there.

Sitting up, Alison saw that Julie was awake too. Julie told Alison that in the brief time they had both been napping, she had heard the very distinctive sound of footsteps and creaking on the upstairs landing.

"It sounded as if somebody was rushing to the bathroom in a hurry," she explained.

Once their three friends were awake, Alison asked them whether they had used the bathroom during the early hours. That would certainly account for the hurried footsteps and creaking. Yet one by one, the three women flatly denied ever having gotten up or leaving Diane's bedroom after bedding down.

Who, then, had Julie heard moving around at the top of the stairs?

Sarah's expression paled, and she immediately asked Hayley and Emily if they were *sure* that they hadn't gotten out of the bed to go to the toilet at night, while she was sleeping on the floor alongside them. Both women insisted that they had not. "But someone must have?!" Sarah went on to explain that while she was snugly tucked up inside her sleeping bag on the floor of Diane's bedroom, she had suddenly heard movement coming from somewhere between her and the open door to the landing.

The movement had brought her back to wakefulness, but she didn't quite put two and two together, putting down the rustling of her sleeping bag to either Hayley or Emily getting back into bed after a trip to the bathroom.

After excitedly comparing notes over a hot cup of tea, the women packed up their gear and left the house in the cold light of morning.

"My two adventures there will certainly not be my last," Alison says as she looks back on her time at the Black Monk House. "It's one of those places where you can't help but feel that you always have unfinished business. No other haunted property has ever had an effect on me like 30 East Drive, and I can guarantee you that the place hasn't seen the last of me…"

CHAPTER TWELVE

This House is Evil

The Black Monk of Pontefract case returned to the public mass consciousness following the release of *When the Lights Went Out* in 2012, but 30 East Drive itself didn't really make it into the spotlight once more until a visit from the TV show *Most Haunted* aired in 2015. While the house address wasn't exactly top secret (readers of Colin Wilson's *Poltergeist!* could find it listed in the pages of that particular book, not to mention numerous articles in the media) the film had been shot on soundstages rather than on location, and an entirely different house was used to stand in for the exteriors.

It's safe to say that *Most Haunted* is a controversial show, to put it mildly. The programme is extremely polarising. To its army of loyal and devoted fans, Yvette Fielding, her husband Karl Beattie, and their colleagues can do nothing wrong: their tried and tested method of going to haunted locations, turning out the lights, and running around in the dark screaming and swearing has attracted a very sizeable viewing audience. Yet to its detractors, the programme is seen as nothing more than paranormally-themed melodrama, scripted, faked, and willing to do anything necessary to convince its viewers of the existence of ghosts.

As with so many things in life, the truth probably lies somewhere in the middle. There have been many instances in which the *Most Haunted* team have been caught out, such as the 'Kreed Kafer' saga which saw the sacking of supposed psychic medium Derek Acorah: In brief, resident parapsychologist Doctor Ciaran O'Keeffe deliberately planted false information about a spirit named Kreed Kafer in a place where he knew that Acorah would hear it. When Acorah subsequently claimed to become possessed by that very entity, O'Keeffe revealed that no such person had ever existed… not only had he himself made it up, but the name was an anagram of 'Derek Faker.' Acorah was let go, and yet it barely seemed to dent the enthusiasm of the *Most Haunted* fans – at the time of writing, some ten years later, the show is still going strong.

Despite claims to the regulatory body OFCOM, *Most Haunted* escaped sanction because it was declared to be "*an entertainment show, not a legitimate investigation, and should not be taken seriously*." (Our italics). All of which makes the show's credibility a little hard to swallow when it comes to the quality of their results.

The first episode at 30 East Drive begins in a rather unconventional way. Whether you believe that the paranormal activity featured on the show is genuine or not, one thing cannot be denied – they know how to edit a show meticulously. No sooner has the title sequence rolled than our host, Yvette Fielding, explains that they are going to show her standard opening piece to camera, but then continue on past its intended stopping point because of what happened next.

First, we get a smooth tracking shot throughout the house, taking us through the living room from the kitchen, into the hallway, and finishing at the foot of the stairs. Director Karl Beattie can be heard calling "Action!" as the camera pans up to the top of the staircase, where we see Fielding giving her opening monologue on the upstairs landing. No sooner has she finished than we hear her excitedly ask, "Did you <expletive deleted> see that!?!" Crew are heard exclaiming wildly in the background. She claims to have seen a bright blue marble flying through the air at high speed, coming from the living room wall and heading straight for Beattie and the cameraman.

Fielding insists that the marble physically emerged *out of the wall itself,* behaviour that is not uncommon in many other poltergeist cases (or, for that matter, in 30 East Drive itself). If she truly did see what she claims to have seen, then the marble would have had to have entered the living room/hallway wall just in front of the structural wall that separates number 30 from Carol's house next door and passed cleanly through the solid brick.

Marbles and other similar objects have been thrown at numerous visitors over the years, and a spot of target practice seems to be a favourite pastime of some of the resident spirits. Objects are also picked up by unseen hands and then dropped onto the floor from a great height. The long-term neighbour and caretaker of 30 East Drive, Carol Fieldhouse had called in the police after a particularly noisy outbreak of activity from inside the deserted house; a loud bang from upstairs resulted in her 999 call. So strong was the house's reputation, we are told, that the responding police officers refused to come inside!

"Can I just say; it's only going to get worse." Fielding claps her hands gleefully.

There may be a problem here. Assuming that the show was shot in sequence, as is strongly implied, then her opening comments give us cause to doubt the authenticity of what is to follow. "Welcome to an investigation that was far from the ordinary, and far from *anything that we were prepared for*." These were Yvette Fielding's exact words as she filmed her intro piece to camera at the beginning of the show. How did they know *at the beginning of the investigation* that it was going to be 'far from anything that we were prepared for?' The investigation hadn't happened yet! One is tempted to conclude that either the show was being shot out of sequence, or that no matter how active or quiet the house was during the course of their stay, *Most Haunted* was going to come away with 'results' no matter what.

Then again, when Karl Beattie called Bil Bungay out of the blue from outside the house, in a heightened state of excitement, asking "What is this place?? We haven't even unloaded the van and it's happening!" – perhaps the team had fortuitously arrived to film on a 'night of feast, rather than famine,' and the intro sequence was indeed shot after the team all realised they had stumbled upon something. It would also account for both Yvette

Fielding and Karl Beattie resolutely claiming it to be "the most haunted house in Britain," having investigated hundreds of allegedly haunted properties.

Yvette goes on to explain that the night ahead of them was so intensely frightening that "none of us would ever be the same again." On a Steadicam swoop through the house, the viewer is given a quick tour of the ground floor as the cameraman weaves his way from room to room. On replaying the footage and paying particular scrutiny to the living room, we see that everything is apparently normal in there, and the couch is completely clear. This will be important just a few moments later, when Karl Beattie seems to find *a big kitchen knife jammed in between two of the cushions* (right), its blade pointing straight up into the air. It is either a chilling threat to the *Most Haunted* team, or an extremely theatrical piece of fakery for the TV audience.

One common complaint surrounding the house is that knives of all descriptions tend to be targeted by the entities there; they have been known to disappear from kitchen drawers, only to turn up later in the most random of places – or even worse, be thrown at visitors. Indeed, as we heard in Chapter Eight, Steve and his guests found two kitchen knives on the stairs minutes after going up and down the (empty) stairs together.

Karl further goes on to say that the knife blade is freezing cold to the touch. Generally, apported objects are reported to be warm, as though some sort of energy exchange has just taken place.

Things take another turn for the bizarre when an ornamental crucifix appears to fall onto the bed from on top of the windowsill in the master bedroom. It is captured on camera by Stuart Torevell, yet crucially we never see the object begin to fall. Stuart's reaction, however, is either that of an accomplished performer or of someone genuinely flummoxed by the cross suddenly hopping off the windowsill onto the bed – he certainly seems taken aback. As Stuart turns his camera to show us the bigger picture, it's evident that there is little if any space to hide a complicit member of the crew, and we would most certainly have heard such a person run for cover in this creaky house – yet the bedroom stays absolutely silent, save for Stuart's perplexed murmurings. Frustratingly however, *the cross was thrown just off camera* (left), making it impossible to rule out the possibility of Stuart somehow having thrown the crucifix himself. Given that he was behind the camera at the time and was some distance away from the cross positioned at the centre of the windowsill, plus the fact that it was thrown towards the headrest and not directly towards Stuart (not a case of invisible thread) it is difficult to see how.

A series of plastic balls are placed in a circle in the centre of Phillip's bedroom, sitting on the pink carpet in the full gaze of a locked-off camera. Employing such items as control objects is a very common technique for paranormal investigators to use. The experiment would yield spectacular results. When the footage is checked, the balls are seen to move in a host of different directions, as if an invisible child happened to be playing with them, rolling them across the floor as a part of some game. The curtains are not blowing, indicating a lack of breeze to explain the movement.

Aiden Sinclair is an internationally-renowned illusionist and has appeared on the television show *America's Got Talent!* He specialises in the performance of paranormally-themed phenomena as part of his live stage show *Illusions of the Passed*, convincing a disbelieving audience that they are interacting with the spirits of the dead. We showed Aiden the footage of the balls moving in Phillip's bedroom and asked whether it was something that he could fake himself, if he chose to do so.

"Absolutely. There are a couple of techniques that spring to mind. One would be using magnets inside the balls themselves, manipulating them from the floor below by running other magnets along the ceiling downstairs. You could also use compressed air to the same effect."

However, just because something *can* be faked, does not necessarily mean that it *was* faked. Carol Fieldhouse was inside the house during that particular part of the *Most Haunted* shoot and confirms that she witnessed no trickery on the part of the team in this regard. They appeared to be every bit as shocked at the phenomena as she herself was. The subsequent discovery of a *subtle shadow figure stood in the doorway* (overleaf), caught by the remote camera monitoring the ping pong balls, further adding to the belief that balls were being moved by something paranormal in nature.

It isn't long in the episode before the team start to hear noises coming from somewhere else inside the house.

"This house is evil," Fielding insists.

"We haven't even started, and I think we should leave," Beattie counters, "I've got a real feeling that we should leave." He then begins to hear whispered voices in Diane's bedroom. The crew describes an oppressive atmosphere throughout the house, something that many visitors to 30 East Drive have experienced, including both authors of this book.

The next section of the programme involves them trying to communicate with any entities present by means of automatic writing. The responses to their questions appear to indicate the presence of a 'Carl Anthony,' aged 52; a priest said to have died in 1633, and one who – when asked what he wants Yvette and Karl to do, responds with "*GET OUT!*" Whether this is genuine spirit communication or something else; like the subconsciousness of those attempting communication, is left to the viewer to decide.

A blue marble being used as a control object on the master bed is found bouncing to a halt at the foot of the main staircase. Loud, rhythmic knocking sounds are heard from the ceiling above the master bedroom (surprisingly, nobody goes up to investigate the attic for a rational explanation for the banging), and the entire team feels the floor vibrating beneath their feet.

The *Most Haunted* team decide to go lights out. Karl Beattie goes upstairs on his own, leaving the rest of the team downstairs in the kitchen. He says that he is 'more scared than he has ever been,' which is quite understandable considering that he is roaming around in the dark in one of the world's most haunted houses.

The door to Phillip's bedroom closes itself, apparently of its own volition, while he is checking the closet that contains the water heater. Something is thrown off camera whilst Karl is in the master bedroom; a doll from the dresser is then found lying face-down on the floor behind where Karl was standing at the time. Karl finally decides to call it quits, and comes back downstairs, appearing to be thoroughly shaken by the experience.

After a recap of the occurrences so far, Episode Two hits the ground running.

Refusing to let anybody go upstairs on their own, Yvette insists that everybody goes up together. Stuart is suddenly taken ill – a not infrequent occurrence on *Most Haunted* – and the floor is felt to vibrate.

Karl is seen to collapse and spends the next few minutes in the arms of his colleagues, who say that he has turned cold and clammy. He appears to be in a stupor and unresponsive to calls to wake up. At one point, somebody claims that he is not breathing, and the idea of performing CPR is floated. At no point does Yvette Fielding suggest that somebody call 999 and get an ambulance for him – hardly the actions one would expect from somebody who was genuinely worried for their spouse.

Much is made of the fact that Yvette Fielding specifically asked whatever haunts the house to "do something to Karl" while he was alone upstairs.

"We need to get him out," somebody calls out, and the team promptly spends the next few minutes ignoring that advice. The drama quotient goes through the roof at this point, as others claim to be drained and overcome. Everything is shot by flashlight and infrared light, yet even in the middle of a supposed medical emergency, nobody thinks to turn the lights on and take a proper look at Karl, who suddenly comes around and sits up, clutching at his head.

Heading back downstairs, the team check to see whether they can catch any EVPs. Their findings might best be described as 'doubtful,' although Ms. Fielding confidently declares that they "seem to be getting some communication."

The team hears running water. On heading across the landing to the bathroom, they find a tap running, noting that the old taps are stiff and require force to open and close. Ping-pong balls begin to appear on the landing and also in one of the bedrooms, though this doesn't actually occur on camera.

Downstairs, objects are thrown in the darkened living room while most of the team is gathered around the couch, whilst upstairs – *at the same precise moment* – there is a loud scream as

Stuart and Karl sustain what appear to be rope burns on their forearms.

"That's like he's branded you," Fielding declares, "in the same place." The injuries are indeed at the same location on the two men's' forearms, which are *placed side by side for comparison; and they are all but identical* (right). It is worth noting that Bil had the subsequent opportunity to speak to Stuart Torevell about this specific event, as Bil had his doubts. Stuart had no hesitation in discussing the incident, and showing Bil the scar on his arm, which was still healing after a couple of months. It was without a doubt, the result of a deep burn.

Stuart went on to show Bil the series of photos that he had taken of the wound as it healed. When he scrolled quickly through them in order, it looked almost *like a video of the healing process* (left), such was the frequency with which Stuart had taken them.

"Why would anyone take daily photos of a self-inflicted wound?" Bil mused, "A painful, self-sacrificial deed that would have had to have been agreed to by both parties, purely for dramatic effect? And how would you actually inflict an *identical* wound on both arms in what seemed like a split-second? Even taking into account film editing and trickery – it seems a stretch that Stuart and Karl would agree to such a deep burn that would lead to permanent scarring. Then there's Stuart dropping an expensive camera. The idea of agreeing to be painfully and permanently branded is one thing (and pretty unbelievable), but we have yet to meet a cameraman that would *ever* agree to dropping their camera; they are fragile, expensive and are their livelihoods – they treat them with utmost respect.

Listening to Stuart, one could hear and see how intrigued he was by what he would have us believe was a poltergeist-inflicted wound.

Despite declaring 30 East Drive to be a "house of horrors," Fielding and her team elect to remain there and to go lights-out once more. Stuart Torevell returns to provoking the entities within the house, challenging them to "give us your best shot." Karl and Stuart claim to hear a cry, which they quite reasonably believe at first to have come from Yvette – who promptly denies having cried out.

A framed photograph is found lying on the floor in the living room. Beattie cries out in pain and clutches at his head, claiming that a second framed picture has hit him on the scalp. "It's a picture frame of an old lady," Torevell says helpfully, completely unaware of the fact that the lady in the photograph is actually Jean Pritchard herself, standing in front of the house and holding a copy of Colin Wilson's book. At the time of writing, this picture resides in the area of the kitchen.

Stuart now reveals that the living room makes him feel angry, annoyed, upset "… just not a happy bunny." Cue yet another scream and round of head-clutching. Yvette and the team come racing downstairs, demanding to know what happened. The ring of heavy iron keys, which are usually kept in the kitchen as an exhibit, are found on the floor next to him, the implication being that they were thrown with force straight at Stuart's head.

Karl Beattie gathers the team round in a circle and asks whether they may have bitten off more than they can chew, admitting that part of him wants to get in the car, leave, and never, *ever* come back (which is ironic, considering what would happen at Halloween). His wife agrees, and the team begins to pack up their equipment and call it a night.

In a voiceover, Fielding closes the show by stating that in over 350 investigations with *Most Haunted*, 30 East Drive takes the crown as being the most violent, evil, and haunted place they have ever visited, and cautions those who visit in future to take the greatest of care…

Well, where to begin? Firstly, it's important not to confuse the activities that are seen on *Most Haunted* with genuine paranormal investigation. Remember that OFCOM declared *Most Haunted* to be "*an entertainment show, not a legitimate investigation, and should not be taken seriously.*" (Our italics). The sad fact of the matter is that no matter how much genuine activity the team experienced at 30 East Drive, it is all tainted with the certainty that at least some of it is overplayed, exaggerated, and downright made up.

It must also be pointed out just how much of *Most Haunted's* so-called 'evidence' is in fact subjective in nature. People falling down, feeling dizzy, nauseous, angry, and even collapsing – are all impossible to verify as being genuine phenomena. The fact that so many visitors to 30 East Drive have had similar experiences is supportive, but simply means that the performers on *Most Haunted* have probably done their homework on the location before visiting.

So, not an investigation, merely entertainment. One other point of contention that we have is the way in which the *Most Haunted* team behave. They display little to no manners and show absolutely no respect for the entities with whom they are supposedly trying to interact. Swearing at them, calling them names, dishing out insults and constantly taunting them is something on which most professional paranormal investigators would frown. Assuming that the spirits of 30 East Drive are intelligent and able to communicate (as the vast majority of evidence suggests) why then would somebody think that hurling verbal abuse and making haughty demands to "do something!" is an acceptable way to interact with them?

Bil Bungay has a specific code of behaviour for those entering 30 East Drive, one to which all visitors must adhere, or risk being thrown out and permanently banned from entering the property. In addition to showing respect for the immediate neighbours and other residents of East Drive, he also insists that under no circumstances does anybody anger 'Fred.' Despite being a rational man by nature, he is not willing to tempt fate when it comes to upsetting the house's most infamous permanent resident.

The long and the short of it is that everything that happened to the *Most Haunted* team during their stay at 30 East Drive must be taken with a huge grain of salt, as it is impossible to separate fact from fiction.

The two-part episode that took place at 30 East Drive was a massive ratings winner, igniting a wave of interest in 30 East Drive that still hasn't abated today, years later: which meant that Antix productions didn't have to look too far in order to select a venue for their Halloween 2015 *Most Haunted Live!* special broadcast. Little did anybody know at the time that it would be their most controversial episode yet.

On Halloween night 2015, the *Most Haunted* team returned to 30 East Drive for a 2½ hour live broadcast.

Host Yvette Fielding seems genuinely terrified as she awaits her turn to go into the house. There are histrionics as host Rylan Clark-Neal enters the house during the daytime and feels something vibrating under his feet.

Entering the house during black-out conditions, Yvette indicates that a statuette of a saint or *monk fell and broke* (right) earlier that day. As things get underway, the sound of multiple knocks is heard coming from the walls in Phillip's bedroom. A domino appears from nowhere in the master bedroom, something for which 'Fred' is renowned.

"It smells like a rancid turd in here," may just be the defining quote of the show.

Gathering around a table in Phillip's bedroom, the team (joined by comedian Paul O'Grady) begin to verbally abuse and insult the monk, who they are still convinced goes by the name Carl Anthony. Karl Beattie claims to hear a *growling sound, like the one that he heard in the master bedroom during his first visit* (left), from somewhere outside the room, a not-uncommon occurrence at 30 East Drive. Then a blood-curdling shriek from Yvette heralds the discovery of a knife sitting on a pillow in the same bedroom, a knife that was secured in a box downstairs earlier that night. A table lifts up into the air, although it is impossible to tell whether one of the sitters is lifting it with their leg or not.

Things become even more dramatic when Karl tells everyone that he was pulled upstairs by something unseen. The video camera at the base of the stairs did record the incident, showing Karl being yanked forcefully from the landing back toward the doorway of

Phillip's bedroom.

The Internet went into a frenzy when some eagle-eyed viewers pointed out that there appeared to be what looked like a piece of rope attached to Karl's belt – a rope that was taut, as though being pulled from the other end. *Most Haunted* fans leapt to the defence of Karl Beattie, while others seized upon the finding as proof that the whole thing had been faked. Some sceptical viewers went further, insisting that Karl had thrown the knife onto the pillow earlier that night when entering the master bedroom.

Karl and Yvette took to social media in order to defend themselves, claiming that the 'rope' attached to Karl's belt had a perfectly natural explanation – it was in fact a camera cable.

When the dust settled, neither side was convinced. The fans mostly remained fans and the sceptics remained sceptical of *Most Haunted's* credibility. The only real loser was 30 East Drive, which was unfortunately caught in the middle: Some of those who denounced the validity of the *Most Haunted* 'investigation' also tarred the house with the same brush, claiming that it wasn't haunted at all. This is a true instance of throwing the baby out with the bathwater, and at the time of writing, *Most Haunted* have not returned to number 30 to film there again.

Bil was there that night and has this observation to make: "After the painful amateur dramatics had concluded, and I had successfully resisted the temptation to rush into the house and put an end to it all – particularly when Fred Batt, the resident *Most*

Haunted 'psychic,' had mauled the house with some supposedly-exorcistic religious incantation – I went in to survey the damage. The house was a mess, especially the front room, which had had a pane of glass in the double doors broken by Stuart's shoulder." (Remember the screws chucked at Bil in Chapter Three?)

"I found myself standing with Scott from *East Drive Paranormal*, apologising to 'Fred' for the harassment he had endured. It was my fault that they were in the house after all, but after their previous visit, I had sincerely thought that they would play it as straight as I had felt that their initial visit had gone.

"It was then that I noticed that the ornaments I had placed on the windowsill in the master bedroom literally minutes before the broadcast began: *an angel playing an organ and an old clock – had been turned around* (right) and now had their backs to the room, as if in silent protest to the charade that had played out just a few minutes earlier. In hamming it up that night, the *Most Haunted* team missed the real activity that was happening all around them, which was a darned shame for them and for all of their viewers.

"As for Karl being pulled up the stairs by 'an entity'… well, let's just say that that's a whole other story."

The truth of the matter is that even if one hundred percent of the findings from both *Most Haunted* shows turns out to be untrue (a finding that the authors of this book consider to be unlikely) then we are still dealing with a minor blemish when compared to the avalanche of eyewitness testimony and evidence gathered by scores of other investigators both before and after the show.

At the end of the day, once the controversy had subsided and life returned to its usual baseline of 'abnormal normal' at 30 East Drive, the accounts of paranormal activity there kept rolling in...

CHAPTER THIRTEEN

Living with the Dead

The front door to number 30 was opened by Scott, a member of *East Drive Paranormal*, who was in the process of tidying the house up a little after the last group of visitors had left earlier that morning. He offered *Richard Estep* (left) and his team (Linda, Andrew, Jason and Charlie) a cup of tea, which they all gratefully accepted – even the Americans, who were more coffee people (Richard is originally from the U.K.)

While they stood around drinking tea and waiting for Bil to arrive, Richard asked Scott whether anything unusual had happened in the house that day.

"Not today, but yesterday I saw Phillip's bedroom door close on its own." It was said in a completely matter-of-fact way, one which implied that doors closing on their own was all in a day's work at 30 East Drive. "I wasn't going to sit on my own in the house after that, so I waited outside for the guests to arrive. Just last week I saw a marble come bouncing down the stairs. Nobody else was in the house."

Scott went on to warn Richard, who would be the key holder for the duration of their stay, to keep the house key on him at all times, due to 'Fred''s apparent fascination with stealing them.

"On my very first day in this house, a marble came flying out of nowhere and hit me in the chest," he said, handing the key over. Richard made a point of placing it in the thigh pocket of his trousers and sealing the Velcro flap shut. "I'd been sitting on the bedroom floor, taunting 'Fred' to do his worst to me. I don't like to do that anymore."

He went on to talk about an EVP session that had been conducted upstairs. They were using an *Ovilus* (a talking dictionary which reacts to energy changes) which came out with the words "Feed me," and at the same time all in the room heard a growl that they are absolutely certain was animalistic, not simply somebody's stomach begging for food.

Charlie the freelancer had wandered off upstairs for a quick look around. He came thudding down the main staircase enthusiastically.

"I'd take it a bit slower if I were you," Scott cautioned him. "The other day, my sister-in-law was pushed down those stairs."

"I hope she wasn't hurt," Jason said.

"She had three scratches running down her side, but it wasn't from the stumble."

[Owner's note: We genuinely advise that visitors to 30 East Drive hold onto the bannister when they descend the stairs. We regularly get reports of people being shoved in the back as they

descend; most recently a group hosted by Cole Siddons had a team member pushed resulting in a bad ankle strain *(right)*]

Conversation turned to the controversial episodes of *Most Haunted* that were filmed in the house, particularly the part in which a carving knife was found by Karl Beattie sticking up from between two cushions on the sofa. Richard asked whether that had seemed genuine to Scott.

"I don't know for sure," he replied, "but I will tell you this. One day, Carol and me were standing in the kitchen. She opened the door to the living room, and there was a knife laying on the ground in front of the radiator. Neither of us had put it there. We tend to keep sharp things hidden in this house. 'It' really doesn't like Carol; it's got a thing for her. She comes inside the house to clean pretty much every day, but never, ever goes upstairs on her own. 'It' frightens her. Nor will my mother, after she saw something in the bathroom."

"What did she see?" Richard asked.

"A black shadow figure sprawled face-down on the bathroom floor in front of the toilet."

Pulling out his phone, Scott showed the visitors a piece of video footage taken during one of his own team's investigations. The *hood of Kenny, one of the investigators, was tugged on by something invisible* (left) – it was a marble that had apparently fallen from the ceiling.

"I've been in this house countless times and it still scares me. You don't want to get him... to get *'It'* riled up."

"'Him' or 'It'?" Jason asked.

"There are multiple spirits in this house," Scott claimed. "Some are nicer than others. Do you believe in portals?"

"I believe that there's some evidence to support the theory," Richard responded carefully.

"There's at least one portal in this house. Maybe as many as three, some psychics have said. The spirits come and go as they please."

Linda asked whether the identity of any of the spirits was known, to which Scott replied that aside from 'Fred' (about whom there was a lot of disagreement and controversy) he knew of a young child that was mainly active upstairs, and also believed that Joe Pritchard was sometimes around.

Everybody's ears perked up. It was a matter of common knowledge that Joe had died in the house, but why would he choose to stick around?

"It was his house," Scott answered. "*His.* Nobody else's." His implication was that Joe was being territorial, keeping an eye on his old home. The idea was an intriguing one.

Richard decided to try a spot of light provocation. Raising his voice, he declared that 'Fred' sounded like a bit of a bully to him, and bullies didn't impress him at all: Scott agreed. They had no idea that before the day was over, they would have gotten a violent response to those comments.

"Too many people come in expecting stuff to be flying all over the place," Scott went on, "but sometimes it's subtler than that. Whatever it is sometimes like to toy with your emotions. We've had a lot of people run out of here in tears without being able to say why they were so upset."

Charlie went around the house with his mobile phone, shooting video footage for future baseline reference. He was a little on edge when he came back, reporting that he felt a little strange, as though he were covered in static electricity somehow. The air didn't feel particularly ionised, but the investigators concluded that jet lag was just as likely an explanation as anything paranormal – Charlie had just made the long flight across the Atlantic and was running on fumes.

Jason went upstairs himself and felt nothing. He placed a *Rem-Pod* at the top of the stairs. This device detects electromagnetic energy and is believed by some members of the paranormal research community to be able to detect some kind of spirit energy: The theory is a controversial one, but all of the investigators present had seen the *Rem-Pod* behave oddly in haunted locations where no sources of EMF should have been present. Mobile phones and Wi-Fi networks can trigger them, and so the team was diligent about switching their mobile devices to airplane mode when using *Rem-Pods* and other EMF meters.

Only a few minutes after it was placed, the *Rem-Pod* began alarming. It was detecting some form of electromagnetic energy, but what was the source? There was no wireless network router in 30 East Drive for it to have picked up, so the airwaves should have been dead. Looking outside, they made certain that nobody was wandering past the house while talking on a mobile phone either. When it went off a second time, Jason went back upstairs to check on it. All was silent.

Just then, Bil Bungay arrived. He and Richard had spoken several times via Skype and email but had never met in person.

"Hello 'Fred,'" Bil said, nervously entering his own house, "It's only me. Please don't freak me out, I don't think your landlord's heart can take it."

As handshakes were being exchanged and introductions made, the *Rem-Pod* squealed again from the deserted upper floor. Perhaps 'Fred' was getting in on the greetings. Jason went to investigate. The second he stepped foot on the stairs, it stopped. Jason went back to speak to Bil and the *Rem-Pod* sounded again – back he went, and once again it shut up when he started up the stairs. It seemed as if something might be playing games with them.

"These are new," Bil pointed out, taking a knee and looking at some scratch marks that were at about ankle height on the kitchen door. They were much too defined to be the simple scuffs that everyday wear and tear brings to any house.

"They look like a dog made them," he went on, "or some other kind of animal, but we rarely have dogs inside this house. Most of them are frightened of coming in. These scratches are on the outside of the door, which suggests that this creature, whatever it was, was trying to get *in!*"

"It surprises me that *any* dog has ever set foot in this house, given their sensitivity to ghosts," Richard said. Bil told them about an incident that had taken place in 2015, when the police had been called to investigate claims of a *blue light floating through the lower floor of the house* (right). It had been called in by a passer-by, and although even the Pontefract Constabulary were a little wary of the infamous haunted house on the Chequerfield Estate, they duly sent a canine unit over to investigate. The highly-trained and ferocious German Shepherd adamantly refused to come into the house.

As the afternoon was wearing on and nobody had eaten since breakfast, it was agreed that the team would go out for an early dinner and leave the house empty but locked up tight. Before leaving, the investigators made a sweep of the house, making sure that everything was in order and taking a slew of reference photos. Without telling any of the others, Richard hid a digital voice recorder at the top of the stairs and started it recording... just in case 'Fred' or one of his friends decided to come out and play while they were gone.

It turned out to be an extremely prescient move. The team was out eating for a little under an hour. When they came back, Bil and Richard were the first ones to walk through the door. Bil called out a greeting to 'Fred,' which has become something of a tradition every time he comes back to 30 East Drive, and suddenly stopped dead in the doorway that separated the kitchen from the hallway. Richard almost ran into the back of him.

Somebody had been busy while the house was empty. Laying on the floor was the mirror which had hung on the wall at the bottom of the stairs. It had been there for several years without interruption, held up by a sturdy piece of rope that hung from a nail. The nail was still in place, but the rope had snapped in two, as though the mirror had been given a sudden violent jerk.

Earning us seven years' bad luck, the glass had cracked all the way through, and *the mirror was up on its side some way from the hook that once held it* (right). Bil and the visiting investigators looked at one another, all thinking the same thing – 'Fred.'

Except, that was too easy a conclusion for them to jump to so early in the game. Was it possible that the rope had been fraying over the years and had now given out completely, breaking of its own accord – in other words, was this simply the right time for it to go, making this a coincidence rather than a paranormal event?

In a word, no. Few seasoned paranormal investigators put much stock in the concept of coincidence: in other words, poke around enough haunted houses over the years and one tends to see things that stretch the possibility of coincidence to its breaking point. The mirror had been hanging on the wall for years without ever falling off. Along came Richard and his fellow investigators from across the pond. They are in the house for less than an hour before Bil arrives. That time is spent talking about 'Fred' and his many antics. Then the house is empty for, once again, less than an hour, and suddenly *that* is when the mirror decides to fall and break? After discussing the ins and outs of it, all of the investigators agreed that the timing made that explanation suspiciously unlikely and the odds unbelievable.

Even so, it didn't necessarily follow that 'Fred' (or some other entity) was responsible. There was an even less pleasant possibility – fraud. Although Richard and Bil held the two sets of master keys to the house, was it possible that somebody else had gotten their own key somehow, or gotten in through one of the windows? Again, unlikely, for all of the doors and windows had been locked.

It was now that Richard got to play his trump card, in the form of the hidden digital voice recorder. If there had been an intruder of the flesh and blood variety, no matter how quiet and sneaky they tried to be, the sound of their gaining access to the house and approaching the mirror should have been picked up by its extremely sensitive microphone.

Retrieving the voice recorder from its hiding place at the top of the stairs, Richard plugged in some headphones and began to play the file back. Everybody waited with bated breath. He could hear the front door being closed and locked as the laughing investigators disappeared for dinner. Then, for the next thirty minutes... nothing. The occasional sound of a car passing by outside was picked up, along with the usual ambient sounds of an estate during the daytime – people walking their dogs or heading back from the shops.

Finally, *there came an almighty thud and crash* (right). Richard played it back again two or three times, then began to pass the headphones around so that everybody could have a listen for themselves. There wasn't the slightest hint of a door or window opening to be heard during playback, nor the sound of footsteps on linoleum or carpet. Neither was there the creaking of somebody furtively coming down the staircase or walking on the floorboards above. The investigators had searched the house from top to bottom before leaving and knew beyond any shadow of a doubt that nobody could have hidden themselves anywhere inside it prior to them leaving to get food.

Nevertheless, just to make sure, they spent the better part of the next hour trying to sneak in and out of the house as quietly as humanly possible. As the smallest and lightest person present (and therefore the one likely to make the least noise) Jason had the fun task of trying to open the front door and tip-toe his way into the hallway. The experiment proved conclusively that no matter how slowly one opened the door, how carefully one tip-toed, shuffled on hands and knees, and even crawled on their belly, it was all but impossible to do so quietly enough that the digital voice recorder wouldn't pick it up.

The investigators were thoroughly convinced that whoever (or *what*ever) had broken the mirror, it hadn't been a human being. That really left two options: a suspiciously-timed 'accident...' or 'Fred' and/or his fellow entities.

If they had been asked to place a bet, everyone present unanimously agreed that they would put their money on it being the latter.

During this episode, another curious thing happened, but something that Bil is always reluctant to discuss because of how easy an event it is to poo-poo. Upon returning to the house to discover the broken mirror lying in the corridor, Bil left Richard and his team to discuss the damage, to establish their own point of view away from Bil's instincts for what he felt to be the work of a resident entity. Bil took to Carol's favourite seat in the corner of the front room – not because it is a particularly comfortable seat per se, but because it allows the occupant to *view the whole room* (left), a little of the kitchen and the doorway to the corridor: in that house it's comforting to have your back to the wall! He took to replying to a text he had received. As he was typing, Richard called for Bil to come and join in the discussion about the mirror, to which Bil immediately got to his feet.

Still consciously engaged in typing his text, Bil walked to the corridor finished the text and hit send as he got to Richard, and placed his heavily cased phone into the pocket of his shorts (remember, you are always on high alert at 30 East Drive and consciously aware of everything you do). The discussion about the mirror continued a little before Bil decided to return to the relative comfort of Carol's seat.

As one does, Bil went for his phone in his pocket to check to see if he had received a text in response to the one he had sent – only to discover that his phone wasn't in his pocket. These days our phones are our lives, so Bil understandably panicked and automatically assumed it had fallen out of his pocket onto the chair. Sure enough, there it was – BUT, it wasn't lying on the chair where he expected to find it, *the phone was stuffed firmly down the side of the chair* (left). Understandably, Bil's first thought was that it was his weight that had opened up the side of the chair and his phone had indeed fallen from his pocket and slipped into the gap, closing and gripping the phone as Bil stood to go and speak to Richard. But he was *100% certain* that he was sending a text as he got to Richard!

It subsequently occurred to Bil that whatever had apported the phone from his pocket, had the temerity to properly mess with Bil's mind, by reintroducing the phone at a location that was bound to make him look the fool. "There is no way I can tell this story without looking like an idiot," Bil thought. "Things fall out of pockets and end up down the sides of chairs all the time." Yet he knew, with *absolute certainty,* that he had the phone in his possession when he got to Richard.

Bil, Richard and his team tried to replicate the circumstances that may have resulted in the phone falling out of Bil's shorts and into the side of the chair, to no avail. Not only was the phone too far forward in the chair in relation to Bil's pocket, but Bil would have had to practically invert in order for the phone to drop out. It seemed highly unlikely that this was a simple accident, and more than likely the work of an unseen prankster possessing some incredible powers/properties.

If the broken mirror was the first sign of 'Fred's displeasure at our presence, more was to follow in short order. Not long after we had gotten back, Charlie was standing at the kitchen sink, in the very same spot where Bil had been the target of a flying domino attack a few months before. The rest of the team was scattered around the house, setting up equipment and generally getting a feel for the place.

Minding his own business and thinking about nothing in particular, he suddenly began to feel himself losing his balance and beginning to tip backwards. "It felt as though somebody was holding on to both of my heels," he explained later, "not letting me take a single step back. It was really weird. I've never felt anything like it before in my life."

Discussing it later over a cup of tea, Charlie was insistent that this hadn't been a problem with his sense of balance or a figment of his imagination: he was convinced that he had experienced a very real phenomenon of some kind, and was a little disconcerted when Richard pointed out that if this was indeed 'Fred' playing his usual games with the newly-arrived visitors, he had obviously waited until Charlie was separated from the rest of the group before pouncing.

Talking among themselves (but all too aware that the entity or entities might be listening) the investigators debated whether this was the result of their ghostly host simply being playful, or perhaps whether he could be angry at their presence? Coupled with the broken mirror, Charlie's experience looked to be more of a threat than a prank.

The team didn't know the half of it.

Charlie was standing in the kitchen just a few minutes later, a few steps away from where he had felt his legs being pinned to the floor. The other investigators were taking a break and enjoying a snack when he suddenly complained that his back felt as though it was on fire.

When asked to lift up his shirt, a series of parallel scratches were plainly visible, turning the skin of his back an angry red in colour. The marks ran diagonally across the mid-to-lower portion of his back and looked as though they had been gouged there by a set of very sharp nails… something that nobody in the group, least of all Charlie, had. Close to ten inches in length, *the three scratches looked very painful* (left).

The team immediately set to documenting the scratches with cameras, including the thermal camera, which showed that the flesh around the marks was extremely hot and irritated. A cynic would say that Charlie simply scratched himself, yet he would have had to have done so in full view of his fellow investigators. There is also the fact that Charlie has never been caught faking evidence before or since on an investigation, and there was no reason whatsoever to doubt his integrity. Given the length and angle of the wounds, it would also have been rather difficult for him to scratch himself, not to mention the fact that like many men, Charlie had short fingernails.

At the time of writing (some two years after visiting 30 East Drive) Charlie has yet to be scratched again at a haunted location, and the authors have it on good authority that he's very happy with that.

A steady stream of uninvited visitors interrupted the American team during their stay, mostly those who were curious about the house and its fearsome reputation. Some would walk up to the front door and brazenly ring the bell and ask politely (in most cases) if they might be allowed in to have a look around. On one particularly memorable occasion, a pair of teenage girls hammered on the front door early in the evening and bolted, engaging in that time-honoured tradition practiced by British kids across the land – playing 'Knock door run' at the most haunted house on the estate.

Richard's brother, Matt, dropped in for a quick visit. An infantry soldier by trade, Matt wasn't somebody who scared easily, but when he walked through the front door of 30 East Drive his usual happy-go-lucky demeanour changed. It was almost imperceptible at first, but as Richard took his brother on a room by room tour of the house, Matt began to tense up and assumed the body language of somebody who was on their guard. When all was said and done, he stayed inside for just a few minutes, took a few souvenir photos to prove that he'd been inside one of the world's most haunted houses, then left.

After giving his brother a hug, Matt said in all seriousness that there was something very wrong about 30 East Drive, something "evil," as he put it. Considering the fact that Matt has seen more than his fair share of violence and trauma, it was quite the comment, and it stayed on Richard's mind for quite some time after he turned around and locked himself and his group back inside the house again.

Keeping with the 'feast or famine' reputation, after the initial rush of paranormal activity immediately after their arrival, Richard and his team now found things trending more toward famine. They were still gathering evidence, just not in the quantity or with the consistency that some other teams had in the past. That was all par for the course with a location like 30 East Drive, and there was always an element of testing one's luck involved with visiting it. 'Fred' didn't seem to care that they had flown thousands of miles to come and interact with him. The only thing to do, the team members agreed, was to keep their expectations under control, continue to conduct experiments, and hope for the best.

Sometimes they were gathering evidence without knowing it. During one particular EVP session that was conducted upstairs in Phillip's bedroom, Richard, Jason, and Andrew sat in the dark for half an hour, calling out and asking questions. The house remained stubbornly quiet. It was only after playing back the recording that they realised they had captured the sound of a voice, one that was speaking indistinctly but was most definitely not one of the three men. After repeated listening and analysis, the voice sounds like it is saying, "Uh huh," or something very similar. Earlier that evening, they had asked whether Emma or Emily were around and willing to talk to them. Could this be a reply from one of the two young girls that are said to also haunt 30 East Drive?

Richard submitted the recording to American EVP expert Tim Woolworth, founder of *ITC Voices,* an online repository of information concerning techniques for communicating with discarnate entities. What follows is Tim's opinion:

"What you have here is a classic example of a Class C EVP – even with headphones, you would be hard-pressed to find two researchers who would hear this EVP in the same way. What I am hearing is a muffled male voice, possibly adolescent. The content is what is in question. I listened to this through several variations: as it was recorded, amplified by 10 decibels, pitched down 35%, and reversed. To the best of my ability, my best guess (and I do mean GUESS, as this is not a clear EVP by any means) is, 'He knows you.'

"Now, the interesting part is that when you reverse the message, to my ears it becomes a Class A that states, 'Anyone?'

"Reverse EVP is a phenomenon that I look into every time I record an EVP or Ghost Box communication. Quite often, you will find messages both forward and in reverse.

"Finally, I listened to the two minutes of audio before the EVP in question, <u>and</u> after the EVP for context. You also have captured a clear Class A EVP of a male voice saying, 'I hurt...'"

This was a new and interesting perspective from an expert source. *"He knows you,"* sounds a little ominous at first, particularly if the 'He' in question is 'Fred.' Then again, the investigators had been camping out on his turf for the better part of a week, so it would make sense that 'He' would know them by now. The same could be said of Joe, if indeed he was still around and guarding his home.

"Anyone?" is a fairly generic word, whereas *"I hurt"* tugs at the heartstrings initially, engendering a sense of compassion for the one that is hurting... until, that is, it is considered with a slightly different emphasis; could it mean that the person speaking *hurts others*?

Andy Evans and Steve Hemingway came to visit one afternoon. Both had written books about their experiences at 30 East Drive. Andy's book, *Don't Look Back in Anger,* is an excellent chronicle of his experiences there when the house had just been purchased by Bil and was in the process of becoming more active, and Steve's *Living Next Door to Malice* also provides some interesting food for thought. In addition to sharing their thoughts about the haunting and their own involvement with it, Andy and Steve sat down with the American team for an impromptu live EVP session with an *Acoustic Echo Box*. As the entities inside the house (particularly 'Fred') should be very familiar with both men after the many days they had both spent there, anticipation was running high among the members of the group.

The session, conducted around the kitchen table, yielded one very interesting piece of evidence: a male-sounding voice came through the speaker, apparently saying the words "*Richard Estep*." Richard was taken aback by what sounded exactly like his first and last names being spoken one after the other. He was immediately suspicious, however, of the brain's desire to hear apparently meaningful words in nothing more than random patterns. Although everybody present agreed that it certainly *sounded* like "*Richard Estep*," an objective third party opinion should probably be sought.

EVP expert Tim Woolworth's verdict was as follows:

"Before the audio in question, there is a female voice stating, 'Cannot leave.' *As for the name part, getting your name called is quite a common occurrence for ghost boxers* [i.e. Those who use ghost boxes, not the spirits of former pugilists – the authors]. *Several times during a session, for those who have been in the field for years, is not unusual. It is, on the other hand, highly unusual for a ghost boxer's first and last name to be said together coherently in a natural speech pattern.*

> "In this clip, I quite clearly hear 'Richard.' The second part is a little murkier. At first blush, one could easily hear 'Estep' as the following word. When one begins to parse the communication, one has to evaluate syllables to be sure of the content. In this instance, if you listen for syllables, there are there are quite possibly five syllables present. Listening, you will hear two syllables in 'Richard' then two short monosyllabic words, followed by another monosyllabic word that is drawn out over reverberation.
>
> "After listening to ghost box communication for over eight years, I am of the opinion that the communication is more likely to be 'Richard it is' *(or possibly* 'Richard it has'*)* 'stopped.'"

After the session was over, handshakes were exchanged, and the two men said their goodbyes. Richard's team spent a final, quiet night in the house, a little disappointed that they weren't going out with a bang, but at the same time very pleased with some of the experiences that they had documented. The broken mirror, Charlie's feeling of having his feet held fast, his scratches, and the EVP evidence would have made their long journey well worthwhile.

None of them could have known that in less than a week, paranormal activity inside 30 East Drive would transition from famine to feast... and then to downright explosive.

CHAPTER FOURTEEN
Don't Mess with this House

Phil Bates has spent many nights investigating 30 East Drive, and was kind enough to give Richard and his colleagues a guided tour of the place. He would repeat this courtesy for the TV cameras the following week by showing Nick Groff and Katrina Weidman around (next chapter).

Phil's friend Darren, who would grow up to become Carol's partner, lived in the house next door to number 30, the house which is now her home. Phil lived five minutes' walk away, but the boys would regularly play together inside the house. He confirms the fact that it is the entire structure (not just the half that bears the number 30) that is haunted.

On more than one occasion, the two boys would see people walking through the gate of number 30, yet when the tenants came home there was nobody inside the house: could they have been seeing apparitions?

"May was the first person to live at 79 Chequerfield Road next door," Phil explains, "but the Farrars lived at number 30 prior to the Pritchard family moving in. Both ladies, Jean and May, were very resilient. They *had* to be, in order to deal with what they had to for all those years. I still remember the time that everything in one of the upstairs bedrooms was chucked out of the window."

Standing in the lobby, Phil begins to talk about the reputation of the house. "A lot of people around here find the place fascinating but won't come inside. That includes the police. Scott and I were standing outside just a couple of weeks ago, having a quiet smoke, when two cop cars pulled up outside. We watched the police officers sit there watching us for a few minutes, then came on over to us.

"One of them was very cocky. He asked me if everything he'd heard about this house was true, and I said that yes, it was. He asked if I was sure and I said again yes, I was positive.

"The big one asked if they could go in and have a look around, so we let them in. I warned them that it was at their own risk, which the big fella scoffed at, but the smaller one asked me if it was seriously that bad. I levelled with him and told him that yes, sometimes it really could be.

"The two coppers had a look around the upstairs. As they were coming back down the stairs, the one that hadn't taken my warning seriously was at the back. Something gave him a shove, pushing him forward down the stairs. Then marbles came out of nowhere and went flying toward his mate.

"They left straight away, and I could tell that they were a bit shaken up. Their shift finished at one o'clock, so I invited them to come back afterward and have another look around then. One of them said that he'd rather face off against an armed robber than go back inside 30 East Drive. Needless to say, they never came back..."

Phil opened the door to the small brick room next to the downstairs lavatory. "This is the coal house. Take a look at this door. It's the original one, never changed since the Pritchards lived here."

Phil likes to point out that there is no lock inside or outside the coal house door. The door opens very easily by simply lifting the latch and pushing on it. On the occasion when Joe Pritchard was trapped inside the confined space, alone in the darkness with whatever it is that haunts 30 East Drive, there is no easy explanation for why a man of his stature – he was a coal miner, strong from years of performing manual labour at the coal face – should be unable to get it open... Unless something stronger than he happened to be forcing it shut. If so, there was no way that another member of the Pritchard house could have been the culprit, for the combined strength of Jean, Phillip, and Diane would not have matched his, especially with the extra strength that Joe would have possessed thanks to the adrenaline running through his system.

What manner of force can keep a door closed in the face of a fully-grown man's best efforts to open it?

"The smells that you get in this place are unbelievable. A wet dog smell, or some other kind of animal. Sulphur's one. The other common one, pardon my language, is shit. Urine as well, and neither of them are coming from the bathrooms or toilets."

Sulphur of course has satanic connotations, and the word

'demonic' is one that is bandied about all too easily in the paranormal field these days, primarily because it's good for book sales and TV ratings. Is it possible that there is a simpler explanation for the stink of faeces and urine that has troubled a number of visitors – such as a problem with the drains?

Bil has had the drains checked by a qualified plumber and has the bathroom and toilets cleaned regularly – no problems have been found with them at the time of writing.

Sticking with the possibility of a demonic/inhuman entity manifesting itself, Phil says that harsh and guttural growls have been heard coming from the coal house on several occasions and recently a *loud clear angry banging was recorded* (right) coming from the coal house.

"Some of the places in this house are more active than others. If you want to refer to them as portals, that's as good a word as any."

When asked which of the rooms is the most paranormally active, Phil says that the upstairs bedrooms are all candidates, but that the activity seems to vary, moving from one to another. It would be tempting to think that the master bedroom (the room in which the Black Monk first appeared at the foot of the bed) was the main hotspot, but both Phillip and Diane's bedrooms also have a long history of documented phenomena.

"You have got to respect this house and the things that reside within it," he explains, obviously very passionate when it comes to this particular subject. His tone then becomes cautionary. "It has a habit of playing with your emotions. Trust me – *don't mess with this house.* Respect it on all levels, or you'll be sorry."

This is sound advice for anybody who sets out to investigate claims of the paranormal but is doubly true in a place such as 30 East Drive – which has a reputation for nastiness if the resident entities are provoked.

Painfully aware that 'Fred' might be listening in on their conversation, Richard hesitantly said that he personally (or a member of his team) may have gotten off on the wrong foot with 'Fred' when they first arrived, and that the smashing of the mirror could have been – no pun intended – a reflection of that.

"Possibly," Phil said, "but things have been getting stranger than normal around here for the past few weeks. We've had odd marks turning up on our team members, marks that we can't explain – in each case, they've been the three stripes. You know the ones."

He was referring to the theory held by some members of the paranormal research community that three scratches are demonic in nature. The theory has been popularised by the television show *Ghost Adventures,* which has claimed that the number three mocks the Holy Trinity. Richard is sceptical of that particular theory, but nevertheless maintains an open mind on the subject.

"We've also had random scratch marks turn up on some of the doors and skirting boards," Phil went on, "when we know full well that nobody has been in the house. Where have they come from?"

"I've absolutely no idea" responded Richard. "After living near it for so long, do you have any ideas as to what it might be? What the cause of the bulk of the phenomena might be?"

"Something demonic," he says without hesitation. "You see, me personally, I have my own beliefs about this house. They say that it's a monk, but I don't believe for a minute that that's what 'It' is. No two days in this house are ever the same. Some people it seems to like... or at least, seems to favour; others it really doesn't like – especially them that drink."

He went on to talk about a female visitor who had gotten a cup ripped out of her hand by an unseen force. Severely shaken, it was only when she had left the house that she was willing to confess that the cup had contained alcohol...

Contrary to this, however, Bil has plenty of anecdotal evidence to support the hypothesis that the presence of alcohol actually results in minimal to zero activity, to such an extent that alcohol is now completely forbidden in the house (not to mention the fact that the combination of alcohol and poltergeists tend to make idiots of the most well-meaning of folk).

Bil has no idea why this should be the case, but he is particularly intrigued by the prospect of there being a connection between the senses being dulled by booze and the decreased levels of paranormal activity. Of course, it makes sense that alcohol dulls the senses, and so it follows that most subtle activity (and much of it *is* subtle) will most likely be missed if guests are inebriated. But given the nature of the house, it would also be pertinent for us to consider a more ethereal explanation.

A religious man might take great offence to the consumption of alcohol, as Phil suggests in his anecdote – yet monks used to brew ale for their own personal consumption, which is one reason why beer brands are literally littered with monk-like iconography. On the other hand, it seems hard to believe a demonic entity would take offence! The more intriguing prospect is this – everything that occurs at number 30 is in some way connected to an extremely subtle extra-sensory perception, or perhaps energy *exchange,* one which lies dormant in most of us. It isn't happening in the 'real world' at all, per se, but the location has some as-yet unknown set of remarkable characteristics that allow for certain people to connect with, or fuel it – perhaps using some dormant sixth sense.

This sense may be so subtle that even the smallest amount of alcohol has the effect of dulling whichever part of it makes a connection – that comes 'online,' if you will – whilst visiting 30 East Drive.

Whilst this particular theory is interesting – it doesn't comfortably account for the physical phenomena that occurs at 30 East Drive (often witnessed by many simultaneously), or any other active location for that matter. We will continue to explore theories such as this at the end of this book.

CHAPTER FIFTEEN
Paranormal Lockdown

Three days after Richard's team left 30 East Drive and travelled back to the United States, a new set of American visitors took up residence inside the house. Along with their Rob their cameraman, Nick Groff and Katrina Weidman would spend around 100 hours locked down, recording their experiences for the TV show *Paranormal Lockdown.*

Although the show wouldn't air until Halloween of that year (it was recorded in July) Richard had the good fortune to bump into both Nick and Katrina at a convention in Atlanta in August, and they spent a few minutes discussing the case. "You must have stirred things up before we got there, because we had some *crazy* stuff going on," Nick smiled. "Just wait until you see the episode!"

The episode begins with some news footage taken at the time of the initial outbreak. "The poltergeist activity inside this house is said to be some of the most vicious in Europe, if not the whole world," announces a news reporter solemnly, standing at the end of the front garden. The house stands behind him, looking the same, bar the modern double glazing replacing the old 50's style single glazed windows.

Nick and Katrina talk about the negative after-effects of an American case that they had just worked, a haunted property known as the Hinsdale House. Paranormal phenomena appeared to follow Nick home, making its presence known with knocking sounds around his house at night. His security camera detected something anomalous in the basement, which he believed was an apparition of some sort.

In an attempt to find answers, Nick sets up a *Portal Wonder Box,* (a portable radio-sized Heath Robinson-esque contraption that allegedly allows spirits to speak from 'the beyond') in his house. Most paranormal investigators will tell you that investigating one's own home is a no-no (after all, you might not like what you find) but Nick is concerned for the welfare of himself and more importantly his family. The device speaks what Nick believes to be the words "Demon," "I'm inhuman," and perhaps most interesting of all, "Pontefract."

Nick states his belief that in addition to an entity from the Hinsdale House, something connected with 30 East Drive may be involved. It must be pointed out that while devices such as the *Wonder Box* are capable of delivering sensational results on occasion, they also make the listener susceptible to the phenomenon of *audio pareidolia* – the tendency to hear apparently meaningful words in nothing more than random sounds. It is impossible to tell which is which, although some of the words that Nick obtains through the box seem to be answering his questions directly, implying an interactive component to the case.

Nick and Katrina visit with Mike Covell, a Hull-based historian, who fills them in on some of the background of the case.

Mike points out that 30 East Drive was not only built close to one of the bloodiest battlefields of the Civil War, but was also built on a junction, which he states were, historically speaking, often the scene of executions and suicides.

They then go to meet with Andy Evans in a local pub. Nick asks whether the story of the Black Monk himself has a factual basis; particularly whether such a character really was hung for raping and murdering a girl. Andy refers them to an old map on which the current location of 30 East Drive is overlaid. "Monks *were* farming all this land. Local legend has it that in the early 1600s, there were monks living in the local priory. One unfortunately had a liking for young girls, and he had raped and murdered a young girl. As legend goes, they threw him in a local well."

Andy says that his map, dating to 1812, does indeed show a well located in close proximity to 30 East Drive. He ventures his opinion that when the initial outbreak of poltergeist phenomena took place during the 1960s, the entity chose to visually present itself as something which ran like a thread through the history of the Chequerfield area – a monk.

This is a very astute observation. No matter what the legend might say, it has little if any proven basis in fact, other than the verifiable presence of monks having lived and worked in the vicinity. However, we do not need to buy into the murdering sexual predator story in order to accept that the Pritchard family really *were* tormented by the apparition of what appeared to be a monk. The dark hooded figure would be a perfect avatar for an inhuman entity to choose as its 'human facade.'

"It's very manipulative," Andy tells Nick and Katrina of the entity in question. "You will find that you will get more activity in, what was, Phillip's bedroom than you will in Diane's." Andy's advice bears out what the authors have learned from their numerous interviews and from personal experience: of the three bedrooms, Phillip's seems to be the most active, followed by the master bedroom, with Diane's claustrophobic little room coming in third place. (Not that Diane's bedroom hasn't seen its fair share of paranormal activity – one night, 'Fred' apparently ransacked it and trashed the bed for no discernible reason).

Andy attributes some of the initial outbreak to the emotional rollercoaster that Phillip was suffering, partly due to the persecution he was said to have undergone from his father.

"My whole entire career has led up to this," Nick remarks as he and Katrina approach 30 East Drive for the very first time. They meet Carol and gain some perspective from her 30 years' worth of experience. "It's a demon," she tells them. "It's not nice. It growls, and when 'It' growls, *you run*."

Inside, they find the pictures on the living room wall hanging askew yet again (it is subsequently revealed that the pictures had been straightened up earlier that morning prior to Nick and Katrina's arrival). Standing near the French doors, Nick feels something moving up his back and catches a glimpse of the light fitting in the hallway moving (although it isn't captured on camera). Then they meet with Phil Bates, who gives them a guided tour, starting with the coal house. He points out that the coal house door is original, and has no lock on; it opens easily.

Taking a seat on the couch, Nick is suddenly overcome with nausea. Standing up to clear his head, he then hears somebody walking down the staircase – of course, when they look, nobody is visibly there. Heading upstairs, Nick feels himself being pushed in the doorway of the bathroom. Shortly after, Katrina claims to see the face of a man in the bathroom mirror that may look like Joe Pritchard, according to Phil.

Katrina voices the opinion that whatever haunts the house could very well be demonic in nature. When the tour is over and Phil leaves, Carol comes over to lock the three of them inside the house for 100 hours. Some paranormal 'reality' shows claim to spend days at a haunted location, but actually only spend a few hours there: *Paranormal Lockdown* has a good reputation for truthfulness, and Carol confirmed that once the front door was chained shut, she did not see Nick, Katrina, or Rob the cameraman leaving the house.

The team then 'go dark' and kick off their investigation. Sitting halfway up the staircase, Nick picks up a temperature drop. Little else of note happens and the team settle down to sleep, with Nick crashing out on the living room couch and Katrina bravely bedding down in Diane's bedroom. Nick awakes with a start as the French door opens itself. This is caught on camera, and clearly nobody was walking on the floorboard that can naturally trigger it – all three of them were fast asleep.

The next day, their investigation resumes in Phillip's bedroom. Nick places a child's plastic ball on the carpeted floor in the middle of the room and asks politely whether it can be moved. Obligingly, the ball moves of its own volition straight away, rolling as if pushed by an invisible hand. The authors of this book have tried similar experiments in Phillip's bedroom, and can attest that this effect is not due to the angle of the floor or anything similar. This is the same room in which *Most Haunted* recorded video footage of several smaller balls spontaneously rolling back and forth across the carpet, adding more weight to the contention that Phillip's former bedroom could be the most paranormally active room in the house.

At the top of the staircase, Rob feels something hit him on the back then hit the ground. True to form for the house, it turns out to be a marble, making Rob just the latest in a long line of targets for 'Fred.'

The remainder of the first fifty hours turns out to be fairly quiet, once again following the pattern for 30 East Drive. Katrina feels nauseous for no apparent reason, another very common experience for visitors to the house. Thumps are heard from the empty upper floor, and a knife is found on the lower staircase, an echo of Steve and his guests' visit. As Nick and Katrina are sitting on the stairs, they hear (and record) what Nick believes may be a growl, although the sound is very difficult to identify.

They begin to conduct some ITC (Instrumental Trans-Communication) experiments with electronic equipment.

"Tell us what you want from us," Nick asks, and is immediately rewarded with the word: DIE. A blurry image which may or may not be a dark figure is captured on a video monitor – it is left up to the reader to judge that for themselves.

76 hours in, and the team are entering the home stretch – their final 24 hours locked inside the house. The stopped clock which sits on the dining room windowsill overlooking the back garden has begun to move again, despite nobody having touched it. Nick starts to feel unwell once again.

Katrina begins to provoke, asking, "Is this the best you can do – make somebody sick? Are you afraid of us? Is that why you're only doing parlour tricks?" She also becomes nauseous on reaching the top of the stairs.

Leaving cameras rolling downstairs, they focus on investigating Phillip and Diane's old bedrooms. Unbeknownst to them, the door that separates the living room from the hallway swings shut all by itself. They smell a strange odour, akin to something burning, and play back their video footage – and are amazed to discover that they have captured a shadowy, transparent figure move past the open door to the hall. It appears to be wearing some kind of white shirt, and the door closes in the figure's wake. It is as though there is a connection between the figure walking past and the closing of the door, even though there is no physical contact between the two of them. Rob, Katrina, and Nick were all upstairs at the time, and with no other flesh and blood person in the house, who could the figure possibly be? It is plainly too tall to be a child yet lacks the classic black hooded look of the Black Monk. Could this be 'Fred' manifesting in a different form, the spirit of Joe Pritchard walking through his former home perhaps, or one of the many 'drop-in' spirits that are believed to pass through the house? It is impossible to say for sure.

At the same time, a number of small black blobs no bigger than mice are seen darting across the living room carpet. Carol states that she had seen the same things in her own house next door, and she is certain she doesn't have mice!

Taken in totality, this is a very impressive set of evidence gathered by the *Paranormal Lockdown* team. Assuming that no fakery was involved (and there is not a shred of evidence that this wasn't genuine paranormal activity); then the combination of visual phenomena in the form of the apparition and the black blobs, plus the door closing after the mysterious figure had just passed by – demonstrate something that is impossible to explain in terms of conventional science. The truth is that either the team are not telling the truth about what happened (and there is no reason to doubt their integrity whatsoever) or this is grade-A evidence of the paranormal. The authors of this book come down on the side of the latter explanation.

Nick then elects to shut himself inside the coal house in total darkness, recording with an infrared light. In seconds he leaves, claiming to have been stabbed in the leg by something. A long vertical scratch mark does indeed run down the length of his lower leg. Angrily he goes back inside to confront whatever it was that scratched him, but after getting no further interaction, cedes his place to Katrina.

It isn't long before she is scratched too, on her right-upper abdomen beneath two layers of clothing. As she is showing the scratches to Nick and Rob, the sound of shuffling is heard coming from upstairs and the smell of sulphur begins to pervade the house. The team heads upstairs to investigate. In rapid succession, the clock at the top of the staircase tips over and loud thumps are heard to emanate from the attic. Gingerly, Nick pokes his head up into the attic and begins to challenge whoever or whatever is making the noises.

Nick declares that they are dealing with "an aggressive demonic presence." At the 100-hour mark, Carol unlocks the door to let them out. Nick and Katrina make no bones about the entity at the centre of the 30 East Drive haunting – "It's definitely evil. It will latch onto you and hit you when you least expect it."

In an interview with Jayne Harris for *Haunted Magazine,* Katrina says that of her entire career in paranormal investigation, the one moment which shook her up the most was getting scratched at 30 East Drive, admitting very frankly that the experience drove her to the brink of tears…

"I think about that night a lot. What I find fascinating is that multiple people have all experienced spontaneous scratches in that house. For fifty years it's been what we would call a violent haunting. *Whether you believe in ghosts or think it's bogus, something is manifesting physically at 30 East Drive!*"

CHAPTER SIXTEEN

A Very Nasty Thing

Long-term neighbour Carol Fieldhouse maintains that activity happens in her own home every bit as much as it does next door at number 30. This makes sense when one considers that the two houses are directly attached, basically one big structure that is partitioned down the middle by a dividing wall. Spirits have never been put off by walls or doors, so why would we expect the paranormal activity to be confined to number 30 alone?

A mother, grandmother and housewife, Carol is a typical northern English, no-nonsense matriarch who has experienced more than her fair share of paranormal events both at home and in the house adjoining hers. Living next door to one of the world's most haunted houses is not for the faint of heart. Slamming doors and cabinets, bangs, thuds, and footsteps regularly occur inside number 30 when the house is empty and securely locked up, all of which can be heard through the dividing wall between the two houses. Most people would have suffered a nervous breakdown after living with ghostly activity for so long, but Carol is made of sterner stuff.

Carol will never forget the first time she encountered the Black Monk in person. As she was lying awake in bed one evening, she could hardly believe her eyes when she saw a black shape crawling along the side of the bed. The black shape slowly raised itself up to its full height, and it was only then that Carol realised she was looking at a cowled figure, one that was both extremely tall and wide. Beneath the hood, the monk appeared to be faceless. She watched in astonishment as the entity walked around the end of her bed and disappeared soundlessly into her fitted wardrobe, without bothering to open the door first.

The following day, Carol took the wardrobe apart and destroyed the pieces. She didn't want to risk even the slightest possibility that the entity was attached to it somehow. Although things quietened down for a week or two, they were soon back in full swing. The paranormal activity does seem to wax and wane over time and can be affected by factors such as the volume of visitors to number 30 or the weather outside, but no matter how quiet things get it seems the haunting is always there in the background, just waiting to flare up again.

The question must be asked: Considering the sheer hell that she and her family went through at the hands of 'Fred' or 'Mr. Nobody,' why did Jean Pritchard remain at 30 East Drive for so many years, long after her husband had died and her children had both flown the nest? The lock she had fitted on the French doors, one that she allegedly kept firmly shut, living primarily in the kitchen/dining area with her parrot, is perhaps a clue to the state of fear she lived in – she evidently wanted to keep something out from the living room next door. Or perhaps she was trying simply to *'keep that bloody door shut,'* the one that was constantly opening on its own?

Carol Fieldhouse, who knew Mrs. Pritchard personally, has no doubt as to why Jean lived alone in the house for so long: Like many matriarchs of her time, Jean was a stubborn woman and not to be messed with. There was no way in hell she was going to let anything drive her out of her own house and home. She was never one to be easily intimidated, even by an entity with a demonstrated propensity toward violent behaviour.

[Authors' note: Given how tenacious Jean was, it is likely that it was her age and all the challenges that brings rather than being forced out by 'Fred,' that lay behind her decision to finally sell the house and to move herself to a local retirement home. In that sense Jean can claim to have beaten 'It' rather than 'It' beating her, an incredible achievement. It is perhaps even interesting to speculate that Jean sold the house reluctantly, it being an unfortunate truth that even those living in an abusive relationship can sometimes miss their tormentors when they are removed from the equation. The sale serendipitously allowed film producer and co-author Bil Bungay the opportunity of buying the house, a house he bluntly refuses to spend the night in. One thing's for sure, in the steadfast, stamina stakes of life, Jean Pritchard surely deserves a medal for her sheer bloody-minded determination to 'not let anything get in the way of her happiness' – *anything living or dead. It's for this, and for easily being the world record holder for living with a*

poltergeist, a fifty-year record unlikely to ever be broken, that we humbly and respectfully have dedicated this book to her.]

"I didn't have a close relationship with Jean, but she was a real icon around the estate. When people asked her why the hell she didn't move out, she'd say, *'This is my home! It's not chasing me out!'*

"There's nothing quite like this house. Every single day without fail when I come into the living room, the pictures are all crooked. I straighten them up, go about me business. Whether or not there's been people in overnight, the next morning, those pictures are crooked again. Cushions like to move themselves as well when the house is empty.

"I've had three people come back here, begging to return stuff they'd taken... well, stolen – 'souvenirs.' They beg me to put it back for them, because something follows them home.

"There was a lady sitting here, suddenly burst out laughing. She said she felt like she was drunk, but she hadn't touched a drop. It was strange. She took it upon herself to take home a little memento, without asking permission, from the house. Now she's having all kinds of problems in her personal life. Is it related? I couldn't promise you, but I think so."

Carol and Eileen, her close friend and member of *East Drive Paranormal* (so called *'East Drive Paranormal'* because of their coincidental location, not their close connection with 30 East

Drive), both have seen something small, black and mouse-sized scurry between the living room and the kitchen. This sounds like what Nick Groff recorded on *Paranormal Lockdown*.

Carol confirmed the existence of a well.

"In the 70s the floor in my front room was bowing upwards. Elsie May Mountain owned my house then. The council came in, drilled down and found a deep drop down below the ground. Darren went down there because Phil Bates dared him to, and he saw the watercourse running underground. They put concrete down over the top of the watercourse in my house after filling it with rubble to stop the damp rising."

The well and watercourse must therefore run underneath both houses. She confirms that a ring was found on the side of the well (though not whether it was on a hand) and that somebody from the council allegedly has it in their personal possession.

"When *Most Haunted* were filming here, a car pulled up outside and an elderly gentleman got out. He said that his name was Leander William Farrar, aka Bill Farrar. When they asked why he had come, he replied that he had come to lay to rest once and for all the claims that the Pritchard family had made it all up."

This is a claim that is still made on a fairly regular basis. 'The Pritchards were in it for the money, the publicity, or a combination of the two,' or so goes the theory. It is a specious argument at best, for it completely ignores the sheer volume and consistency of eyewitness testimony that was documented at the time of the initial outbreak. Colin Wilson spoke to many of these witnesses at first-hand and was impressed with their credibility. And if the Pritchards *did* make it all up, the publicity generated didn't benefit them in any way other than gaining some local notoriety: indeed, some people on the estate avoided them and their house especially because of the ghost stories, and when Jean finally sold the house she sold it well below market value.

"That's why we didn't tell anybody what was happening in our house for years," Carol explains. "We've lived a life of hell, and now I'm past caring. I put it all out there so people can hear the real story...

"When these two houses were first built, Aunt May [Mrs. Mountain] lived over in Pontefract centre. They offered her a house in King's Croft first, but she couldn't afford the rent, so they said, "There's two houses over in Chequerfield, we'll give you one of them." They were so new when she first moved in that they were still putting the doors on.

"Jean was living across the road from here at the time. She wanted number 30, but the council wouldn't give it to her, so she took the place they offered in Chequerfield. Then along came Mr. & Mrs. Farrar; they moved into number 30. A year or so after they moved in, Barbara Farrar ran into Jean Pritchard down at the shops. When she asked her how she was liking her new home, she told her that she really didn't like it at all. In fact, she offered to swap houses with her. Jean could hardly believe her ears, but she wasn't one to look a gift horse in the mouth. 30 East Drive was her dream home, and she was delighted to take her up on her offer.

"Joe and Jean moved in just as soon as Bill and Barbara could move out. They had a relative who lived up the road who liked to read tea leaves, you know, fortune-telling and things like that. Just for a laugh they invited her to come in and do a Ouija board with them. I think they didn't close it down afterward. That's when things really started to happen around the house."

Carol is referring to the theory that Ouija boards must be opened up and closed down properly, with stern instructions given to any spirit communicators that they may not hang around the place where the séance happened and bother the people who lived there. Some claim that Ouija boards are essentially portals that allow, not only communication with discarnate entities, but also permit them to come and go as they please unless the portal is shut down properly. Could this be where the stories of there being portals inside 30 East Drive originate?

"They made tape recordings of strange noises inside the house. I know because Darren once borrowed them and played them for us. I can still remember hearing them today. Really loud banging on the walls, so hard that you thought the walls must have been knocked down. They were bad... no, they were *horrendous.* You could hear Joe shouting and swearing at whatever it was making the racket.

"We didn't speak a lot, me and Jean. The last conversation we had, she said *'Hello'* to me as I was coming back in from the shops one day. We got to chatting, and she told me that she was thinking of putting the house up for sale."

Carol warned Jean that she would have to disclose the haunted history of the home to any potential buyer, otherwise there may be the possibility of her getting sued if the paranormal activity ramped up again. Jean replied that the activity *was* getting bad again for some reason.

The two ladies talked about the strange and disturbing events that were going on in both of their respective houses. "I've being fighting it all these years, love," Jean told Carol, plainly weary of it all. Since her children had grown up and moved out and the death of her husband, Jean had lived alone (except for a pet parrot) at 30 East Drive, and for many years. Carol went on to explain that Jean had "gotten locks installed on the French doors in an attempt to lock 'Fred' out of the kitchen and keep him confined to the living room." The locks can still be seen on those doors today.

"She lived in the kitchen, with a television in one corner and Skipper the parrot in the other." Although it obviously isn't possible to physically lock a ghost out of a place ('Fred' had demonstrated the ability to gain access to sealed locations before, such as the jigsaw puzzle box that had been taped shut, and more recently 'Fred' had opened the firmly locked, unused front door of the house – the key to which hangs safely on a hook in Bil's house in London), it says a great deal about the amount of fear and stress that Jean must have been living in towards the end of her time at 30 East Drive. Nobody should be forced to live in fear inside the four walls of their own home, which should be a place of security and sanctuary from the outside world. It says a lot for the pure grit, tenacity, and courage Jean possessed that she stuck it out for as long as she did. "I'm going," she told Carol, "before it gets *really bad*."

"I looked at her, and said, 'Jean, will you tell me the truth – did you fake any of it?' She looked me right in the eye and said, 'No, love. *We did not. We had years of hell in that bloody house. Years. We did not fake it.*'" Jean went on to point out that neither she nor any member of her family benefited financially from the publicity (some would say notoriety) that came along with the arrival of 'Fred,' or 'Mr. Nobody.' What would have been their motivation for making some or all of it up or staging it in any way?

As the two ladies continued talking, Carol expressed her own stubborn insistence on staying in her home, no matter what the entities threw at her. But they couldn't help wondering just how bad things might possibly get. Jean told her of the day on which Joe Pritchard had undergone his terrifying experience inside the coal house.

"He came out of there a different man. It broke his spirit. Joe's character completely changed overnight: he went from being a loving husband to a person that nobody understood any more, not even Jean." When asked to clarify exactly what happened to Joe in the coal house, she explains, "Until that day, he blamed Phillip for everything that had been going on. He wasn't really the rough and ready sort of bloke that most miners wanted for a son; Phillip was a little more sensitive than that, and it didn't sit well with his dad. Joe used to give Jean a hard time for supposedly pampering their son, and suspected that Phillip was engaged in some sort of 'tit-for-tat' exchange with his overbearing father.

"When Joe opened the door to the coal house to find his NCB [National Coal Board] jacket buried in the coal, he immediately cursed Phillip. But then 'It' happened. Well, what *exactly* happened Joe would never speak about to anybody – not even to Jean. But he was in a proper state and was covered in bruises. It was a physical attack and it scared the life out of him. He tried to talk Jean into moving to another house, but she wouldn't have it. She refused to let 'It' drive her out.

"A couple of years later, we hadn't seen Jean for quite some time. She liked to keep herself to herself. Me and my family kept hearing the sound of a television blaring out through the joining wall. We thought that perhaps one of Diane's children had moved into number 30 to look after their grandmother. Then Phillip Pritchard came over on one of his rare visits and we asked him about it. I said, 'Phillip, I keep hearing the telly at full volume. Is your mum alright?'

"Phillip went pale and gave me the strangest look. He said that Jean had moved out months before and that number 30 had been empty ever since. 'She can't have!' I said, not able to believe it. 'We hear her moving about in there all the time. We can even hear Skipper the parrot calling out her name! I heard it just the other day.'"

"'But Carol, Skipper went to an animal sanctuary months ago...'" came the reply.

"He went out, mowed the back garden, put the lawn mower away and then said, 'You won't get me back in that house again for love nor money!' This is a grown man in his sixties. He was terrified that 'Fred' was starting back up again.

"We had no idea that she had moved out. None. It sounded like the house was still being lived in. We couldn't believe it when Phillip told us."

When asked about some of the more interesting antics that 'Fred' had gotten up to over the years, Carol talks about the time when Jean Pritchard went upstairs one day only to find all three of the family's mattresses had been stripped and flipped, the sheets tugged off and scattered about the bedrooms. It must have looked as if an enraged drill instructor had just conducted an inspection in there.

Hearing Jean's scream, May came over from next door to find out what was the matter this time. Sympathetically, she helped Jean remake the beds one by one. May's daughter Doreen Mountain offered to finish tidying up. As Doreen came downstairs, she noticed that a potted plant had appeared at the top of the staircase and was swaying from side to side, as if invisible hands were playing with it.

Not fazed, Doreen said, "Go on then, do your worst," at which point the potted plant rose up into the air and came floating down the staircase, leaving a trail of soil running down every successive step. The plant then settled gracefully onto the carpet at the bottom of the stairs in front of Doreen. Even the down-to-earth Doreen found herself impressed.

One morning, Doreen awoke at five o'clock to a loud commotion outside her bedroom window. Looking outside, she saw Joe Pritchard standing in his back garden screaming and shouting at the top of his voice. For a moment she thought that Joe might be drunk, but it was then that she noticed the piles of debris that littered the grass of number 30's back garden. In the dark, it looked like a mixture of dark wood and broken glass.

"It's that f—g thing!" he roared. "It's only gone and chucked the f—dressing table through the window!"

'Fred' seemed to have taken a liking to chucking the contents of the house out through the windows. At the time of writing, Carol has only found one window cleaner willing to service the windows of her house and number 30, stating that most of them steer clear of the house because of its reputation. Jean Pritchard had less of a problem engaging the services of a window cleaner back in the 1970s. One morning the window cleaner knocked on the back door of number 30 and told Jean that she ought to go and close the rear-facing upstairs windows.

"Why, what's up?" a puzzled Jean asked. She went to the rear window and was mortified to see that the contents of both hers and Phillip's bedrooms were now scattered across the back garden. The kindly tradesman helped Jean carry each and every piece of furniture back into the house again after the windows were closed. He was apparently made of sterner stuff than his assistant, a young lad who turned on his heel and fled when he saw the latest goings-on at the Chequerfield Estate's most haunted house.

As Carol was telling Richard the story of the window cleaner, they were both sitting in the living room of number 30, along with several members of *East Drive Paranormal*. No sooner had she spoken the window cleaner's name than a loud bang came from somewhere upstairs, which everybody knew to be empty. Carol simply smiled in a way that seemed to say, 'See? Here we go again...' (The sound was successfully recorded in the background when Richard played back the audio file from his digital voice recorder for transcription).

"Whether people like it or not, it *happened*," Carol insists firmly, "and it's *still* happening in this house and in mine next door. Only a couple of weeks ago, I was getting my grandkids ready for school and we heard a massive bang coming from upstairs. None of us went upstairs to look. It's an almost daily occurrence. We've almost gotten used to it... *almost*."

Turning to the subject of spirit portals and the claims made by some that there are up to three of them inside the house, Carol refuses to say where they are ("Find 'em yourself!") but is willing to talk about some of the entities that are associated with the house.

"There are the regulars like Joe and the kids, and there are ones that like to drop by and visit. I don't know if the watercourse attracts them, or if there are ley lines that do it. Some of them come by and leave again, but one or two have come through a portal and decided to stay.

"Joe is here. He is *definitely* here," she insists, referring to Joe Pritchard, the family patriarch who died in the house, "he has not left here."

"Is he earthbound?" Richard wanted to know.

"Somebody's just shouted 'No!'" Carol said. None of the others in the room heard anything.

"I don't feel that he's earthbound either. We've met his spirit in here before. The energy that he gives off is *not* nice or friendly... it's more a case of *'Get out of my house!'* He wasn't a nasty person by nature, but maybe the coal house changed all that. But we've also come inside number 30 many times and he *hasn't* been here, so we know that he's not living here permanently.

"The two little girls are also definitely here. Believe it or not, you'll also hear animals in here. Farmyard animals. We've heard cows mooing before. I know how it sounds, but we have."

"Is there anything truly malevolent or malicious here?" Richard asked.

"YES," Carol replied without hesitation. "There's one thing, but I'm not even going to mention its name. There are pictures of it. [She is referring to the pictures of the dark shape captured upstairs, and on the staircase]. It's not human, and it never has been. It can shift its shape."

When asked whether the paranormal activity has increased since Mrs. Pritchard sold the house and moved out, she is very emphatic that it has. "When Bil first started letting visitors inside the house, we had some people that abused it. They played with Ouija boards and never closed them down properly – that's why he had to ban them. We think they've opened up more doorways that things have come through, like that bloody elemental in my house."

Carol may be referring to an entity in her home that is not human, "We know it's never lived on the earth plane; it's a load of energies that have gotten together and somehow made a *thing* – a *very* nasty thing."

CHAPTER SEVENTEEN

I've Just Seen the Black Monk!

For the seven members of *Spookspy Paranormal Investigation*, hunting for ghosts was (and at the time of writing – is) a fun pastime; a social gathering with a bit of adrenalin thrown in for good measure.

So for them, being offered an opportunity to spend the night at 30 East Drive, 'The most haunted house in the UK,' to raise money for a good cause, was a veritable win win situation: have fun and help people at the same time. And like previous forays into other allegedly haunted locations, fun was all that the group (like many visitors before them) were expecting at this location – after all, there surely couldn't be any truth in the stories could there? Believing in ghosts was one thing: seeing ghosts, let alone communicating with them – the stuff of movies and imaginative literature.

With it being November, it was dark and cold when the team arrived. 30 East Drive was illuminated by the soft, yellow light of the lamp post on the street outside, giving it a nightmarish quality – that disconcerting feeling where you can't quite pick out the exact detail of the environment in which your mind has randomly placed you, often the uneasy prelude to some disturbing event.

Straight away, the whole group sensed an ominous feeling emanating from the house. But an ominous feeling was to be expected given the reputation of the place, and was therefore all in the mind, surely?

Then again, this was a house that had the reputation of converting many rabid sceptics into believers…

As Pete Barry turned the key in the door, all seemed normal. This was a run-down, musty old council house in need of a little TLC. Taking no chances, the group immediately huddled together to perform a protection spell, before ferrying in and unpacking their ghost hunting equipment and supplies for their 18 hour stay.

The house seemed quiet as the group set out in pairs to set up a number of trigger objects and other experiments for the evening. The newest device in the group's arsenal was the *GeoBox*; a cool, retro-looking, radio-like spirit box, that allegedly uses energy levels in order to trigger spirit voices. On switching the box on, it almost immediately spoke the word "Diane," followed soon after by "666" and "demon." Quite understandably, this put the whole team even more on edge, but it was then the clear, precise utterance of the words "black monk" that completely blew the team away.

While 'Diane,' '666,' and 'demon' could easily be construed as being relevant to number 30, given its past history and reputation; the icing on the cake had to be 'black monk.' This completed a sequence of inordinate improbability, one which went far beyond mere coincidence.

[Authors' note: To appreciate the significance of the GeoBox responses, and to pre-empt that oft-levelled accusation of 'coincidence' at such events, let's for a moment consider the probability of these specific words being heard almost immediately the GeoBox was activated.

For the sake of argument, we have eliminated '666' and 'demon' from the debate; because they could be considered relevant to ALL haunted locations. We will only concentrate on three words uncannily pertinent to 30 East Drive – home to the Black Monk and once home to Diane, the young girl the poltergeist allegedly terrorised back in the 60's: 'Diane, black and monk.'

If you've ever played a lottery, we can say with a high degree of certainty that you haven't won the jackpot. That's because the probability, or chance, of you selecting all 6 numbers from 49 numbers with only 6 numbers called – is 1 in almost 14 million. Nigh on impossible odds. So, for the sake of our example: if the GeoBox consisted of only 3 uncannily pertinent words out of 49, the odds of getting them straight off the bat are precisely 1 in 18,424. The Oxford English dictionary actually has about 220,000 words. So, assuming the GeoBox has access to them all and 1000 of those words were uncannily pertinent, the odds of just three of them appearing straight away, one after the other are 10.68 million to one. Just shy of winning the jackpot in the lottery. Nigh on impossible odds.

Even if you massively slash the numbers of words available to a HUNDREDTH of the number in the OED to 2200 words, AND assume that ALL the words were 'ghost location' relevant, e.g. 'ghost, scared, dark, dead' etc. including words and names specific to 30 East Drive ('Jean, Joe, Diane, Phillip, Pritchard, Pontefract, council house' etc.) the odds of 'black, monk and Diane' appearing are still eye wateringly high at a million to one precisely. BUT the odds of 'black and monk' appearing IN ORDER rather than say 'monk, black,' or 'black, 666, monk' are almost off the scale at 1 in 48.4 US billion (1 in 48 400 000 000). i.e. the odds of the two most pertinent words for 30 East Drive being heard in the right sequence following each other are so extreme, that one can't help but feel that coincidence plays no part whatsoever.]

The group immediately armed themselves with an *SLS camera* (Structured Light Sensor), a camera that has cleverly adapted *Microsoft Kinect* technology to highlight forms that are invisible to the eye. Without much ado, stick figures showed up in various parts of the house; one waved at the camera when asked to do so, another played the piano next to a group member plinking away at the keys. On a separate visit, *Ghosts of London* captured extraordinary footage of *a stick figure form apparently turning and stepping to the top of the stairs* (right) when asked to do so. Though sometimes a simple camera phone is enough to capture a *figure loitering at the top of the stairs* (right) – like this footage by Claire Cowell of *East Drive Paranormal*; the figure looks like it was surprised to see Claire at the bottom of the stairs filming and quickly steps out of view.

Calling out, the most basic of 'ghost hunting' techniques, came next. The group asked out loud for the spirits to "knock twice if there is anybody here." The reply was instantaneous – two big knocks, each loud enough make the whole group jump. Could it have been a water pipe? Or someone next door or outside playing tricks, one of the group playing a pointless joke even? Anything remotely mundane? Perhaps… save for the fact that the group continued to get loud, concise, *intelligent* knocked responses to their questions for the *rest of the night.*

The first spirit to make its presence known claimed to be 'Diane.' This entity seemingly found herself attracted to one young lad in the group, because everywhere he went she followed along. Naturally the assumption was that 'Diane' was in some way connected to Diane Pritchard, but at the time of writing, Diane is, to the very best of our knowledge, thankfully alive and well. So, the group assumed that Diane was perhaps the chosen persona of an unidentified entity within the house.

This may have been a trick employed to deliberately confuse the team. The Christian and Jewish bibles hold that some demons have the ability to impersonate others if it suits their purposes *('There is nothing surprising in that, for the Adversary himself masquerades as an angel of light' 2 Corinthians 11:14)*. Whether you believe this or not, the unseen entity continued to knock intelligently all around the house, in response to the questions posed by the team. These knocks sounded from the ceilings, the walls, the floors, and several different rooms.

Whoever (or whatever) 'Diane' was, they seemed to be very frightened of something… but of what? Of the visitors themselves, or something else? At around midnight, all communication with 'Diane' stopped abruptly, in the same way a child might cease speaking if an authority figure came into the room. Pete wondered if there wasn't a sinister reason for the sudden silence, and delicately asked the obvious question, "Is *HE* here?"

The response came immediately in the form of three series of six loud bangs. Six. Six. Six. The number of the beast.

After that, the style of communication seemed to change. The questions being posed still continued to be answered accurately, but there was a greater intensity of response than before. The responses now somehow felt angry and aggressive in nature. Still, no matter which bedroom the group went into, the responses followed.

After an exhilarating couple of hours spent communicating

with 'Diane,' followed by the arrival of what seemed to be a new entity, the group was beginning to tire. They declared that they were going for a break, only for the entity to knock loudly twice – the agreed-upon signal for *NO*.

The group chose to ignore this and went downstairs anyway. Straight away, loud, aggressive banging and crashing sounds were heard coming from somewhere upstairs. With all seven members of the group accounted for downstairs, it seemed obvious to all that this was 'Fred' – or whoever the newcomer was – having some kind of a tantrum.

The bangs that began coming from the living room sounded far from agreeable, leading the group to conclude that it was perhaps unwise to continue to refer to the entity as 'Fred,' just in case it was felt to be demeaning. Instead the group called out the name they had heard on *Most Haunted* – 'Carl Anthony.'

"Is Carl Anthony your name? Knock once for yes," Pete asked. He was rewarded with a single, loud knock. After that, the tone of the responses seemed to soften just a touch.

Little did the group realise that this was the calm before the storm.

The group had placed two *Boo Buddies* (teddy bear-type trigger objects) at the top of the stairs, one which lit up when it sensed energy, and one with an audible alarm. The second bear kept triggering constantly, so, fearing a malfunction, and given the fact that it was now the early hours of the morning and the neighbours were sleeping, the audible bear was reluctantly switched off.

As two of the group members conducted a private vigil in Diane's bedroom, that all hell broke loose. In the space of just thirty seconds, the bear that had been switched off suddenly began to alarm again: the left-hand tap in the bathroom turned itself on, and one of the lads came screaming out of the bedroom in a state of blind panic – saying he had just been scratched or burnt. He immediately lifted up his shirt. His fellow investigators could clearly see three round burns that were causing him no small amount of pain.

Pete turned the tap off with some difficulty (it takes a little strength, due to the tap's stiffness), and as the group hurried down the stairs, the bear that had sounded its loud warning alarm was checked again – to "turn it off properly this time!" but they were shocked to find that it was *still switched off.*

Not to be put off, the group took it upon themselves to confront the entity with some blunt questions. They weren't happy that the young lad had been physically assaulted for a second time, having earlier received an inexplicable scratch on his face. Pete and his team suspected that he was being targeted and wanted to know why, and more importantly – *by what.*

The validations the group received were, to put it mildly, phenomenal. Sitting in the relative comfort of the living room, enjoying the false sense of security that it provides, Pete asked 'Carl' when his life was taken. Asking for specific yes or no answers, a date of 1633 was arrived upon.

"Did you rape and murder young girls?" was worryingly followed by a single knock, signifying YES.

"Do you regret your actions?" Two knocks for NO.

"Why the obsession with marbles, Carl? Did you use them to entice your victims?" That earned a single, affirmative knock.

"How many crimes were you accused of?" was answered with an astonishing *58* knocks, all counted by the group.

"Is the well a portal for you to come and go through?" One knock. "Is the well under the floor in the kitchen?" Two knocks.

For the group, this was almost more surprising than all of the incredible responses they had already had; having assumed the well to be under the kitchen floor.

Earlier that night however, a female guest had claimed to have felt that the carpet in the middle of the front room was wet and squelchy, despite the fact that, when she bent down to feel it, the carpet was bone dry.

"Is the well under the living room floor?" There came a loud and instantaneous single knock for YES. This paranormal affirmation lends credence to the accounts of Darren Burke and Phil Bates, who said that they saw the well under the buttress of the semi-detached property many years earlier; when it was revealed and subsequently capped.

Pete and the group went on to gradually uncover the story that 'Carl' came to Britain when he was just 11 years old and was originally from Rome. It also amused the group that, whenever there was a gap in asking questions, they would always hear three bangs, implying that 'Carl' was impatient for the next question. Could it be that he was actually enjoying the dialogue?

'Carl' was even prepared to play a game where Peter would ask how many fingers he was holding up (the entity always answered correctly), after which 'Carl' was invited to knock once to signify the number of guests that were present in the house. The knocks always got that right, too.

These are admittedly trivial questions by any standards, but the spirit entity seemed to welcome the distraction, and participated wholeheartedly. This seems par for the course with whatever it is that haunts 30 East Drive. One can't help but feel that it even likes to show off for the sake of it (out of pure boredom, one imagines), such as the time it *made a stack of polystyrene cups on a kitchen surface* (left) in the blink of an eye, the witness having wiped the surface down mere seconds before.

As the group started to pack away their things, getting ready to depart, the taps and bangs continued unabated upstairs. It was as if whatever had been communicating with them was frustrated that they were intending to leave.

Pete wondered if a connection had been made that night: a connection not only between the entity and the group, but perhaps between him and it too. Heading back into the front room one last time, Pete thanked 'Carl' for giving them a truly amazing night. He then rather cheekily asked, "Hey! Bang five times, just for me?"

For the first time that visit, he received no response, so Pete concluded that the entity only wanted to communicate with the group as a whole... either that, or perhaps it preferred to only show off in front of the female guests?

Pete turned to head back into the kitchen, on his way out of the house for the last time: Suddenly, five loud bangs came from directly underneath the floor of the front room.

It had been easily the most memorable night of their lives. With so many intelligent responses we might be forgiven for thinking that while knocks, bangs, stick figures and so forth, are all incredible – they would pale in comparison to witnessing a full-bodied apparition: in other words, actually *seeing* the entity.

We close this chapter with Pete's own words...

"After a long night, and with dawn fast approaching, our team settled down in the front room for a little nap, to refresh ourselves a little before our long journey home. I was just about to doze off when I suddenly awoke with a start.

"There in the dim light, between one of my colleagues sat in a chair a few feet away and I, was the distinct impression of a man in dark robes, crouching down – then the apparition was gone. I couldn't help myself but call out to my exhausted colleagues that *I had just seen the Black Monk of Pontefract*!"

CHAPTER EIGHTEEN

What the Heck is It? Part 1

Was *Poltergeist!* the story of the Black Monk of Pontefract, as told by Colin Wilson, a true and accurate account of the terrifying events that plagued the Pritchard family at 30 East Drive? The authors of this book believe that it was. It is beyond any doubt that Colin travelled to Pontefract in order to meet the Pritchards, interviewing them and other witnesses to the paranormal phenomena which took place there.

The *Battle of Chequer Field did indeed take place on what is now the Chequerfield Estate* (right). Many battlefields the world over have a reputation for being haunted – Edge Hill in England and Gettysburg in the United States being just two of the better-known examples. A great deal of blood would have been shed in the vicinity that would one day become known as East Drive, and where one finds violence, trauma, and other strong emotions, one also often finds ghosts.

It is also true that an *orchard known as the Gill Croft once stood on the site* (right) and was likely frequented by local monks, so it is no great stretch to believe in the existence of a phantom monk haunting the vicinity. Several contemporary witnesses claim to have seen what was specifically described as the apparition of a monk.

However, there is little more that urban-myth to support the theory of the Black Monk being the spirit of a murderous monk. The most common variation of the tale is the gruesome, sensationalist one which claims that the monk in question abducted, raped, and killed young girls and, when evidence of his vile crime came to light, the local people gathered together in a mob. After a spot of vigilante justice was carried out, the enraged mob dumped the monk's dead body down a large well – a well that can now, it is claimed, be found beneath the living room floor of 30 East Drive, and the directly-connected house next door.

We spoke with the neighbour Darren Burke, who clearly recalls a time many years ago when some work was being done on the floor in the neighbouring house of the semi-detach – number 79 Chequerfield Road. Long re-sealed, he confidently claims that the well sits directly beneath the dividing wall that separates the living room of number 30 from Carol's house, with the fireplace having been built directly on top of it.

While there is no reason to doubt the existence of the well, the same cannot be said of the monk's violent demise. During the era of the English Civil War, life was both short and extremely difficult for all but the privileged few that comprised the gentrified upper classes. We take a constant supply of clean drinking water for granted today, but back then it was an entirely different story. The last thing that somebody would want to do with a well would be to contaminate it by tossing a body down there and allowing it to decompose. It would be just as easy to hang the miscreant from a branch of the nearest tree or beat him to death on the spot than to go to all the trouble of poisoning the water supply: That is unless (as has been speculated) the murderous Cluniac monk had himself already poisoned the well by disposing of the bodies of his victim, or victims – a plausible theory given the speed with which one would want to cover ones tracks after perpetrating such a terrible and shocking crime.

The story of the monk's supposed brutal demise first gained widespread attention when it was published in Colin's book. Colin Wilson was an excellent writer, a skilled researcher, and a rational man who possessed great integrity. His reputation for checking into the background of a case was well-founded, but in this particular case we believed that he may have made an error by using just a single source of information. Several investigators have scoured the local historical records since the case first came to light, each of them trying to find evidence that might support the story of the monk's death. To our knowledge, none of them have been successful thus far.

If we look at the facts in the cold light of day, we are forced to admit that the likelihood of a monk having been executed on or near the current site of 30 East Drive is slim indeed. While this does not mean that the house is not haunted (or that the murderous events themselves didn't happen), it does put into question the most commonly-accepted origin story. Although it makes for a great yarn, as anybody who has seen the movie *When the Lights Went Out* can confirm, no facts have been discovered to support the hypothesis of a Cluniac monk hell-bent on the sexual assault and murder of young girls… though one has to consider the reputation the Catholic church has to this day of quietly covering up the actions of twisted representatives so as to protect itself.

Regardless, it is no reason to be discouraged, because it allows us to examine some other possible explanations for why 30 East Drive is reputed to be one of the world's most haunted properties.

Sticking with Colin Wilson's account of the haunting for now, one thing that stands out is the fact that he chose to label it as a poltergeist outbreak. It is easy to see why poltergeist episodes tend to be relatively short in duration (lasting weeks to months, rarely more than a year), and can often be very violent in nature, with phenomena ranging from broken crockery at the low end all the way up to physical injuries being inflicted. (Legend has it that in the case of 50 Berkeley Square, London, the entity that once resided there was even allegedly responsible for deaths). Such cases are generally the shooting stars of the paranormal world, burning brightly and spectacularly but fizzling out after a relatively short amount of time.

As stated earlier in this book, the haunting of 30 East Drive doesn't really fit that profile at all. Although the initial outbreak(s) were only a few years long, there are multiple witnesses who state that the house has remained active for *decades* afterward, albeit at lower levels of intensity. According to our interviews with some of those who knew the family, even when Jean Pritchard was the sole occupant of the house after her other family members had either left or passed away, the haunting didn't abate entirely. There are no other poltergeist cases on record that we are aware of in which the activity lasted for so long.

Although the poltergeist phenomenon has been with us for many years, it still continues to defy explanation, despite the best efforts of such luminaries in the field as D. Scott Rogo and Guy Lyon Playfair. A number of theories have been advanced in an attempt to explain just what is going on with the "noisy ghost" cases that still occur in all corners of the world.

Broadly speaking, there are three types of haunting: haunted places, haunted objects, and haunted people. Most cases that are given the label of 'poltergeist' tend to fall under the last of those categories.

One of the most popularly-held beliefs about poltergeist outbreaks is that they usually centre around a child or a teenager on the cusp of puberty. The theory holds that because most such children are not only emotionally volatile but also undergoing complex hormonal growth changes, some form of psychic energy is generated – energy that can be used to power the ofttimes terrifying phenomena that can occur.

The classic focus of such cases is often an adolescent going through extreme emotional stress: physical stressors, brought on by their time of life, in combination with a stressful home environment, such as autocratic parenting or divorce in progress.

Poltergeist hauntings also tend to be intelligent and interactive. There has been much debate among paranormal investigators regarding the nature of the intelligence behind it all: Some believe that opportunistic spirits of the dead are to blame, latching onto the child focus and leeching their energy away in order to manifest paranormal phenomena. Others believe that the invisible force terrorising such families is a tangible manifestation of the focal person's own subconscious. Sometimes the force is playful, taking apparent delight in pranking and playing tricks, whereas at other times it seems to be downright malevolent, lashing out violently in order to terrify or inflict harm.

"The short answer is that there are two possibilities," Guy Lyon Playfair, author of *This House is Haunted,* said in interview with Steven Volk for *Sceptico*. "Either they are some kind of discarnate entity, which I certainly don't rule out, or else they are an entirely unknown force that emanates from the human mind. How it works, we simply don't know. We can only observe its effects. I think there's quite strong evidence that it's some kind of so-called spirit or discarnate entity, kind of drifting blobs of ex-intelligence if you like."

In the Enfield case[a] (superscript QR references can be found at the back of the book) to which Playfair is referring, the entity that many believe to be at the heart of it all was a man named 'Bill,' who died in the house several years before the family moved in. This differs from the case of 30 East Drive, as the Black Monk would have died *centuries* before the Pritchard family took up residence there – *if* he even existed in the first place. Playfair offers no opinion as to how long the hypothetical "drifting blobs of ex-intelligence" might hang around, but it seems unlikely that they would last for hundreds of years.

Where the Pritchard family was concerned, there are two possible candidates for being the focus of a poltergeist outbreak – Phillip and Diane. Of the two, Phillip seems to be the most likely choice. Going back to the first day of recorded paranormal activity, the only two people at 30 East Drive that day were Phillip and his grandmother – the rest of the family were away on holiday, including Diane, upon whom the poltergeist was to perform its most violent act; it was Diane, not Phillip, who was dragged upstairs, kicking and screaming, by an invisible force. If the poltergeist was indeed a subconscious manifestation of Phillip's own personality rather than a disembodied spirit, could this have been a brother's resentment for his sister manifesting itself in a very disturbing way? How many older children are jealous of the younger sibling stealing all the attention?

On the other hand, if there really was a discarnate spirit manifesting at 30 East Drive (perhaps using the energy of Phillip and/or Diane as a power source) then it showed an alarming willingness to target members of the family in a particularly vengeful way. Consider not only its treatment of Diane, but its assault on Joe Pritchard in the coal house. In both cases the entity's intended target could have been seriously injured, although as is typical with most poltergeists, the actual bodily harm suffered was relatively minor.

Our limited understanding of such phenomena makes it impossible to say if what happened at the Pritchard's home was some inexplicable, but nevertheless real, entity putting in its first dramatic appearance, perhaps feeding off the energies freely emanating from two angst ridden adolescents, the manifestation of a child's subconscious mind, or something altogether different. And let's not ignore the similarity in the Enfield case; the presence of not one, but two children coming of age.

Given that one of 30 East Drive's first residents, Bill Farrar, has emphatically confirmed that his family were troubled by something unseen almost as soon as they moved into the newly finished house, something ultimately intent on harming their baby daughter, we can at least say that the East Drive case already challenges the assumption that 'adolescent energy' is the catalyst for such manifestations, but may more accurately suggest that whatever 'It' is can access energy from other sources, running water being the next best candidate, but can effortlessly and efficiently harness the energies emanating from adolescents: the entity was already there when the Pritchards moved in, it simply needed Diane and Phillip to come of age in order to fully power-up. Additional support for this theory is the growing amount of activity since Bil opened the house to guests – is this because we all have energy that the entity can more easily harness than that from water, albeit not to the degree of the power ball of energy that adolescents seem to possess? One is good, two is phenomenal – perhaps allowing the entity to switch between power sources as and when they are available, allowing it to maintain a more consistent presence.

It is also important to discuss the controversial idea that a long-dead monk would or could lay dormant until 30 East Drive was finally built and occupied. If so, where was he waiting? In the well – like the creature in the movie; *The Ring?* Was a ghostly monk sighted by farmers working their crops centuries before the idea of the Chequerfield Estate was dreamed up, or scaring the life out of passers-by seeking to quench their thirst at the now-safe well (one assumes that the bodies of the monk and his victims long decayed and the water once again purified)? If the presence of a poltergeist isn't already controversial enough, the concept of the 500-year-old spirit of a monk waiting patiently to make its appearance is really taking the proverbial biscuit.

Perhaps then, it is an entity with a more recent antecedent? But while the house was built on the edge of a battlefield, we have no record of there being any specific deaths having taken place there in the few hundred years afterward. The only person known to have passed away at 30 East Drive is Joe Pritchard, and while there are those who have claimed to have made contact with Joe's spirit at the house in recent years, he died long after the first appearances of the Black Monk were reported, allowing us to definitively conclude that Joe is not the subject behind the Black Monk activity. We must however be careful not to assume that whatever has been identified as Joe is the spirit of Joe rather than an imitator: Was 'Bill,' the former resident of the Enfield house ever the real Bill and source of the poltergeist phenomena, or was it the voice of a clever 'all-knowing' impersonator; a demon hell-bent on conning us with its mimicry? But then again – what would be the point?

Regardless of the likely catalyst for the Black Monk, the fact remains that not everything about the Black Monk case is text book. We now know for certain that the entity didn't dissipate to nothing as per the general consensus of the 'life' of poltergeist manifestations. Judging by the lock on the French doors between the kitchen and the front room, and rumours that Jean avoided certain rooms in the house, it seems reasonable to speculate that the poltergeist remained in residence with an increasingly elderly Jean. How active it was is open to conjecture, given Jean isn't available for comment. Perhaps the Black Monk was constantly harassing her in a 50-year battle of wills – two determined entities refusing to yield one iota to 'their house'… or perhaps 'Fred' went into a state of hibernation, laying mostly dormant during those wilderness years, forced to consume a low energy, youth free diet?

Thanks to conversations with long-term neighbour Carol Fieldhouse, we know that both 30 East Drive and her own adjoining home next door experienced paranormal activity throughout that time period, though certainly nothing on the scale or intensity inflicted upon the Pritchards when the whole family was in residence, or the increased levels that have come along with the resurgence of public interest in the house. By all accounts, 'Fred' was not something that Jean Pritchard liked to discuss in her later years, particularly while she was still living in the house – it would seem that she lived in a state of perpetual uneasiness with 'the ghost,' arriving at a sort of uneasy 'entente cordial' with 'It.'

With the emergence of 30 East Drive back into the public consciousness thanks to the cinema, subsequent DVD, and now Vimeo release of *When the Lights Went Out* in 2012, and visits from *Most Haunted, Paranormal Lockdown* and many other broadcasters worldwide, the house has become a point of interest for the paranormal community again. A whole new generation – the majority of whom will have never read Colin Wilson's book – have been introduced to the story of the Black Monk, and now flock to the house in droves. Each and every one of these visitors is a potential energy source, that could be used by entities still present in the house in order to manifest paranormally.

The existence of this steady stream of regular visitors brings with it another fascinating possibility. Since 2012, everybody that comes to 30 East Drive is fully versed in the story of the Black

Monk, particularly the parts that concern his supposed crime and execution. Many focus their efforts on trying to interact with the monk in some way, such as: calling out, attempting to record EVPs and using all manner of specialised recording equipment in an attempt to get him to manifest.

All of this sustained and focused mental activity raises the possibility that over the past few years, all of those thoughts have coalesced into a 'thought form.' Many cultures around the world have them: For example, in Tibet they are known as the *Tulpa*[b]; an entity which one creates simply by thinking about it. These invisible beings seem to take on a life of their own, sometimes interacting with their creators by answering questions or manifesting physically.

Perhaps the most famous example of this is the so-called *'Philip Experiment'*[c] which took place in Toronto, Canada in 1972. Carried out by a psychologist, mathematician, and a number of their acquaintances, this ground-breaking piece of paranormal research yielded extraordinary results, the implications of which are still being discussed and debated today.

The Philip Group had one single, clear goal: to create a fictional character, someone who had never existed in real life, and see whether it was possible to communicate with him by paranormal means. They devised an extensive backstory, placing their invented nobleman, a man they chose to call Philip Aylesford, in the 17th century and deciding that he had served in the English

Civil War (shades of the Battle of Chequer Field!) where he had spied on behalf of King Charles II.

It goes without saying that no good ghost story would be complete without death and tragedy – preferably both – and this was no exception. The group decided that their poor unfortunate subject had taken his own life after the love of his life was tragically put to death.

After a few unsuccessful sessions gathered around the séance table, it wasn't long before Philip put in his first appearance. Knocks and raps came out of thin air, seemingly on demand, accompanied by cold draughts and other physical phenomena such as a table being moved. A number of the sitters became convinced that there was an invisible presence in the room with them, presumably that of Philip himself. A sceptic would quite rightly point out that the sense of presence could be explained quite easily by the fact that all of the sitters were either hoping or expecting their 'artificial ghost' to turn up in the séance room, but the other physical phenomena are a little harder to explain away.

While some people believe that the Philip Experiment was nothing more than an exercise in mass delusion, others are equally convinced that the group genuinely conjured up an interactive thought-form of some kind. If that was indeed the case, what is to prevent something similar having happened at 30 East Drive? 'Fred' has been ascribed both a name and a personality (that of a lustful, angry monk) along with a backstory that involves his untimely death and unfinished business – all the classic elements of a good ghost story. Whether 'Fred' was real or not during the Pritchards' initial tenure in the house, they put a label on 'him' in an effort to take the unknown and make it a little less scary. Throw in the unsourced backstory, not to mention a lot of very consistent and very focused thinking about 'Fred,' and you have all the ingredients necessary for a thought form to be created.

With nobody but Jean Pritchard and one or two friends and neighbours around to devote any serious attention to it, the thought form may have lain dormant until she moved out of the house and Bil Bungay took over ownership of the property. Carol Fieldhouse, who was keeper of the keys during the fallow period when the house was empty, still experienced paranormal phenomena there and heard the sounds of both movement and a TV playing (despite there having been no TV in the house) which suggests that 'Fred' wasn't entirely out of the picture.

Then came the 2012 resurgence, and hundreds (soon to become thousands) of people crossing the threshold of 30 East Drive, all of them thinking about 'Fred' and wondering whether they would have their own personal encounter with the Black Monk of Pontefract. That would constitute the equivalent of an all-you-can-eat buffet for a thought form, a continual source of energy for the entity to feed upon.

We find the theory to be a credible, yet things aren't necessarily as simple as that. One simple obvious consideration is that the Philip experiment requires one certainty – that the observers must want 'Philip' to exist, to make an appearance, to be present 'and real,' whereas based on Colin Wilson's thorough account of the Pritchard's tenure and comparatively recent first hand and anecdotal comments, we can confidently assert that the Pritchards had no such desire, and the Farrar's before them: for them the haunting was random and spontaneous, occurring without forethought and caused a lot of fear and physical and psychological stress, the last thing they wanted to disrupt their modest happy lives was a 'Philip' (noting the difference in spelling for Phillip Pritchard!).

One of the aspects of the 30 East Drive phenomenon that some visitors find to be frustrating is its 'feast or famine' nature. On some nights the house seems to be very much alive, with the sounds of disembodied footsteps, growls, and other strange noises being heard, along with flashes of light and investigators being scratched. On others, the house is as quiet as the proverbial grave.

Despite an ever-present sense of there being 'something' in the house – a feeling which may be paranormal, psychological, or a mixture of the two – nothing spectacular happens. The authors of this book have experienced 30 East Drive in both scenarios and find that the unpredictable nature of the house is all part of its fascination. One never feels quite alone in there, particularly after dark.

The energy levels inside the house seem to run in random peaks and troughs over time, and it is almost impossible to predict which nights will be quiet and which will be almost explosive. There is no discernible pattern to it. When Richard moved into the house for five days with his small team, for example, most of the paranormal activity took place during the earliest part of their stay. As the week wore on, the house got quieter, not busier, the opposite of what one might expect. Despite having captured some interesting evidence during the earlier part of the week, the trip ended on something of an anti-climax. Yet after just two days without any occupancy, when Nick Groff and Katrina Weidman moved in for their own five-day lockdown, the paranormal activity came thick and fast. Had Richard and his team simply helped to 'charge the battery' for Nick and Katrina, or are there other factors at work?

Sensitive, psychic, gifted – call them whatever you wish, some people seem to be more attuned to the paranormal than others. Whether or not they actually *attract* that kind of experience is debatable, but certain individuals are more likely to encounter the ghostly than the next man or woman. Scientists and paranormal investigators have spent years debating exactly what it is that makes such people so predisposed. Genetic, physical, mental, and emotional factors may all play a role, but so too must the natural environment – the weather, humidity, and temperature must be taken into account. It has also been theorised that certain types of minerals may contribute, along with standing or running water, power-lines and a myriad of other variables.

No single factor is more important than location, however, and the best way to improve your chances of encountering the paranormal is to spend time in a place that has a solid track record of other similar happenings. 30 East Drive is unquestionably such a place and has been for more than sixty years.

When asked to explain why he thinks that 30 East Drive is such a haunted place, Phil Bates likes to advance the theory that involves the watercourse running underneath the property. He likes to point out that in all of the books that have been published so far which talk about 30 East Drive, none of them refer to the discovery of a medieval ring down in the well, underneath the buttress of both houses. As a young boy, Phil played in the house next door with his friend Darren and claims to have witnessed with his own eyes the well being dug up and concreted over.

Would the discovery of the ring lend credence to the story of a monk's body having been thrown down the well? It would if the well was opened up and excavated, but there is no likelihood of that happening any time soon. The authors are unaware of the existence of any other eyewitness in addition to Phil and Darren, and while we do not doubt their word, more concrete evidence is required before the complete truth of the matter can be fully known.

"A lot of the furniture in this house isn't original," Phil explains. "The settee. The chairs. A lot of it was brought in by Bil, and with the energies inside this house, you really have to ask yourself how much of the paranormal activity that goes on really originates here, and how much of it is attached to the stuff that has come in from the outside?" It is a very good point, and one that many people overlook in their eagerness to ascribe the cause of the haunting purely to 'Fred.' Haunted objects are a not-uncommon thing.

Richard once investigated an abandoned hospital outside Salt Lake City whose chapel was said to be haunted by the ghost of a very angry old man. Some of the pews in the chapel were purchased from a funeral home which closed down after a fire. Several visiting psychics claimed that one of the pews was what had brought the man's spirit along with it, and that he had actually watched his own funeral while sitting on it. The anger, they said, came from a combination of unresolved issues left over from the man's physical life and the sheer helpless impotence of watching his body be cremated in front of his very eyes.

Whether you believe in such things or not (and it does beg the question of just how many thrift shops and charities stores might be haunted), the possibility of 'spirit hitch-hikers' is one that should not be discounted. We have already mentioned that there are three broad types of haunting: haunted places, haunted objects, and haunted people. One is forced to wonder just how many of the visitors to 30 East Drive unwittingly bring along their own spirit attachments with them, and of those, how many stay behind and manifest to interact with future visitors instead of going home with the people who brought them.

Colin Wilson ascribed much of the paranormal activity to the land itself, believing that East Drive and its surrounding environs can act as a sort of natural battery which, under the proper circumstances, may be used to fuel paranormal activity. Writing some thirty-plus years later, Andy Evans proposed the repeated use of Ouija boards inside the house opened up doorways to another realm, doorways that may never have been closed. These portals may allow disembodied entities to come and go as they please, either dropping in for a brief visit or sticking around for months, if not years at a time.

Phil Bates sees merit in both arguments.

"I don't believe that it's the house itself," Phil says. "I think it's the land that it's built on. Cromwell would have been encamped somewhere around here, and I think the smells of sulphur and the noise of dogs barking in this house when there's no dog here might be residual leftovers from those days. There's the fact that Joe died in the house, and I think he's still resident here as well.

"Andy Evans is a man who has done a lot of research into this property, for the book he was writing. He discovered a map that shows that there was once a croft or an orchard here."

[Authors' note: During our research, we discovered that 30 East Drive sits on an area surrounded by ancient springs *(right) making the area perfect for growing an orchard or locating an encampment – though it's interesting to note that there is no 'pump' located directly on 30 East Drive itself, on a map dating from 1932, suggesting that the well that eyewitnesses claim lies under 30 East Drive had been lost over time, or was perhaps considered unsafe for drinking, and so was capped, grown over, and forgotten.]*

Phil continues: "We've also been monitoring activity in relation to weather patterns, and we've found that on the days and nights when it's raining cats and dogs, the level of activity tends to pick up. I think there's a relationship between bad weather and the intensity of the haunting, but we're still trying to figure out why.

"Do I believe there's a demonic entity here?" Phil asks rhetorically. "Yes… Yes, I do."

CHAPTER NINETEEN
What the Heck is It? Part 2

"Physics extends beyond what is scientifically known today. The future will show that what we now call the occult or the supernatural is based on a science not yet developed."

Nikola Tesla.

For six decades now, and in three distinct phases, 30 East Drive has been the subject of intense interest. Phase one occurred during the Farrar tenancy, an intense and stressful experience where the malign presence first began to make itself felt in the brand-new house. The final straw came when it started to physically harm Bill and Barbara's baby.

Phase two spanned the residency of the Pritchard family. Jean, Joe, Phillip and Diane, along with many visitors to the house, all witnessed some of the most incredible poltergeist activity ever recorded, as expertly documented by Colin Wilson in his book *Poltergeist!*

Phase three still goes on today. This new chapter began when advertising agency founder, movie producer and tech entrepreneur Bil Bungay produced a movie called *When the Lights Went Out*, focusing on the Black Monk of Pontefract, and subsequently ended up buying the house, with the singular aim of using it to promote his movie. It was never his intention to own the house, certainly not to keep it. But, as seems to be the case for many of today's visitors, he has since developed a deep connection to the place – a connection that he will freely admit goes beyond mere intrigue. "There's something extraordinarily profound about 30 East Drive, something beyond our current understanding of the way things are, but nevertheless something very real. It's almost as if whatever is in the house is calling to you," Bil says. As a result, he has become absolutely determined to find an explanation for what is actually happening there.

Like most people, Bil was initially a sceptic (as opposed to a non-believer: in the truest sense of the word, sceptics aren't prepared to declare an absolute position either way, because they simply cannot be sure without irrefutable evidence). The stories with which Bil was regaled by his copywriter Pat Holden when they both worked together as juniors at a London advertising agency were fascinating, but utterly fantastical. "Who in their right mind would believe such nonsense? But then again, who wouldn't want to make a movie about a punching, kicking, screaming poltergeist moving into a cramped little council house?"

Pat, whose mother Renee Holden spent a lot of time at 30 East Drive with Jean during the worst of the activity, subsequently became the director of *When the Lights Went Out*. Bil assumed the role of producer.

Bil's initial plan (and sole reason for buying the property) was to have a premiere for two competition winners in the actual house that the movie was about, and, once that was all said and done, do the place up and sell it. "I had read that poltergeist hauntings tend to dissipate, gradually winding down to nothing once the malcontented-adolescent-focal-point of the haunting has either grown up or moved on," he explains. "As far as I was concerned, the house was no longer paranormally active, and hadn't been for over forty years... assuming that it had ever actually been active in the first instance."

That remained Bil's stance until he began to witness the activity for himself. The first peculiar occurrence was his phone dying in an instant, dropping to zero from a 75% charge. Then came the disembodied footsteps and the knocks, followed by the gate, which he had deliberately and consciously obstructed with a concrete block, somehow opening a full 90 degrees.

Perhaps the most notable incident took place on Valentine's Day 2016. On that day, in broad daylight, he was bombarded with a constant torrent of small objects over the course of two hours. Once you witness such a thing, three things tend to happen.

Firstly, *everything* you have ever thought the world to be is blown apart in an instant. It is simply beyond the rigid, blinkered conventions of our current level of science for an object to somehow materialise out of thin air. Many scientists take the line that because this theoretically cannot happen, therefore it *does not happen.* THEY'RE WRONG.

Secondly, an inquisitive mind is then compelled to question

what incredible process is actually involved in the apportation of solid objects? The only logical answer, once you accept that such a thing not only can happen but has just physically happened to you, is to reason that a type of energy is involved which lies beyond the understanding of our current scientific frame of reference and ask *what the heck is a poltergeist anyway*?!?

Finally, you write a book!

After considerable reflection and debate, the authors feel that there are no less than eight potential explanations that merit serious consideration (though there are doubtless many more) when one is attempting to formulate some plausible hypotheses which may potentially warrant further investigation and experimentation.

Let's begin with the elephant in the room…

1: It's all one big hoax.

It is understandable and altogether reasonable that a sceptic could look at 30 East Drive and declare that the whole thing is most likely an elaborate scam, one shamelessly perpetrated by a savvy businessman – and, what's more, one who also happens to be both a movie-maker and an image specialist.

One would think that if anyone knew how to cook up an elaborate hoax, one which would have to employ world-class theatrical effects in order to create the sheer variety of phenomena reported by visitors to 30 East Drive, then that man would be Bil Bungay. But therein lies the rub: In order to create a fraud that was robust and elaborate enough to explain away the multitude of bumps, bangs, footsteps, thrown objects, moving items, scratches inflicted, ice cold columns and drafts of air, shadow figures, voices, responses to any number of detection devices – not to mention scores of intelligent EVPs – it would require a set-up that was so sophisticated and costly that no investor would ever seriously consider taking a punt, especially considering that to get found out (which would be inevitable) would result in a catastrophic fail (never use rope...) and subsequent media exposure and ridicule.

We must also take into account the fact that the technology to, for example, get an object to apparently materialise out of thin air, be propelled in the specific direction of a particular witness, and then have the object miss the target by the barest whisker, would be incredibly complex. If the technology existed (and it doesn't – in the public domain at least), one could imagine it costing millions, likely billions to develop, access and implement – assuming you had access to it in the first place. But even if such technology did exist, one would need a permanent team of on-site specialists in order to implement and manage it, and indeed, each of the other technological set-ups required to perform each specific event.

As anyone that has visited 30 East Drive will be willing to

attest, it's a very small house. We are not talking about a darkened Victorian-era parlour turned séance room here – many of the reported phenomena take place during the daytime hours, when there are no dark places in which a hoaxer could hide either themselves or the tools of their trade.

By all means call it a scam or a hoax if you are so inclined – but rest assured, you would be doing so without considering the logistics of just how elaborate that scam would need to be in order to explain the full body of reported phenomena. We are talking Oscar-worthy levels of illusion here. Remember that even the Disney Imagineers take immense pains to conceal the mirrors on attractions such as the Haunted Mansion, experiences which cost millions of dollars to design and successfully implement in its theme parks.

The doubtful cynic should also take note of the fact that there is no sign on the 30EastDrive.com website or on the door of 30 East Drive itself that proclaims the familiar message which one so often sees preceding paranormal TV shows such as *Most Haunted*, one which states some variation of, 'this experience is intended for entertainment purposes only.' This is because *nothing* at 30 East Drive is rigged, *nothing* has been engineered to create fake frights or drama, and most pertinently of all, Bil has a strict policy of banning anybody who is suspected of carrying out fakery inside the house... or, for that matter, anybody who disrespects its ghostly residents.

The most important message on the website is one that offers the exact opposite of a disclaimer – it in effect states that paranormal activity can in no way be guaranteed, because '*this isn't a theme park attraction!*' So, those visitors that insist on pulling up the carpets or peeling back wallpaper to check to see if there are hidden devices creating footsteps, knocks, bangs etc. – the owners politely ask you to please stop doing so. When Richard Estep and his team moved in, they checked all over for any suggestion of fraud, and found nothing. Neither did Nick Groff and the crew of *Paranormal Lockdown*, or any of the dozen or so professional film crews that have visited, or indeed any of the thousands of visitors to the property.

Whatever the explanation for the bizarre events taking place inside this modest ex-council house finally turns out to be, trickery will *definitely NOT* be the answer.

2: It's spirits of dead people.

"There is probably no heaven, and no afterlife either."
                                             Professor Stephen Hawking.

Broadly speaking, this book will probably be read by two types of reader: Those that believe in the existence of ghosts and are fascinated by the subject, and those that are sceptical of their existence and are reading the book either out of curiosity or in search of the truth. Bil has at one time fitted into both groups. His early experiences of no less than three inexplicable 'events,' that he has often thought about in the context of 'ghosts,' piqued his interest in the possibility of such things.

On one such occasion, Bil is convinced that he saw his dad walking towards Bil's house the week after he, his mother and his brother Gus had buried him, and notably – the day that Bil was heading back to work after the funeral. "He seemed as-happy-as-Larry, clad in his distinctive country attire, a style that was very much out of place in London, especially during the 7am office worker commute time."

Bil's second sighting was of a young female 1920s era-styled tennis player stood on a dilapidated tennis court near a rundown stately manor house. An old tennis net lay rotting on the court, weeds sprouting through a multitude of cracks in the broken surface. She held an old off-white wooden racket and evoked the distinct impression that she was longing for a tennis partner to turn up.

Most impressive, however, was hearing the very distinctive sound of combat boots stomping angrily down an isolated corridor in an abandoned former army base. Significantly, this event was witnessed by his brother and two friends in addition to Bil himself. "We ran into the corridor to escape, expecting to get collared by a khaki-clad officer arriving directly outside the room we were in," Bil recalls, "only to find a completely empty corridor. There was just one door leading in and out of the building. We waited outside the long wooden hut for ages for someone to appear, but to no avail." Pertinently, Bil and his brother knew the exact sound of army boots on a wooden floor, as for the first 18 years of their lives their father was in the army.

Yet despite all three of these experiences being as real as it gets, Bil's innate sense of scepticism held firm. Perhaps, he tried to convince himself, he was simply hallucinating (despite the fact that no mind-altering substances were ever involved), or maybe the sightings could be put down to a trick of the light. After all, the idea that the dead might possibly live on seemed like a bit of a stretch. At the very least, one would surely need to have religious faith in order to believe that when we die some element of our spirit 'lives' on, and the belief that 'souls' can get lost enroute to heaven or hell – purgatory perhaps – before believing in ghosts. Nevertheless, Bil's primary fascination with 30 East Drive involves the very crux of this debate. He has become increasingly curious to know whether the house may hold *proof* of the existence of an afterlife; some profound form of ongoing consciousness beyond our earthly bounds. Imagine for one moment that such did turn out to be the case: the broader ramifications for human society and culture, particularly such institutions as the various churches and religious faiths of the world, would be huge – their adherents would presumably flock to number 30, as it would validate the core tenet of their belief systems.

But let's be realistic. Our materialistic scientific community[d] is supremely confident that it has satisfactorily proven that, in order for us to possess the very consciousness that allows us to contemplate the question of an afterlife in the first place, we require highly-evolved anatomical structures and physiologic processes; the body and brain, the very peak of human evolution, working in perfect union. They rationalise that, when we die, the biological machine which gives us life and, more importantly, consciousness, decomposes into its constituent matter, and we no longer have the apparatus required to contemplate, feel, have a sense of identity and so on. When the plug is pulled, the mind is gone. All that makes us 'us' disappears, lost for all eternity, our atoms going back to whence they came.

But despite this apparently rational assertion, and the wealth of evidence that has been captured and recorded with technology of various types, powerful eyewitness testimony, and the authors' own personal experiences; it isn't unreasonable for us to conclude that, on balance – ghosts (or some inexplicable phenomena that we like to term 'ghosts') do indeed actually exist. And if that is the case, the next question surely becomes: Given that such phenomena exist, *exactly how and where* do they exist?

As we have already mentioned, the belief that ghosts are the spirits of the dead is, in most cases, closely associated with a belief in an afterlife; a god, along with heaven, hell, and other similar concepts. The authors consider themselves ill-equipped to debate the veracity of millennia-old belief systems: but Professor Stephen Hawking, undeniably one of the finest minds that has ever existed – *was* a man uniquely qualified to do exactly that…

"When people ask me if a god created the universe, I tell them that the question itself makes no sense. Time didn't exist before the big bang, so there is no time for god to make the universe in. We are each free to believe what we want, and it's my view that the simplest explanation is; there is no god. No one created our universe, and no one directs our fate. This leads me to a profound realisation – there is probably no heaven, and no afterlife either. We have this one life to appreciate the grand design of the universe, and for that I am extremely grateful."

If Professor Hawking's assertion is correct (and who are we to disagree?); then what of the mass of evidence that we have on hand that points towards the mysterious phenomenon that we refer to as 'ghosts'? If they aren't the spirits of the dead, and it isn't possible for us to live on after the death of our physical bodies – then what are they?

It's interesting to consider this question in light of Einstein's First Law of Thermodynamics: *If energy cannot be created or destroyed – what happens to our energy when we die*? Obviously, the majority of our energy is locked up in our physical bodies and is 'recycled' back into the food chain when we die: but what of the so called 'weight of the soul'; the 21 grams that Duncan MacDougall (somewhat inconclusively) concluded in 1907 to be 'the weight of the human soul'? If this is the case, then does our surplus energy indeed miraculously manifest itself into the form of a 'ghost' (contrary to Professor Hawking's conclusion), or transition into an 'afterlife' on some other plane of existence? And if *this* is the case, why aren't there billions of ghosts – with 155,000 new ghosts being 'born' every day – rather than the relatively few (and seemingly static) numbers of cases of hauntings that are currently reported? It may be that the 'soul', if it truly does exist, is composed of some type of energy that is as yet unknown to modern-day science.

For many years, the prevailing wisdom has been that the human mind arises from the brain. In other words, brain creates mind. Once the body dies and all blood flow to the brain irreversibly ceases, the organ from which all thought and consciousness springs falls silent forever, and our personality is wiped out.

Now, however, an increasing number of medical professionals are challenging this point of view. In the literature of resuscitation, both in the pre-hospital and in-hospital settings, there are an increasing number of documented cases in which a patient in cardiac arrest is successfully revived after a prolonged period of time, only to have recollections of an out-of-body experience. Such experiences are often very lucid, and those who undergo them have repeated verbatim, to a shocked resuscitation team, some of the words and phrases that were spoken over their supposedly dead body. None of this should be possible when there is no blood supply to the brain. This would be the equivalent of switching off your laptop, removing the battery, letting it sit for an hour, and then firing it up again, only to find a brand-new text document sitting open on the desktop, containing an hour's worth of writing. The laptop had no electrical supply, nothing to power the memory and the central processing unit. A text file (and one which makes perfect sense at that) could not, by any method explainable by current scientific principles, have been created during that time. And yet, there it sits, defying explanation.

An interesting new theory posits that, rather than being the generator of consciousness, the brain is actually a receiver, in the same way that your television set is a receiver for signals that originate elsewhere. In other words, the brain is more of an antenna than a processor. How else can we explain the lucid out-of-body experience in situations during which the brain has no supply of oxygenated blood? Then again; if all we are are 'receivers' – then what of 'free will'?

Until we discover the truth, perhaps it's wise for us to exercise caution and not automatically conclude that the paranormal phenomena in question are necessarily connected to or are proof of an afterlife.

3: It's 'demonic.'

Demons are a millennia-old feature of religions from all around the world, often placed as the evil counterpoint to the central deity. In Christianity, demons are a form of corrupted spirit which serve the fallen angel Lucifer, otherwise known as Satan.

While not demonic in nature, some dark entities (the souls of the wicked deceased, which roam the earth and like nothing better than to torment the living) often act very much like them. The difference being, bad people are said to remain bad people, even after death, but they are still *people*. Demonic entities, on the other hand, are not, and never have been, human.

Christian writings also describe the Nephilim[e], who were said to have come into being because of a union between angels and humans, but their bodily parts were wiped out during the Great Flood. Their spiritual part supposedly now desires re-embodiment. And then there are the fallen angels who sided with Lucifer when he was cast out from heaven, after his major falling-out with God.

One class of demon that appears in the Christian Bible are the 'Se'irim'[f]. They are physically described as 'shaggy goats' or 'hairy beings' – a hybrid creature, half-man, half-beast. This seems to bear an uncanny resemblance to *Lisa Manning's description of the beast* (right) she saw looking down at her from the upstairs bedroom window of her new Coventry end-of-terrace council house, after one terrifyingly active day – one in which she and her children were forced to climb out of the ground floor window of their house, as all other exits were blocked by some kind of unknown force.

Could it be that whatever resides at 30 East Drive is demonic in nature? A lot of visitors certainly believe this to be the case. The violence alone seems to lean toward there being a powerful entity, one that is hell-bent on creating as much fear and terror as it possibly can. It has been known to give voice to unmistakably evil intentions, physically harmed Diane Pritchard (most notably when it dragged her upstairs by her throat and hair) and more recently has scratched and burned numerous visitors – intriguingly, the scratches having three scratch lines as if the result of a creature with a three fingered claw and not the five you would expect from a 'human-like' presence.

A number of visitors to 30 East Drive have reportedly been possessed, followed home, and have had their lives turned upside down – particularly those that have *innocently taken 'souvenirs' from the house without permission* (left). Lisa is convinced that her boyfriend was possessed on at least one occasion – his eyes somehow changed enough for her to know that something was seriously wrong with him – "They weren't his eyes," she recalled.

It is also interesting to note that in the Bible, Enoch blames the Nephilim for the corruption of humans – sin originates when 'angels descend from heaven and fornicate with women, birthing giants as tall as 300 cubits.' The figures witnessed at both 30 East Drive and in Lisa's old house in Coventry are described as being seven feet tall. Perhaps not 300 cubits (almost three times as high as Nelson's Column) but nevertheless giant compared to the average human. Of course, the description of what resided at Lisa's house and what resides at 30 East Drive do differ somewhat; so, we should not automatically assume that they are the same thing, but could it be possible that we are actually dealing with a demonic entity or entities at 30 East Drive? If that is indeed the case, then it naturally begs the question of why such an evil entity hasn't gone to hell, or whatever appropriate place exists for such beings?

The word 'demonic' is one that is grossly overused these days, and we have the so-called paranormal 'reality shows' to thank for that. It is more frequently used by American paranormal enthusiasts than their British counterparts, primarily because the United Kingdom is a great deal more secular – or at least, less overtly religious. Does one need to believe in religion in order to believe in the existence of demons? Not necessarily.

Some paranormal investigators who are avowed atheists or agnostics still hold the opinion that non-human entities do indeed exist. They take the view that such entities are the spiritual equivalent of sharks and tigers, paranormal predators that are capable of causing great harm when they interact with human beings. It isn't necessary for somebody to put faith in a particular belief system in order for them to accept the possibility of non-human entities existing (see: 'Creatures from other worlds' below).

4: It's Psychokinesis.

A blend of two Greek words: psyche – meaning mind, soul, spirit or breath – and kinesis, meaning motion or movement. Psychokinesis is a term coined to describe the ability to move objects with the mind. But a panel commissioned in 1988 by the United States Research Council to study paranormal claims concluded that:

'Despite a 130-year record of scientific research on such matters, our committee could find no scientific justification for the existence of phenomena such as extrasensory perception, mental telepathy or 'mind-over-matter' exercises... Evaluation of a large body of the best available evidence simply does not support the contention that these phenomena exist.'

However, theoretical physics is entering a new era of understanding about the nature of 'things' – specifically matter – at a quantum level[g], which confidently asserts that we do indeed have an influence on the way in which matter behaves, and we have experimental proof of this. But as far as our ability as a species to influence events 'in the real world,' through the simple act of observation, goes – only anecdotal, experiential 'evidence' exists, at best. This fragile 'evidence' is, needless to say, undermined by simple coincidence, acts of persuasion, probability, and so forth.

We are still waiting for tangible proof of the ability to influence the physical world by mental effort alone. Nevertheless, could it be that 30 East Drive has some unknown peculiarities that allow it to somehow 'power our thoughts' into physically moving objects, creating bumps, bangs, footsteps etc.? It is true that Bil had longed to see an object materialise in thin air, to experience 'a poltergeist' first hand – so perhaps the power of his will alone manifested the event into actually taking place?

5: 'They' are real and alive in our three-dimensional* space but exist in a way that is beyond our ability to perceive.

*Deliberately three-dimensional and not including our fourth dimension (time) because such entities, it would seem, occupy a place where time, in the way that we understand it, just doesn't seem to apply. After all, *ghosts don't age.*

Despite being born with the most complex and advanced processor that has ever existed (to our knowledge), there are many concepts that we humans struggle to grasp. One difficult concept is the idea that there are other ways of viewing things in our three-dimensional day-to-day space. You've only to watch a David Attenborough documentary in order to begin to appreciate the sheer breadth and diversity of animal life which shares the same three-dimensional space as us. This multitude of life may occupy the same up, down, and sideways dimensions as we do, but views it in a very different way.

For example, the tiniest of creatures perceive the world as something other than massive – they perceive it as being *completely normal* to them (size is, after all, relative) and yet there is no doubting that from their perspective, we would be seen as truly massive. An ant's reality would be a land of giants, but to the microbe, the ant is the big guy. To a blue whale, the largest of human beings is relatively tiny. By the same token, we would be too big for the microbe to even begin to comprehend us – like early man attempting to comprehend our planet and its place in the greater universe.

Also, within the confines of our three-dimensional world, there exist multiple fields of view that aren't scale related at all. Bats, for example, *'see'* the nocturnal world using 'echolocation' (contrary to popular wisdom, a bat's day-time vision is every bit as good as our own) – they emit an ultrasonic sound wave that bounces off solid objects, allowing the bat to form a picture of them. Bees see on the ultraviolet spectrum of light, which means that they can detect the most healthy and profitable flowers on which to land in order to extract nectar. This principle is as beneficial to the plant or the flower as it is to the bee. Birds use magneto-reception to orient themselves during migration, being able to perceive the Earth's magnetic fields. Many snakes see temperature, meaning that they can spot the heat that prey emit day or night. The Trap Door Spider can feel such subtle tremors with its feet that it can know the precise location of its prey even when the spider is deep in its hole – with the hole covered.

Many animals seem to possess a kind of 'sixth sense,' the ability to be able to predict earthquakes, fires, tsunamis and so on: Flamingos flew to higher ground, elephants ran, dogs refused to go for their daily walks and zoo animals rushed to their shelters – well before the Christmas tsunami hit the Sri Lankan and Indian coastlines, for example. Very few wild animals died in this terrible event, despite it having taken a serious toll on the local human population.

There are many documented examples of family pets seemingly possessing the ability to anticipate an event in advance of its occurrence; foreseeing an epileptic seizure well before it occurs, for example, or the onset of hypoglycemic shock in a diabetic. We know now that this seemingly magical ability is down to a highly evolved olfactory system – an incredibly acute sense of smell in relation to our own.

Other frankly 'alien' perceptive abilities in the animal and insect kingdom include the fly's ability to taste with its entire body and see things in slow motion, and a fish in the deepest depths that uses the largest organ on its body to see in the darkest of depths – *its skin*.

Not modes of perception per se, but worthy of mentions in the context of how alien creatures can be on our own planet:

The *Turritopsis Nutricula* (an author favourite): A Hydrozoan jellyfish that defies aging through the act of love making – every time it mates it actually becomes physiologically more youthful; the only thing that can end its immortality is a predator. And Australia's *Mary River Turtle,* that uses bimodal respiration; the ability to ingest oxygen using two methods: breathing air like us and a remarkable ability to extract oxygen in water via its cloaca (genitals).

The point is that there are many, many ways in which to perceive things that exist in our world and indeed many unusual ways to exist (it's estimated that 86% of all plants and animals on land and 91% of sea creatures have yet to be discovered). We have five amazing senses, but *only* five. For us to assume that everything that there is to perceive can only be perceived with our five senses is not only naive, but *fundamentally incorrect.*

Could it be that whatever resides at 30 East Drive, is an extraordinary as yet undiscovered species, or race that is simply beyond our field of view?

In all fairness, science has satisfactorily proven that there are fields of perception beyond our own. This has resulted in many practical devices which have increased our sensory capabilities, or perhaps more accurately, have translated the formerly unseen into a form that our five senses can now comprehend.

So much depends on the way in which our brains choose to interpret the information with which they are supplied: If you think colour is what you perceive it to be, ask someone that is colour blind whether they agree. Or ask the incredible Neil Harbisson[h], who became a certified 'Cyborg' after fusing a camera permanently to his skull. The camera creates specific vibrational frequencies when it sees colours – he literally *listens to colour!* What's more, he actually has a significantly greater perception of colour than ordinary humans have. But we digress.

Many of the technological devices we now have access to have been inspired by nature, such as sonar (acoustic location), night vision (infra-red), electromagnetic field readers (EMF), high speed cameras, motion detectors, thermal cameras – to name but a few.

Hopefully, the sceptical reader will appreciate the pertinence of this next point. Many of these 'sensory extensions' have been widely adopted by the paranormal community, and some in addition have actually been developed by the paranormal community (e.g. *Alice box, Parascope, Kinect SLS camera*) – not because the community is necessarily factoring in our sensory limitations, but that they understand that whatever it is they seek to witness is something that isn't visible to us – something beyond the conventions of our three-dimensional existence. This is why they experiment with as much of what science and engineering has to offer, in the hope of finding a way of connecting with the unseen.

Sadly, the scientific community has a low opinion of all things paranormal. Scientists fear being ostracised by their peers for taking on this much under-studied sector – rather ironic given the number of scientific thinkers that have been actively persecuted by religion and politics for their discoveries throughout history; time subsequently vindicating the majority. This is why the two communities so rarely, if ever, see eye to eye. However, there is one fundamental thing upon which both groups agree – that *we are simply not engineered to perceive everything that there is to be perceived.* Indeed, both science and the paranormal communities are fundamentally in the business of unravelling the mysteries of the universe.

6: 'They' exist in another dimension or parallel universe.

If getting our collective heads around our inordinately complex three-dimensional universe with the aid of our five basic senses isn't a difficult enough task, imagine if you will, the mind-boggling place that exists inside the head of Professor Michio Kaku. Professor Kaku is a world-renowned Japanese American theoretical physicist. He is one of a growing number of exceptional minds that have *calculated* that there are probably as many as *eleven* different dimensions, as compared to the modest three we have been discussing so far.

Many of those dimensions are incredibly small, and operate at the quantum level, meaning that they are impossible for us to see, but at least one of them (the eleventh) is theorised to be infinitely large in size.

What is most fascinating about cutting-edge theoretical physics, in particular M-Theory (unifying all consistent versions of Superstring Theory), is that it is now becoming increasingly clear that our concrete, observable, and convenient three-dimensional space is actually a very confined place.

Nevertheless, we have evolved in such a way as to comfortably occupy 'up, down and sideways' – dimensions that are very real and familiar to us. So why is it so difficult for us to imagine a fourth dimension (still ignoring 'time' as our actual fourth dimension for the moment) let alone an additional *seven*?

Here is a paraphrased analogy that Professor Kaku offers in order to help us grasp the concept of a fourth dimension. Imagine a fish swimming in a pond. It swims in a three-dimensional space familiar to the fish and to us. But if you catch the fish and lift it out of the pond, it says "What the heck?" It has left its three-dimensional space and entered a broader, fourth dimension – one that we know exists because we occupy it! What's more, the fish cannot survive in 'our dimension'.

Of course, what cannot be ignored here is that at this juncture (and not for the last time) religion and science might become awkward bedfellows, primarily because proving that life can exist on a scientifically-plausible 'other level' would give the religiously-inclined great comfort and validation.

Or perhaps we should be considering the possibility of a

parallel universe, or universes? This is not to be confused with higher dimensions. A dimension is; a facet that defines our own reality, however surreal that might appear: A parallel universe, on the other hand, is an entire alternative field of existence hovering fractionally above our own plane of being. Determining the existence of such a plane is one of the great preoccupations of cutting-edge physics today.

The Large Hadron Collider, located at CERN in Switzerland, is the largest, most expensive machine ever built. It was developed with a single, fascinating objective: to locate the Higgs-Boson, otherwise known as the 'God Particle.' Without going into too much detail here (the subject has been covered in great detail in other books) in essence, the experiment was designed in an effort to prove a theory presented by physicist Sir Peter Higgs back in the mid-1960s that hypothesised that dark matter – all the stuff in the gaps in space – is insufficient by itself to keep everything bound together. Given that gravity is too weak to be responsible all by itself, the question becomes, what exactly is hidden in those gaps?

Higgs posited that there may be a hidden something that gives fundamental sub-atomic particles mass, but until fairly recently it hasn't been possible to either observe it or to prove its existence using experimentation. Finally, after a 50-year wait, Sir Peter Higgs got to witness the discovery of a brand-new particle at the LHC on July 4th, 2012, when a collision was created between protons colliding at something near the speed of light. It was subsequently named the Higgs-Boson.

The discovery of this 'God Particle' has many potential ramifications, not least the possibility we may never have existed without it, for it is suggested that the Higgs-Boson may have been the catalyst for the Big Bang itself. One such significance is that the discovery of this hidden energy field (christened the Higgs Field) could perhaps serve as evidence of a parallel universe: an alternative plane of existence, situated just above our own three-dimensional, observable universe. The Large Hadron Collider is now being used to experiment with mini-black holes with the specific objective of proving the existence of such parallel universes.

Could it be that whatever 'haunts' 30 East Drive doesn't actually occupy the house at all, but rather occupies a parallel world, one from which it can interact with us, but we can less frequently interact with it?

Let's go back to Professor Kaku's analogy of the fish in its pond for just a moment, the one where we are conclusively living in a fourth dimension from the fish's perspective. Now imagine taking the fish's little castle house out of the pond and placing the castle at the opposite end of the pond. As far at the fish is concerned, the object simply relocated from one end of the pond to the other in an instant: but in actual fact the castle exited the fish's three-dimensional space and voyaged via a fourth dimension (a parallel universe) before re-entering the fish's three-dimensional environment once more, all in the blink of an eye. Could this be an explanation for the poltergeist's ability to apport objects?

The first object that Bil had thrown at him on Valentine's day was a domino. Could it be that the poltergeist simply took the domino via a fourth dimension or a parallel universe and re-entered the object in our three-dimensional space in a different location? A bit like taking a pebble from the fish pond and throwing it at the fish from the pond's surface? Bearing in mind that, just as the analogy implies, the fish couldn't see who moved his little castle, but we could see the fish the entire time; *the poltergeist could see Bil as clear as day, but Bil could not see it.*

We can't be sure one way or the other, because as far as we know, nobody has yet to see an object actually disappear in front of their eyes; eyewitnesses tend to catch sight of them when they reappear, sometimes in thin air. However, when Bil was bombarded by small objects on Valentine's day, his distinct impression was that there was likely *no time* between the objects disappearing from the house and reappearing in thin air. When Jean Pritchard held a box of eggs firmly shut in order to prevent them from being dropped in front of her eyes in the front room of 30 East Drive, the eggs simply disappeared from the box and seemingly in the very same instant, materialised before her astonished eyes before being dropped onto the floor – she would open the box after each egg was dropped to discover another egg missing.

An unmissable big yellow balloon that Bil observed in the front room one minute, *materialised in the middle of the kitchen floor just moments later* (right). There is simply no way it could have been blown without being seen. As suggested at the beginning of this subchapter, it would seem that whatever is apporting objects not only isn't bound by the confines of our own three physical dimensions, but also isn't bound by our fourth – *time* – either. The entity can take an object and instantaneously put that object in another place. Alternatively, as has also been observed, it can take an object and keep it until such time as it chooses to reintroduce it back into the house, such as *the piece of newspaper from the 1970s that appeared from nowhere* (left) and was witnessed by several recent visitors, and medieval keys that were seen falling from a new chimney breast by none other than Jean Pritchard, adding more grist to the legend of 'It' being an evil medieval monk (once a resident of the local Pontefract Priory) behind the haunting.

Lastly, a few visitors to 30 East Drive have reported feeling as though they have been followed home from the house by something. This is an occupational hazard for paranormal investigators. There is a small amount of anecdotal evidence to suggest that something untoward has happened to a number of visitors, though that may be entirely coincidental:

Paranormal investigator Kevin Warrener had every reason to feel "genuinely scared" after his first visit to 30 East Drive back in September 2015. Immediately after his visit he was checked into A&E with an unexpected broken ankle. Immediately following that; a random 'sick note' from the University of London mockingly appeared in his trainer – he has no way of getting such a note, and no idea where it came from or how it got into his shoe. As he sat down to write about his experiences at 30 East Drive, a large bird flew at speed directly into the window he was sat in front of, leaving a dust impression on the window pane. The 'atmosphere in his house changed' and other inexplicable things started to occur; a hair brush that always stayed in the exact same location completely disappeared – eventually turning up in the bath, a large random spring (dangerously) appeared inside his wife's pillow, and most dramatically: On a subsequent visit to another location, one where Kevin wasn't expecting much in the way of physical activity, he was 'stormed' by an invisible force and hit by a 'red hot flying marble' – a signature move of the Black Monk of Pontefract. Kevin was absolutely convinced that the Black Monk had latched onto him and followed him home, and even on to another location.

Yet another visitor, Patrick Jackson, returned to the house bearing flowers by way of a peace offering, after enduring what he could only describe as "a month of sheer hell" after spending a week at the house. He heard an aggressive male voice shouting in his ear, accusing him of all sorts of obscenities. Is it possible that whatever resides at 30 East Drive has the means of being able to transport itself at will, free of the physical constraints that bind the rest of us? It is also interesting to note that Patrick was 'rewarded' for his floral offering with *a marble delicately balanced on the curved top of his small black knapsack* (right), a gesture that intriguingly suggests that whatever 'It' is may be aware of our true intent and motivation for being at 30 East Drive and will react accordingly.

Finally, Jordan Parker and his mother reported that their car was swarmed with bees shortly after leaving 30 East Drive (monks would keep them for their honey production, and Jean Pritchard once had to deal with a swarm of bees – as depicted in the film *When the Lights Went Out*).

On the discovery of the Higgs Bosun and the Higgs Field, it was also established that a certain particle – the photon – remains massless, meaning that it can pass through space in the blink of an eye. Could it be that the entity known as the Black Monk somehow possesses the ability to transport itself near-instantaneously to anywhere it chooses, due to having either harnessed technology or possessing innate abilities that allow it to travel completely unimpeded? Or do the specific characteristics of the dimension/parallel universe it occupies allows it to possess the ability to move at will between dimensions? This admittedly reads like the stuff of imaginative science fiction writing but given the advances that are taking place in theoretical physics right now, it is not necessarily as absurd as it might sound at first.

When Bil invited some movie distributors to view *When the Lights Went Out*, on not just one but *two* occasions, in two completely different viewing rooms, power to the viewing suites was shut down completely (and only to those specific suites); at the point where the poltergeist first began to make its presence fully felt and ten minutes before the second viewing. In both instances, the power supply couldn't be restored, so the viewings had to be abandoned. This was an event that hadn't happened even once in all of Bil's years spent screening movies and adverts in viewing suites, and yet here it happened *twice in two different suites on different days* (left and right), affecting two entirely different sets of infrastructure and equipment. A remarkable 'coincidence' if ever there was one. Bil to this day still treasures an email from his co-producer – top Hollywood producer Deepak Nayar – stating that "If the viewing fails for a third time, I am taking my name off this movie!" It's important to add that to 'create a failure' in the viewing suite for the purposes of a PR stunt would be beyond madness given the lengths movie makers have to go to get distributors in the room. In the third and final (successful) viewing the numbers of potential distributors was cut to a small handful – a complete disaster by any standard.

Considering the possibility that whatever entity resides at 30 East Drive has the ability to be anywhere it chooses in an instance, in defiance of the conventions of 21st century science, and to perceive external events (things that happen beyond the confines of 30 East Drive) that are related to it and can then engage and interact with whichever ones it chooses, is this perhaps an early example of 'It' making its presence and feelings felt? Is it a possibility (however extraordinary) that it was the entity that scuppered two separate screenings of a movie that focused upon it? Could it be that it truly isn't bound by time and that it had the foresight to know that the movie would bring the world to its doorstep – so it tried to maintain a peaceful environment at its erstwhile sanctuary by scuppering the entire enterprise? And it came *very* close to achieving that, having reduced potential distributors to single figures.

Perhaps more alarming still, Bil wonders whether he has inadvertently summoned something untoward into the movie itself by attempting to depict the nefarious deeds of the Black Monk on film – is the movie itself haunted? Leaning very much toward the 'extraordinary coincidence' camp at the time, Bil took it upon himself to turn the event into the PR event that it had never intended to be, by having a *gathering of 'vicars' to come and exorcise the movie* (left), resulting in a very amusing image!

Please let the authors know if you have ever had anything paranormal occur whilst watching *When the Lights Went Out*!

7: 'They' are creatures from other worlds in our universe.

"We could be in the middle of an intergalactic conversation... and we wouldn't even know."

Michio Kaku, Theoretical Physicist.

Before you poo-poo the alternative life form or 'alien' hypothesis as a possible explanation for the strange events unfolding at 30 East Drive, ask yourself this one question: What's stranger – believing in ghosts, or believing in aliens? The bodiless, on-going existence of dead people, or the possibility of other life forms that have evolved in the same way as us but located elsewhere in an infinite universe?

The finest minds working at the cutting edge of theoretical physics and astrophysics posit that extragalactic civilisations probably do exist, or more accurately, that they *actually do* exist. This is based upon a simple principle: if the universe is infinite, then everything is possible. Add to that the accepted figure that our universe is some 13.7 billion years old, and that we as a species are a mere 100,000 years old (we have existed for only 0.0015% of the life time of our planet) and you have all the information you need to reach an informed conclusion about the prospects of there being many *much* more advanced civilisations – comprised of life forms that are millions of years more advanced than us – elsewhere in the universe.

These civilisations could have long ago cracked the seemingly intractable scientific conundrums that we have only just begun to contemplate: Interstellar travel, time travel, eternal life, telepathy and so on. Of course, the question of how *they* might get to us is a complex one, but it is interesting to note that none other than NASA themselves have recently announced the discovery of magnetic portals in space[i], some no more than 10,000 miles from Earth. Portals that open and close, seemingly at random that may offer a direct path to and from the sun some 93 million miles away, and presumably from there to other planets in our solar system. Is it possible that whatever is at 30 East Drive is a visitor that arrived via portals to our planet, and that the house happens to possess the exact (energetic/magnetic?) qualities for it to be a convenient 'local portal' for interstellar visitors? Although it may sound far-fetched, these visitors may possess advanced light bending or 'cloaking' technology that allows them to hide from view when it suits their purpose to do so.

Lisa Manning lived with a kicking, scratching, punching, and frankly downright evil poltergeist at her home in Holbrook, Coventry. Her deeply traumatising experience had many uncanny similarities with those surrounding 30 East Drive and the Pritchards, except sadly she was unable to stay at the house. The entity became too violent, and her young children were increasingly brutalised. Their first dog was thrown down the stairs so violently it needed to be put down, while the second – the replacement puppy – inexplicably had its hind legs broken.

Lisa actually describes having seen 'It' on one occasion: "It was about 7 feet tall and looked like an animal," she said. This sounds much like the description of a demonic entity, and those of a religious disposition may well default to that as an explanation. Yet isn't it equally likely (or at least no less believable) that it's another species, one which has developed elsewhere in our infinite universe and possesses similar characteristics as us?

The likelihood is that if we do get visitors from afar (and there is plenty of evidence to suggest that we already do) it is entirely plausible that they would look nothing like us, or even anything like the appearance that Hollywood's special effects artists have imagined for them... unless, of course, they were a derivative of us, or vice versa. They could also theoretically be human beings from the future of our own timeline, but that's a whole other story!

8: It's self-determined reality; an invention of the subconscious.

"It is not possible to formulate the laws of quantum mechanics in a fully consistent way without reference to consciousness."
                    Eugene Wigner, Nobel Prize winner in Physics.

To say the brain is incredibly complex is a massive understatement. A billion neurons making parallel calculations (not linear, like your average computer) make the human brain the best processor on the planet by a factor of 10,000, when compared to the world's fastest supercomputer.

It seems entirely feasible that such a magnificent thing would be capable of creating any sort of imagined reality and convince you of the reality of those events with utter certainty. But even taking into account such well-documented phenomena as visions, hallucinations, and lucid dreams, grasping the idea that the brain can manifest a physical object out of thin air and then propel it at the observer is another thing entirely.

Of course, given that everything we perceive is simply a product of how our brains choose to interpret its various sensory inputs, it is entirely feasible that it could convince us that we are actually holding something that isn't actually there. Virtual Reality and 3D movies prove that our brains can suspend disbelief long enough for us to believe that we are being bombarded by objects when we really are not; or being shot at in a battlefield – when we are in actual fact, in the comfort and safety of our homes. Yet when other observers simultaneously witness the exact same thing, either visually or physically, it becomes extremely improbable that the entire event is imagined... unless, of course, *life itself* is somehow a trick or a creation of the mind; a simulation as hypothesised by the *Matrix* trilogy of films.

Indeed, theoretical physicists are fascinated by something truly unbelievable called quantum consciousness. This discovery in quantum mechanics (the study of the incredibly small-scale universe) suggests that we may influence outcomes by simply being an observer. Experiments using electrons have conclusively proven that the mere act of observing an experiment somehow physically influences the behaviour of the electron. The question then becomes: If there is no observer to bear witness, what is the electron doing? Does it even exist? And if that's the case, does it then follow that the observer actually determines whatever it is they wish to see?

At a quantum level, particles can be in two (or more) places at the same time (that's two places *anywhere in the universe*). Perhaps more accurately, they can be in an infinite number of places at the same time. This has been proven experimentally: When individual photons are fired in a single stream at a card with two slits in it, the photon (impossibly) passes through both slits at the exact same moment; this is known as the Double Slit

Experiment. It is conceivable that when a poltergeist apports an object, it doesn't take the object via a different universe at all, but rather possesses the means to simply tap into the incredible peculiarities that pertain to our own universe on a quantum level, and simply 'makes it exist' in a different place instantaneously. Even stranger still, what of the possibility that the aforementioned object already exists everywhere at once – so it simply interrupts one version of the object in question, allowing it to manifest elsewhere?

It is worth pointing out that, given the fact that we are incredibly complex, energy-packed biological entities composed of particles, when we interact with each other we almost always alter outcomes – *we influence each other's behaviour*.

Yet again, religion and science become awkward bedfellows. It may be pertinent to quote a biblical verse at this point: Psalm 37:4 'Take delight in the Lord, and he will give you the desires of your heart.' If quantum consciousness does indeed exist (and the Double Slit experiment suggests that this is indeed the case) then life as we perceive it could simply be an illusion, only existing because our consciousness has determined it to be so. If this is the case, then literally all of the factors in your life are decisions made by your consciousness: your partner, kids, job, house, wealth, appearance, mates, interests, car, and so on. And indeed, such fantastical notions as ghosts, poltergeists, aliens, mind-reading, extra-sensory perception... All absolutely real, because it was predetermined by your consciousness, in some profound way, which concretely manifested them all. You desired these things in your life, and therefore manifested them. 'God grants the desires...' For those of you thinking 'if this is true, why haven't I won the lottery yet?', that's because the theory may come with an inbuilt caveat.

The Secret, as its adherents call it, is a principle whereby people mentally imagine the things that they would like to manifest in their lives, from the emotional to the practical, from the basic to the luxurious. Stick a picture of your dream home to your wall, Blu-Tack the image of your perfect partner to your computer, and in time there is every chance that your dreams will indeed come true.

It's an incredible theory, and one that may not be quite as ridiculous as it may seem at first. Bil observes that he considers that there is nothing in his life that is a surprise to him at all – including this book, the movie, the house, his family (and all their nuances), his property, his friends, his businesses and unsurprisingly – a dark foreboding house and its 'resident demon'! Remember Bil's recurring nightmare at the beginning of this book? Does it not seem *remarkably coincidental* that he should find himself the owner of a house containing an utterly improbable, sinfully dark entity, one that is so similar in its silent, brooding threatening presence that one might consider it the *exact same* terrifying entity as the one in his unforgettable nightmare? What extraordinary set of complex circumstances needed to play out for this 'coincidence' to manifest??

And are the 'Tulpa thought forms' and the 'Philip Experiment' (page 298) not perfect examples of quantum consciousness in action? In the case of the 'Philip Experiment' the participants set out to consciously manifest a 'thought form', but inadvertently ended up believing that 'Philip Aylesford' actually existed – at an inexplicably profound subconscious level, and thus (inadvertently) proved that 'ghosts' are indeed simply the result of a subconscious desire: It certainly offers a plausible explanation as to why hardened sceptics and non-believers are unlikely to experience anything 'paranormal'.

Quantum consciousness provides legitimacy for the most challenging of principles and outcomes: telekinesis, mind-reading, miracles, telepathy, ESP, ghosts, and so on – because anything your consciousness desires would manifest itself, in no uncertain terms.

But the effortlessly predictable and fitting nature of all of Bil's experience presents a caveat. Imagining your desires, believing that one day they will manifest (and certainly not ignoring the rational fact that simple ambition has the potential to take you there) does seem to bear fruit, but only when the idea or desire becomes part of your *subconscious* desires and beliefs. It's as if you need to *very deeply* believe in the thing that it then manifests. It has to somehow become 'one with you.' If you *fundamentally* believe you are a loser, you will be a loser. If you *fundamentally* believe you are a winner, then you *will be a winner*. Perhaps Bil's deeply religious upbringing ('conditioning' as he sees it) seeded and subsequently amplified an obsession with 'the darkness' that manifested the demonic nightmare, which ultimately led to the ownership of 30 East Drive – despite it being against his logical better judgment?

For those of a religious persuasion, this principle would lend itself to the belief that it is God that has predetermined every detail of our lives. This may provide some comfort, which is not necessarily a bad thing, but quantum consciousness, backed up by scientific observation, is revolutionary thinking that promises to radically change our view of how and why things are the way they are. The only problem that the authors foresee is that quantum consciousness also simultaneously presents a paradox: for quantum consciousness to exist, it may need consciousness to determine that it exists in the first place. In other words, the very notion of quantum consciousness may be only a construct of the writer's or reader's mind, and just like everything else in the writer's/reader's life, it doesn't really exist at all!

The mind boggles.

A final point remains to be made. When Albert Einstein discovered his equation $E=MC^2$, he also unlocked an incredible truth about the amount of energy locked up in every single atom that makes up everything in our universe. The atom bomb became a tragic proof of that particular concept. And whilst the energy locked up in the atoms that make up our minds and bodies is stable and unlikely to ever blow up, the energy locked up inside the average person is roughly 80 000 times greater[j] than the energy released in Hiroshima and Nagasaki – enough energy to kill everyone on the planet more than twice.

We are energy, incredible amounts of energy that is vibrating at an extremely high level. This energy came into existence 13.7 billion years ago, possibly recycled from a black hole containing the energy of a collapsed universe that exploded, repeating a cycle with no beginning and no end. Time and some extraordinary processes have created forms of energy (including us) that seem to serve the singular purpose of allowing our universe the means of being able to 'experience' life as a conscious form, to be able to contemplate its own existence. If this is indeed the grand purpose, then the fact that everything is imagined is perfectly reasonable, because all that energy wants to do is *experience*.

CONCLUSIONS

"Once you eliminate the impossible, whatever remains, no matter how improbable, must be the truth."

Sherlock Holmes, Arthur Conan Doyle.

Visitors to 30 East Drive go there for three reasons, broadly speaking: to visit the infamous subject of books, newspaper reports, documentaries, movie and urban legend, out of sheer curiosity ('Is there really anything in it?'), and to get the living bejeezus frightened out of them.

There is *no* doubt that there is something extraordinary; something beyond the scope of current scientific understanding – *something paranormal* – happening at 30 East Drive, and many hundreds of visitors, including the authors of this book, are more than willing to support that statement. But without sound scientific support, attempting to provide the answers for what is driving the phenomena is a risky business, and at best can only be conjecture. However, given that it is unlikely that science is going to make an appearance any time soon, and we are all impatient for answers, we'll at least endeavour to create some hypotheses based on the 'evidence' collected so far: it's our effort to advance the debate a little, in the hope of tempting cutting-edge science through the door of 30 East Drive one day.

Fortunately for us, 30 East Drive has now had thousands of

visitors, many of whom (as we have discussed) come armed with an arsenal of 'ghost-detecting' equipment. The stunning array of images, videos, *Kinect* captures, audio recordings etc. they have captured, combined with hundreds of eyewitness experiences and accounts, provide the fuel for debate.

Like good detectives, we are bound by the 'evidence,' we cannot simply omit something because it doesn't fit into an explanation we seek – we *have* to work with it all – in the same way that theoretical physicists need to factor in so many apparently disconnected truths about our universe in order to come up with a unified theory of everything, you cannot simply ignore a piece here and there in order to justify your grand theory.

Our method is admittedly a tad basic (but at least it's simple). We have consolidated and listed some key eyewitness events for consideration below but have also included a few eyewitness accounts from other poltergeist cases: it would seem that there are many similarities between them all, so it makes sense to include them here in an effort to keep the debate as broad as possible. We have then compared them to the theories touched upon in this chapter to see what fits and what doesn't. To reiterate, this isn't a decade long serious scientific study at a quantum level, but it *is* one based on the 'evidence' collected by hundreds of independent witnesses.

Poltergeist activity at 30 East Drive, Pontefract:

Actual voices heard, mainly aggressive male seemingly interacting with visitors

Young female 'heard' via various monitoring devices, often warning of the presence of the male

A monk appearing at the foot of the master bed, in the kitchen and in the front room

Pools of water appearing on the lino

A layer of dust falling from below head height

Gloved hands conducting singing guests from behind the living room door

Medieval keys falling from chimney flue

Eggs being removed from a sealed egg box and appearing in thin air in front of Jean Pritchard

Random objects materialised on the sofa (above right)

Diane's hair standing on end before she was dragged up the stairs, leaving her with hand marks on her throat

Physical objects regularly apported without being seen to float into place

Visitors receiving 'animal-like' scratches on legs and faces

A young girl and a *very tall figure caught on Kinect* (above) that both responded directly to instruction

Visitors receiving deep burns in arms

The sense that you are often being watched

Dark shadows witnessed and photographed

Figure of what appears to be a 'demonic girl' photographed

Water jug filled itself back up again

Ice cold columns of air

Footsteps, thumps, bangs – including rapid loud banging from the coal house

Visitors believing that they have someone with them when they leave, including hearing actual aggressive voices long after departing East Drive

Feeling drawn to the house, as if being called

Shadows of what appear to be Civil War soldiers entering the upstairs cupboard adjacent to the bathroom and *a pike bearing English Civil War soldier photographed* (left)

Cupboards opening and objects moving on command

Intelligent tapping

Responsive stick figures on SLS cameras

Light anomalies visit guest and retreat (right)

Objects going missing – such as keys, later appearing in improbable places such as inside broken vacuum cleaner

Poltergeist activity at Lisa Manning's old house in Coventry:

Large heavy objects apported, including a glass ashtray thrown with velocity at Lisa, missing her by a whisker

Lisa's boyfriend apparently becoming possessed by something

Cutlery draws opening and all the cutlery being ejected

Kettle being constantly thrown

Dog seemingly thrown or kicked down the stairs

Second dog (puppy) having its legs broken

Blasts of cold air

All doors and windows held firmly shut

Toothbrush and other objects floating outside window

Physically seeing the entity on the top floor, it being described as "7ft tall and looking like an animal"

Poltergeist activity at Enfield, London:

Girls being physically lifted from their beds

A girl seemingly being possessed by the cause of the manifestation – a former resident

IN SUMMARY

[Key: ED = 30 East Drive, Cov = Coventry, and En = Enfield]

Broadly speaking, what we are trying to assess:

Is about 7 feet tall (ED, Cov) but...

Appears as a smaller form (a girl?) (ED)

Seems to want to interact and not just observe (ED, Cov, En)

Is sometimes animal-like in appearance (Cov)

Wears some sort of habit-like outfit (ED)

Scratches like an animal, shoves like a human; can make physical contact (ED, Cov, En)

Speaks/shouts aggressively in English (ED, Cov, En)

Sounds predominantly male; a girl has been heard (ED, En)

Is invisible to us unless choosing to be visible (ED, Cov)

Can apport objects (ED, Cov, En)

Can lift heavy objects, including humans (ED, Cov, En)

Has the ability to cause objects to defy gravity (ED, Cov, En)

Is often accompanied by ice-cold columns of air and breezes (ED, Cov, En)

Has been photographed as dense light-trapping black shadows (ED)

Has been videoed as an 'invisible mirage form' (ED)

Isn't always alone; a girl has been present at the same time (ED)

Has been known to be kind to dogs, once refilling a jug of water for one (ED) but also…

Is extremely violent toward dogs, causing deaths (Cov)

May possess the ability to influence events in two distant places at the same time (ED)

Can seemingly travel in an instant to another location (ED)

Seems both mean and playful (ED)

Seems to understand our intent and respond accordingly (ED)

Can 'possess' people (ED, Cov, En)

In order to establish a bold conclusion or two based on probability rather than gut feel or personal preference, we've created a detailed *chart comparing eight possibilities* (right) against the above 'evidence,' agreeing that it is representative of the sorts of eye witnessed themes associated with 30 East Drive. The results of our comparative 'straw poll' assessment are as follows:

1. **IT'S ALL A SCAM** (the ultimate hoax): 31 out of 40 themes could be scammed with some effort, but the circumstances would require the regular participation of a group and would amount to a conspiracy of inordinate complexity. The scam would probably have come to light by now. 8 of the themes are considered impossible to scam, due to the limitations of 21st

century technology and the impartial, spontaneous nature of the witnesses present.

2. **GHOSTS OF THE DEAD** (evidence of life-after-death): 13 out of 40 themes could be ghosts, but that doesn't explain what ghosts are. If they do exist, and the authors have every reason to believe they do, then they are possibly quite different to what is reported at 30 East Drive.

3. **DEMONIC/NON-HUMAN BIBLICAL ENTITY** (a biblical 'fallen angel' – evidence that God exists?): 32 out of 40 themes could be demonic. The 4 themes that weren't considered demonic, seemed too playful for an 'evil' entity, one intent on doing damage. And one theme is to do with ghosts rather than the single representation of (an evil) something. It also begs the question, if this is a demon, then what is a demon and where does it exist? Believers in an after-life would call this as proof of a heaven and hell. The entity that Lisa Manning saw certainly sounds like the description of a demon…

4. **PSYCHOKINESIS** (we have incredible undiscovered powers): 24 out of 40. Psycho or telekinesis have been debated for 160 years with little evidence to support them. But many visitors to 30 East Drive have reported unambiguous physical experiences, including one of the authors. Could it be that those that will an

event enough may somehow manifest what they wish for? It might also explain why some people have no luck whatsoever with events, particularly defiant sceptics?

5. **THEY ARE CREATURES FROM HERE THAT EXIST BEYOND OUR FIVE SENSES** (they're real, we simply can't observe them): 35 out of 40. We have a field of view limited to our 5 basic senses, whereas nature proves there are many, many more ways of perceiving things, and indeed ways of existing. Could it simply be that whatever is in the house exists as part of our world (an unknown species) and our universe, but beyond our ability to see it? The creature however, can see us? The only question is – why aren't we constantly being made aware of 'Them' in other locations like our own homes? Why specifically 30 East Drive and a small handful of others?

6. **THEY LIVE IN A PARALLEL UNIVERSE** (and are trying to make contact): 31 out of 40. You'd think that this conclusion would be an almost identical match to the 'alien species' conclusion above, but a couple of noticeable anomalies occur, namely – the monk's habit. It is hard to imagine that an entity from a completely different universe would end up with the same fashion as us (albeit a centuries old one) and it would be even more remarkable that it would speak English, but then again, it

could maybe learn some basic phrases to challenge us with, like an angry tourist remembering a few choice foreign swear words.

7. **THEY ARE ALIEN BEINGS FROM OUR OWN UNIVERSE** (visiting us/observing us): 36 out of 40. What's more likely? Ghosts of dead people or the prospect of highly advanced visitors from afar that have evolved in the billions of years our universe has existed and have harnessed the technology required to travel to our planet (or are from the future of our own planet – they are us traveling back in time) and possess *'cloaking' technology that prevents us from seeing them* (right)? As crazy as this sounds: NASA have discovered 'portals' a mere 10 000 miles from our planet, could it be that 30 East Drive and other houses that have similar hauntings are 'mini-portals' through space, and significantly, time? The monk's habit in the case of 30 East Drive would lean toward 'It' being one of us, perhaps from the future, as to assume that 'we' would evolve elsewhere in the universe then find our way here would be even more of a stretch, or is it?

8. **SELF-DETERMINED REALITY: QUANTUM CONSCIOUSNESS** (we all subconsciously determine the exact nature of our lives – no matter how bizarre): 40 out of 40. Full marks. Our universe at a quantum level is very strange indeed and is only just beginning to be understood. Sub-atomic particles can

be in two places at the same time (possibly an infinite number of places at the same time) and can reflect the actions of its other particle with infinite distance between. Even time isn't a boundary at the quantum level. This has given rise to the theory of Quantum Consciousness – where the act of us observing will have a very real bearing on the outcome. In other words, what we will to happen, can, and often does happen; observe how we influence each other when we interact. Is it simply that we are observing what we choose to observe at 30 East Drive? And more significantly, in every aspect of our lives? Ask yourself how much of your life is actually uncannily familiar to you; does it not (honestly) feel like you are living the right life for you, that it's a relevant fit – *whether you like it or not*?

Whatever the correct explanation for what resides at 30 East Drive, and frankly it could be any combination of the above, or indeed none of them at all – one thing is beyond doubt, 30 East Drive is an extraordinary place and home to phenomena beyond our understanding. One wonders if what Bil actually bought isn't simply a haunted house (though that prospect in itself is incredibly fascinating) but rather an anomalous glitch in the 'matrix' that could provide some answers to the truth of how things really are?

We invite you to join the debate at the *30 East Drive Owners Page* (overleaf) on Facebook.

On the *website for the house* (below right), and now here in this book, Bil invites theoretical physicists to visit and study the house free of charge. It's the job of science to provide us with answers, *and we, the writers and readers of this book – want answers.*

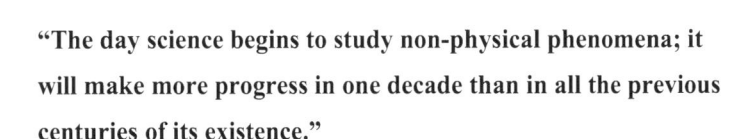

"The day science begins to study non-physical phenomena; it will make more progress in one decade than in all the previous centuries of its existence."

Nikola Tesla.

ACKNOWLEDGEMENTS

To Nelly, Lucas and Carla Bungay for accepting losing their husband/father to this book for a good while.

To Laura, for her unwavering support.

To Lucas for lending his maths skills.

To Jason, Linda, Charlie, Andrew, and Lesley, for joining Richard on the adventure.

To Carol Fieldhouse, *East Drive Paranormal* and the East Drive and Chequerfield communities of Pontefract, West Yorkshire for forgiving the intrusion into their lives, and for appreciating the significance of 30 East Drive in the grand scheme.

To Amy Bowker for patiently proof-reading every word.

To you the reader: Thank you for spending your hard-earned money and valuable time to read this book. It is our sincere hope that you have enjoyed it and would kindly ask you to please consider rating it at the website it was purchased or borrowed from, with our heart-felt thanks.

To all of the paranormal investigators that have visited 30 East Drive – a huge thank you for your patience, time and effort in capturing and sharing the incredible evidence we have had the pleasure of presenting to you in this book. It is by no means everything (in fact we are really only just scratching the surface) so do please keep forwarding everything you capture, including your stories, to **30eastdrive@gmail.com** or show and tell the community on the Facebook Owners page, and perhaps we'll get to collate and present more evidence to you again in the not too distant future.

Finally, at Bil's insistence, we would like to respectfully leave the last word to the Black Monk of Pontefract himself. In September 2018, Paul Hill of *Plymouth Paranormal Investigators* had two team members sit on the same spot Amanda and Gemma had sat when they captured the figure of 'Emma,' standing and staring directly at them from the bathroom doorway. It was 4.30am and in the dim light from the streetlamp they could make out a dark shadow at the end of the corridor, right at the top of the stairs.

They instinctively took a quick sequence of shots – one, two, three. On later examination, the second image clearly revealed what looks distinctly like a *man in heavy robes, like a monk's habit* (left), albeit with the hood down, calmly reading what looks like a book large enough to be a medieval bible.

[a] Page 288
Enfield Poltergeist

[b] Page 293
The Tupla

[c] Page 293
Philip Experiment

[d] Page 313
Materialist science

[e] Page 317
Nephilim

[f] Page 317
Se-irim

[g] Page 320
Weird quantum

[h] Page 325
Seeing with sound

[i] Page 337
NASA: portals

[j] Page 344
We're energy

'When the Lights Went Out'
on Vimeo

CREDITS

n.b. The majority of these are external links so we cannot guarantee that they will work ad infinitum.

For exclusive offers, future updates and prizes

(including chances to win trips to 30 East Drive)

scan the above QR code occasionally

or bookmark it now.

Copyright 2019, Richard Estep & Bil Bungay

All Rights Reserved

OTHER BOOKS BY RICHARD ESTEP

Haunted Longmont

In Search of the Paranormal

The World's Most Haunted Hospitals

The Haunting of Asylum 49 (with Cami Andersen)

Spirits of the Cage (with Vanessa Mitchell)

Visiting the Ghost Ward

Trail of Terror

The Dead Below

The Devil's Coming to Get Me

The Fairfield Haunting

Haunted Healthcare

The Horrors of Fox Hollow Farm

Printed in Great Britain
by Amazon